HIGH COURT
CASE SUMMARIES

ENVIRONMENTAL LAW

Keyed to Percival, Schroeder,
Miller, and Leape's
Casebook on Environmental Law,
5th Edition

THOMSON

WEST

Mat #40604596

© West, a Thomson business, 2005
© 2007 Thomson/West
        610 Opperman Drive
        St. Paul, MN 55123
        1–800–328–9352

Printed in the United States of America

ISBN: 978–0–314–18108–4

 TEXT IS PRINTED ON 10% POST CONSUMER RECYCLED PAPER

Table of Contents

Alphabetical Table of Cases

CHAPTER TWO

Environmental Law: A Structural Overview

Madison v. Ducktown Sulphur, Copper & Iron Co.

Instant Facts: Farm owners sued the owner of two copper smelters for an injunction and damages for injured trees and crops and lost profits.

Black Letter Rule: An injunction against a private nuisance is left to the court's discretion and is not appropriate when the benefit of the polluting company's actions outweigh the harm they cause.

Missouri v. Illinois

Instant Facts: Illinois (D) began dumping its sewage into the Mississippi River, causing possible contamination of the drinking water in Missouri (P).

Black Letter Rule: Proximate cause is an essential element of a public nuisance case.

Georgia v. Tennessee Copper Co.

Instant Facts: Georgia (P) sued copper smelters in Tennessee to enjoin them from discharging noxious gases into Georgia (P).

Black Letter Rule: In a public nuisance action, a state may obtain an injunction to enjoin damage to its inhabitants.

International Paper Co. v. Ouellette

Instant Facts: A Vermont landowner sued a New York paper mill for private nuisance arising from the paper mill's stench.

Black Letter Rule: The Clean Water Act preempts state common law in actions against out-of-state polluters.

New York v. United States

Instant Facts: New York challenged the federal Low–Level Radioactive Waste Policy Act, requiring states to dispose of all low-level radioactive wastes or take title to them.

Black Letter Rule: Under the Tenth Amendment, Congress may not force states to administer a federal regulatory program.

Sierra Club v. Costle

Instant Facts: Environmental group claimed that the EPA had weakened proposed environmental standards as a result of an undocketed meeting with the President, a member of Congress, and the White House staff.

Black Letter Rule: An undocketed meeting between the President and the EPA regarding a proposed regulation does not violate the Clean Air Act or due process.

Chevron U.S.A. v. Natural Resources Defense Council

Instant Facts: An environmental group challenged the EPA's definition of the term ''stationary source'' in the Clean Air Act to include all pollution-emitting devices in a plant.

Black Letter Rule: Courts must defer to agency interpretations of statutes, unless the interpretations are unreasonable.

Madison v. Ducktown Sulphur, Copper & Iron Co.

(Farm Owner) v. *(Owner of Copper Smelter)*
113 Tenn. 331, 83 S.W. 658 (1904)

INJUNCTION AGAINST PRIVATE NUISANCE IS NOT PROPER REMEDY WHEN THE BENEFIT OF THE POLLUTER'S CONDUCT OUTWEIGHS THE HARM IT CAUSES

■ **INSTANT FACTS** Farm owners sued the owner of two copper smelters for an injunction and damages for injured trees and crops and lost profits.

■ **BLACK LETTER RULE** An injunction against a private nuisance is left to the court's discretion and is not appropriate when the benefit of the polluting company's actions outweigh the harm they cause.

■ **PROCEDURAL BASIS**

Appeal from a private nuisance action for damages and an injunction.

■ **FACTS**

Madison (P) and other farm owners (P) sued the Ducktown Sulphur, Copper & Iron Co. ("Ducktown") (D), the owner of two nearby copper smelters. Madison (P) alleged that the smelters emitted large quantities of smoke that injured their timber and crops and diminished their enjoyment of their land. Ducktown (D) argued that it was conducting its business lawfully and by the only possible method. Ducktown (D) further argued that it made every effort to eliminate the smoke, without success, and that there was no place more remote to move its operations. The trial court denied Madison's (P) request for an injunction. The court of chancery appeals reversed and enjoined the operation of the smelters.

■ **ISSUE**

Is an injunction a proper remedy against a private nuisance?

■ **DECISION AND RATIONALE**

(Neil, J.) No, not when the benefit of the polluting company's conduct outweighs the harm it causes. Here, Madison (P) has proven a case for damages. However, injunctions are left to the court's discretion. If we grant an injunction, we will destroy the copper smelters, significantly destroy half the taxable value of the community, and drive more than 10,000 people from their homes. Indeed, the injunction would shut down important manufacturing enterprises worth nearly $2,000,000, in order to protect small farms worth less than $1,000. Ducktown (D) cannot conduct its activities in a different manner and cannot relocate to a more remote place. Thus, an injunction would practically confiscate Ducktown's (D) property without any compensation. We must balance the rights of the parties and, therefore, we grant Madison (P) damages and deny him an injunction. Reversed.

Analysis:

This case arose during the industrial revolution when manufacturing reigned supreme. Thus, the court paid great deference to Ducktown's (D) interests and discounted the farmers' (P) interests. Viewed from a moral perspective, the court's ruling seems grossly unfair. The court's balancing approach may nearly always weigh against an injunction insofar as an injunction would nearly always cripple the defendant's business. Here, Madison's (P) business may have been nearly crippled. It is unclear whether the court granted damages only for Madison's (P) past injuries, thus requiring him to sue again in a couple of years for subsequent damages, or whether the court granted damages for likely future injuries as well.

■ **CASE VOCABULARY**

PRIVATE NUISANCE: Common law cause of action that focuses on conduct that unreasonably interferes with the use and enjoyment of another's land.

Missouri v. Illinois

(State) v. *(State)*
200 U.S. 496 (1906)

VICTIM OF ALLEGED PUBLIC NUISANCE MUST PROVE PROXIMATE CAUSE

■ **INSTANT FACTS** Illinois (D) began dumping its sewage into the Mississippi River, causing possible contamination of the drinking water in Missouri (P).

■ **BLACK LETTER RULE** Proximate cause is an essential element of a public nuisance case.

■ **PROCEDURAL BASIS**

Original action in the U.S. Supreme Court for injunction of public nuisance.

■ **FACTS**

Illinois (D) built a canal to reverse the flow of the Chicago River, thereby causing Illinois' (D) raw sewage to flow to the Des Plaines River which dumps into the Illinois River and then into the Mississippi River. Missouri (P) sued Illinois (D) for an injunction claiming that the sewage contaminated Missouri's (P) water and increased the rate of typhoid fever in the state.

■ **ISSUE**

Is proximate cause an essential element of a public nuisance case?

■ **DECISION AND RATIONALE**

(Holmes, J.) Yes. Missouri (P) itself dumps sewage into the Mississippi, thus it may be responsible in part for contaminating its water. Furthermore, the expert evidence about whether Illinois' (P) sewage actually caused the increase in typhoid fever is very contradictory. In addition, while the number of cases of typhoid fever has increased in Missouri (P) since Illinois (D) opened the canal, typhoid rates have not increased on the banks of the Illinois River, which would be the case if the canal were the true cause. The evidence about the existence of the typhoid bacillus in the Missouri (P) water is also unclear. [Yes, the water is also unclear.] Thus, Missouri (P) has not proven that Illinois (D) is the proximate cause of its water contamination.

Analysis:

Missouri (P) was unable to establish that Illinois (D) was the proximate cause of its water contamination. While it may be true that "but for" the canal, Illinois' (D) sewage would not have reached Missouri (P), the evidence showed that sewage from other sources, including Missouri (P) itself, may have caused Missouri's (P) increased typhoid fever. Thus, the Court did not have to address whether Illinois' (P) dumping was an unreasonable interference with Missouri's (P) drinking water. The Court gave significant weight to the fact that Missouri (P) itself contributed to the contamination of its water. This was important because Missouri (P) was seeking an injunction, an equitable remedy, which is not available when the plaintiff has unclean hands [or, unclear water].

■ CASE VOCABULARY

PUBLIC NUISANCE: Common law cause of action, usually brought by a governmental entity, alleging an unreasonable interference with a right common to the general public.

Georgia v. Tennessee Copper Co.

(State) v. (Copper Smelter)
206 U.S. 230 (1907)

STATE MAY OBTAIN INJUNCTION AGAINST PUBLIC NUISANCE FOR DAMAGE TO ITS INHABITANTS

■ **INSTANT FACTS** Georgia (P) sued copper smelters in Tennessee to enjoin them from discharging noxious gases into Georgia (P).

■ **BLACK LETTER RULE** In a public nuisance action, a state may obtain an injunction to enjoin damage to its inhabitants.

■ PROCEDURAL BASIS

Original action in the U.S. Supreme Court for injunction of public nuisance.

■ FACTS

The Tennessee Copper Co. (the "Copper Co.") (D) was a copper smelter located in Tennessee, near the Georgia (P) border. Georgia (P) sued the Copper Co. (D) to enjoin it from emitting noxious gases into Georgia (P). Georgia (P) claimed that the gases were destroying its forests, orchards, and crops. The Copper Co. (D) claimed that Georgia (P) was guilty of laches.

■ ISSUE

Does a state have standing to sue for injunction of a public nuisance for damage to its inhabitants?

■ DECISION AND RATIONALE

(Holmes, J.) Yes. Although Georgia (P) owns very little of the damaged land, Georgia (P) controls its air, forests and mountains and has the right to pursue an injunction to stop their destruction. It is fair and reasonable that Georgia (P) wants its air and land to be free from further damage. We might rule differently if this were an action between private parties. We do not dispute that the Copper Co. (D) generates large quantities of sulphur dioxide which the wind carries into Georgia and which causes damage to Georgia (P). Finally, Georgia (P) is not guilty of laches. Georgia (P) merely waited to sue until it could determine whether the Copper Co.'s (D) new chimneys would decrease the problems. But, instead, the new chimneys seem to cause the poisonous gases to be carried even further into Georgia (P). We will grant an injunction after the Copper Co. (D) completes the structures it is now building in an attempt to stop the fumes.

Analysis:

Here, Georgia (P) was able to do what the plaintiff in *Madison v. Ducktown, Sulphur, Copper & Iron Co.* [injunction against private nuisance not granted when the benefit of the polluting company's actions outweigh the harm it causes] was unable to do. In fact, Ducktown was one of the defendants in this action. Georgia (P) was likely successful here because it was a state pursuing a public nuisance action, rather than an individual pursuing a private nuisance action. In a public nuisance action, there is less balancing of the costs and benefits of the polluting company's actions. This accords with Justice Holmes' statement that the Court might rule differently if this were an action between private parties. Private parties may usually pursue a public nuisance action when they are damaged in some way that is unique to the damage suffered by the general public.

International Paper Co. v. Ouellette

(*Paper Mill*) v. (*Landowner*)

479 U.S. 481 (1987)

CLEAN WATER ACT PREEMPTS STATE COMMON LAW ASSERTED AGAINST AN OUT-OF-STATE POLLUTER

■ **INSTANT FACTS** A Vermont landowner sued a New York paper mill for private nuisance arising from the paper mill's stench.

■ **BLACK LETTER RULE** The Clean Water Act preempts state common law in actions against out-of-state polluters.

■ **PROCEDURAL BASIS**

Certification to U.S. Supreme Court of private nuisance action removed to federal court.

■ **FACTS**

Ouellette (P) owned land in Vermont on Lake Champlain. International Paper Co. ("IPC") (D) operated a paper mill across the lake in New York. On behalf of 150 lakeshore property owners, Ouellette (P) sued IPC (D), claiming that IPC's (D) paper mill emitted a terrible stench. IPC (D) removed the action to federal court. IPC (D) argued that the Clean Water Act [federal regulatory scheme to control water pollution through permit requirement] preempted Virginia's common law.

■ **ISSUE**

Does the Clean Water Act preempt state common law when asserted against an out-of-state polluter?

■ **DECISION AND RATIONALE**

(Powell, J.) Yes. Although the Clean Water Act does not expressly preempt state law, it does by implication because it is comprehensive and conflicts with state law. Permitting states to impose separate standards on a single pollution source would undermine the Clean Water Act's objectives. Here, Vermont law would circumvent the Clean Water Act's permit system and would upset the policy choices made by New York, the source state. Our ruling does not leave Ouellette (P) without a remedy. He may still bring his action under New York law. Applying New York law would not upset the balance of federal, source-state, and affected-state interests because it would involve applying state law to a source in the state. In fact, New York is permitted to impose higher standards than those under the Clean Water Act.

Analysis:

This action arises in light of the Court's 1981 holding in *City of Milwaukee v. Illinois* that the Clean Water Act preempts federal common law. In that case, the Court held that preemption of federal common law does not involve the federalism concerns that preemption of state common law does. In this case, ultimately IPC (D) settled with Ouellette (P) and the other landowners (P) for $5 million and established a trust fund for environmental projects in the area.

■ CASE VOCABULARY

PREEMPTION: Congress's power under the Supremacy Clause of the U.S. Constitution to supersede state law in a specific area.

New York v. United States

(State) v. *(Federal Government)*
505 U.S. 144 (1992)

UNDER TENTH AMENDMENT, CONGRESS MAY NOT FORCE STATES TO ADMINISTER A FEDERAL REGULATORY PROGRAM

■ **INSTANT FACTS** New York challenged the federal Low-Level Radioactive Waste Policy Act, requiring states to dispose of all low-level radioactive wastes or take title to them.

■ **BLACK LETTER RULE** Under the Tenth Amendment, Congress may not force states to administer a federal regulatory program.

■ **PROCEDURAL BASIS**

Certification to U.S. Supreme Court.

■ **FACTS**

Congress (D) passed the Low-Level Radioactive Waste Policy Act (the "Act"). The Act required states to dispose of low-level radioactive waste by January 1, 1993, or take title to all such waste generated within their borders and become liable for all the potential damages the waste causes. New York (P) sued the federal government (D) claiming that the Tenth Amendment bars it from requiring states to regulate in this field.

■ **ISSUE**

May Congress require states to administer a federal regulatory program?

■ **DECISION AND RATIONALE**

(O'Connor, J.) No. Congress may enforce a program, but it may not require states to do so. Congress may, however, hold out incentives to influence the states' choices. For example, Congress may attach conditions to a state's receipt of federal funds. Or, Congress may give a state the option of either regulating an activity according to federal standards or having the federal regulation preempt state law. These options give the state's citizens the ability to choose whether to comply. They also make federal officials accountable for federal laws and state officials accountable for state laws. With respect to the Act here, the portions that authorize states to impose surcharges on radioactive waste from other states and to deny access to such waste are within Congress's power to regulate. However, the "take title" provision is different. Neither choice Congress offers is constitutional. Congress may not transfer the radioactive waste from generators to the states. This is like requiring the states to subsidize the generators or assume their liabilities. The other choice, regulating pursuant to Congress' direction, would allow Congress to "commandeer" the states, which is clearly unconstitutional. Even though Congress gives the states some latitude in enforcing the Act, the states do not have the option of declining to administer it at all.

Analysis:

This case brings up the issue of federalism, the division of power between the federal government and the states. Justice O'Connor is very concerned with the accountability of federal and state officials and the power of a state's citizens to make their own policy decisions. In 1999, President Clinton issued Executive Order 13,132. It requires the federal government to defer to the states when taking action that affects state discretion, and not to construe federal statutes to preempt state law unless there is an express preemption clause or other clear evidence that Congress intended to preempt state law.

Sierra Club v. Costle

(Environmental group) v. *(EPA Administrator)*

657 F.2d 298 (D.C. Cir. 1981)

UNDOCKETED MEETING BETWEEN PRESIDENT AND EPA REGARDING PROPOSED REGULATION DOES NOT VIOLATE CLEAN AIR ACT OR DUE PROCESS

■ **INSTANT FACTS** Environmental group claimed that the EPA had weakened proposed environmental standards as a result of an un-docketed meeting with the President, a member of Congress, and the White House staff.

■ **BLACK LETTER RULE** An undocketed meeting between the President and the EPA regarding a proposed regulation does not violate the Clean Air Act or due process.

■ **PROCEDURAL BASIS**

Action challenging administrative action.

■ **FACTS**

The EPA (D) promulgated new source performance standards for coal-fired power plants. After the public comment period, the EPA (D) officials met with President Carter, a member of Congress, and the White House staff. The Sierra Club (P) claimed the EPA (D) had weakened the standards as a result of this undocketed meeting.

■ **ISSUE**

Does a post-comment undocketed meeting between the President and the EPA (D) regarding a proposed regulation violate the Clean Air Act or due process?

■ **DECISION AND RATIONALE**

(Wald, J.) No. While the Clean Air Act requires that interagency written comments and draft rules be docketed, the Act does not refer to informal intra-executive meetings and oral comments. The President has sole control over the executive branch and, therefore, must monitor executive agency regulations and be fully briefed about them. The regulations at issue here require weighing environmental, energy and financial considerations. The EPA needs the President's input and ideas. However, there may be times when docketing conversations between the President and federal agencies may be necessary to ensure due process. For example, it may be required when the conversations directly concern the outcome of adjudicatory proceedings where an individual's rights are at issue. Docketing may also be necessary where a statute specifically requires that information upon which a rule is based be docketed. However, absent a specific legislative requirement, courts must be very cautious about requiring additional rulemaking procedures. Whatever was discussed in the meeting, any rule issued by the EPA must have factual support in the rulemaking record and may not be based in any part on any information not in the record. It is possible that Presidential prodding lead to an outcome that is factually based on the record. But such a result cannot be prevented. Rulemaking must be influenced by political considerations and Presidential power.

Analysis:

When important regulations are at issue, how can the President and Congress not be interested? This is particularly true for the President, who may be ultimately accountable for the regulations' results. The Administrative Procedure Act ("APA") and the environmental statutes lay the groundwork for how agencies should act. The APA requires agencies to provide public notice in the Federal Register of proposed rulemaking actions, a public written comment period, and publication of final rules in the Federal Register. Despite these requirements, agencies have considerable discretion over the substance and procedures of regulatory policy. Here, the court defers to the EPA's authority and ability to issue reasonable regulations despite possible presidential influence.

Chevron U.S.A. v. Natural Resources Defense Council

(Not stated) v. *(Environmental group)*

467 U.S. 837 (1984)

COURT MUST DEFER TO EPA'S REASONABLE INTERPRETATION OF STATUTE

■ **INSTANT FACTS** An environmental group challenged the EPA's definition of the term "stationary source" in the Clean Air Act to include all pollution-emitting devices in a plant.

■ **BLACK LETTER RULE** Courts must defer to agency interpretations of statutes, unless the interpretations are unreasonable.

■ **PROCEDURAL BASIS**

Certification to U.S. Supreme Court of decision setting aside EPA regulations.

■ **FACTS**

In 1977, Congress amended the Clear Air Act to include a state permit program regulating "new or modified major stationary sources" of air pollution. In 1981, the EPA promulgated regulations allowing states to adopt a plantwide definition of the term "stationary source." That is, states could treat all pollution-emitting devices in a plant as a single stationary source. The Natural Resources Defense Council ("NRDC") (P) challenged the EPA's definition. The Court of Appeals for the District of Columbia Circuit set aside the regulations. *Is the statute silent or ambiguous? Is EPA's interpretation reasonable?*

■ **ISSUE**

Must courts defer to agency interpretations of statutes?

■ **DECISION AND RATIONALE**

(Stevens, J.) Yes, so long as the interpretation is reasonable. In interpreting an agency's construction of a statute, we follow two steps. First, we look at whether Congress' intent is clear in the statute. If the intent is clear, we must follow it. However, if the statute is silent or ambiguous, we look to whether the agency's interpretation is based on a permissible construction of the statute. Agencies have the authority to fill in the gaps left by Congress in statutes. Here, once the Court of Appeals determined that Congress did not define "statutory source," it should have looked only at whether the EPA's definition was reasonable. It should not have imposed its own judgment on what is appropriate. Agencies have more expertise in technical matters than courts do, and agencies' interpretations represent accommodations of competing interests. Finally, agency decisions should be left to the political process. Reversed.

Analysis:

U.S. Supreme Court decisions regarding judicial review of agency decisions have been somewhat schizophrenic. *Chevron* arose not long after the Court's 1971 decision in *Citizens to Preserve Overton Park, Inc. v. Volpe*, where the Court held that courts must aggressively oversee environmental agency actions. In 1978, in *Vermont Yankee Nuclear Power Corp. v. Natural Resources Defense Council, Inc.*, the Court held that agencies are free to experiment procedurally without strict judicial oversight. While

---

Chevron unambiguously requires deference to agencies' interpretations of statutes, studies have shown that courts, including the U.S. Supreme Court, have not done so. When courts even follow *Chevron*'s two-step procedure, courts take advantage of their right to determine whether a statute is ambiguous, which is often a rather ambiguous task.

CHAPTER THREE

Preventing Harm in the Face of Uncertainty

Reserve Mining Company v. EPA

Instant Facts: The federal government, three states and several environmental organizations sued a mining company under federal statutes and common law nuisance for the company's discharge of taconite tailings into Lake Superior.

Black Letter Rule: When the risk of harm from pollution is potential, rather than imminent or certain, and the polluter earnestly seeks a way to prevent further pollution, a court is not justified in an immediate shutdown of polluter's operation.

Ethyl Corp. v. EPA

Instant Facts: EPA determined that lead additives in gasoline caused a "substantial risk of harm" to health and ordered reductions in the amount of lead allowed in gasoline.

Black Letter Rule: When the purpose of a statute is to prevent harm, agency administrators are rationally justified in taking into account imperfect trends and projections if evidence is difficult to come by.

Industrial Union Dept., AFL–CIO v. American Petroleum Institute

Instant Facts: The Fifth Circuit struck down an OSHA permissible exposure limit for benzene of 1 ppm because the Fifth Circuit found that OSHA had not established that the benefits of the limit were reasonably related to its costs.

Black Letter Rule: Prior to promulgating any toxic substance standards, OSHA must make a threshold determination that such a standard is reasonably necessary and appropriate to remedy a significant material health risk.

Chlorine Chemistry Council v. EPA

Instant Facts: Despite publishing a scientific advisory committee finding that the presence of chloroform in drinking water was unlikely to be carcinogenic below a certain dose range, the Environmental Protection Agency (EPA) (D) promulgated a final rule setting the MCLG (maximum contaminate level goal) for chloroform at zero.

Black Letter Rule: The "best available evidence" rule cannot be rejected because of the possibility of contradiction in the future by evidence unavailable at the time of the action.

Corrosion Proof Fittings v. EPA

Instant Facts: Corrosion Proof Fittings challenged an Environmental Protection Agency's rule, made under the Toxic Substances Control Act, that prohibited future manufacture, processing, importation and sale of asbestos.

Black Letter Rule: To meet its statutory burden under TSCA of showing a reasonable basis for the least burdensome adequate protection from an unreasonable risk, the EPA must consider intermediate level standards, calculate costs and benefits equitable for a sufficient period of time, and analyze the availability and risk of substitutes to toxic substances.

Reserve Mining Company v. EPA

(Alleged Polluter) v. *(Federal Agency)*

514 F.2d 492 (8th Cir. 1975) (en banc)

COURTS MAY NOT ORDER IMMEDIATE SHUTDOWN OF POLLUTER'S OPERATION WHEN THE RISK TO HEALTH IS NOT ACTUAL OR IMMINENT, AND POLLUTER EARNESTLY SEEKS A WORKABLE WAY TO STOP THE POLLUTION

■ **INSTANT FACTS** The federal government, three states and several environmental organizations sued a mining company under federal statutes and common law nuisance for the company's discharge of taconite tailings into Lake Superior.

■ **BLACK LETTER RULE** When the risk of harm from pollution is potential, rather than imminent or certain, and the polluter earnestly seeks a way to prevent further pollution, a court is not justified in an immediate shutdown of polluter's operation.

■ **PROCEDURAL BASIS**

En banc review of a circuit court decision to stay a district court order requiring an immediate halt to the operation of a plant discharging mine tailings into Lake Superior and into the surrounding air.

■ **FACTS**

The Environmental Protection Agency [EPA] (P), Minnesota, Michigan, Wisconsin and several environmental groups sued to stop Reserve Mining Company [Reserve] (D) from discharging taconite tailings into Lake Superior and into the ambient air around its plant. The taconite tailings contained fibers nearly identical to asbestos fibers. All of the evidence showing that asbestos was harmful had considered only airborne asbestos. The district court considered three types of evidence concerning the harmfulness of the fibers discharged by Reserve (D). First, the district court directed a study comparing the presence of asbestos-like fibers in the tissues of Duluth, Minnesota residents (whose water came from Lake Superior) to the presence of such fibers in residents of Houston, Texas (whose water had no asbestos-like fibers). The study looked at the tissues of recently deceased residents who had been drinking Duluth water throughout the fifteen-year operation of the Reserve (D) mine. The study showed no fibers in Duluth residents. EPA (P) argued that the study examined too small of an area of the bodies to be conclusive. The trial court concluded that the results of the test were inconclusive as to the danger posed by the fibers. Second, the district court considered conflicting animal studies; not surprisingly, those offered by Reserve (D) showed that rats *fed* asbestos fibers had not absorbed those fibers into their gastrointestinal tissues, while the studies offered by EPA (P) showed that rats *injected* with the fibers had absorbed them throughout their bodies. Third, the court considered medical evidence offered by EPA (P) showing that workers exposed to asbestos had higher rates of gastrointestinal cancers. Although Reserve's (D) expert proposed that the workers had first inhaled and then coughed up and swallowed the asbestos, other medical experts hypothesized that the cancers could have been caused by ingesting the fibers. The district court found that Reserve (D) violated provisions of the Federal Water Pollution Control Act (FWPCA) that authorize the federal government to sue to prevent discharges that violate state water pollution laws and "endanger...the health or welfare of persons" [FWPCA §§ 1160(c)(5) and 1160(g)(1)]. The district court ordered

Reserve (D) to immediately terminate all discharges into the Lake Superior. Reserve (D) appealed. An Eighth Circuit panel stayed the district court injunction.

■ **ISSUE**

Does exposure to the amount of waterborne asbestos-like fibers discharged by Reserve into Lake Superior cause a legally cognizable risk to health?

■ **DECISION AND RATIONALE**

(Bright, Circuit Judge) No. The probabilities of harm caused by waterborne asbestos-like fibers are too speculative on the record at present to *prove* that they are a danger to human health. Therefore, the district court abused its discretion by ordering an immediate cessation of all discharges, thereby closing down a major industrial operation. The court did not err simply by considering potential as well as actual harm. By using the word "endanger," Congress intended for the EPA (P) and for courts to consider potential harms. Congress intended the FWPCA to be preventative of future harms and not just corrective of existing harms. Furthermore, Congress gave courts a flexible power to give injunctive relief under the FWPCA "when the equities of the case may require" [FWPCA § 1160(c)(5)]. The problem in this case, however, is that the evidence is not strong enough to warrant an immediate injunction. The probability of harm occurring cannot be determined as "more likely than not," and the level of harm cannot be stated precisely. The tissue study (comparing residents of Duluth with those of Houston) is inconclusive. The tissue study does not prove that Reserve's (D) tailings are not harmful, but indicates that they cause no immediate health crisis. The animal studies gave directly conflicting results, but provide some support for the hypothesis that the asbestos-like fibers can penetrate the gastrointestinal tissues. The strongest evidence of harm is the study showing increased gastrointestinal cancers among asbestos workers. This theory "rests on an tenable medical hypothesis." None of the evidence of harm is strong enough, however, to warrant an immediate shut down of Reserve (D). In fact, the harms caused unemployment to Reserve's (D) workers may outweigh the benefits of an immediate shutdown. Reserve (D) testified that it is willing to adopt new procedures and construct facilities at its plant to properly dispose of the taconite tailings. We hold that Reserve (D) shall be given a reasonable time to make changes to its plant and operations to permit it to cease discharging tailings into Lake Superior.

Analysis:

It is always difficult for courts to deal with laws that attempt to prevent future harm. We all know that if we tried to live a completely safe life, we'd never leave the house or get into a car. To determine whether the activity is worth the risks, we probably all do instinctively what the district court did in this case: we ask what the chances are of something bad occurring and how bad that thing will be if it occurs. We might take a 50% risk of stubbing our toes, but not even a 1% risk of falling off a tall building. In this case, the consequences of the harm, gastrointestinal cancer, were very bad. But the circuit court was not at all convinced of the probability of the harm occurring. Naturally, Congress did not say in the Clean Water Act, "By 'endanger' we mean a 51% chance of a small harm, or a 10% chance of a big harm." By their nature as human beings, legislators and judges may be risk takers or risk avoiders who would interpret the term "endanger" very differently. This may be one reason why the Eighth Circuit chose to examine this case *en banc*. The Circuit Court added another level of consideration to the case, however, when they looked at the consequences of closing the plant, i.e., unemployment. It may be legitimate to ask whether Congress intended for the EPA or the courts to look at circumstances beyond the health threats caused by pollution when deciding whether to enjoin polluters. Nevertheless, the circuit court clearly considered the economic impact in determining that at least an *immediate* shutdown was not warranted. It also appears from the circuit court's decision that on appeal Reserve (D) strengthened its arguments about finding safe alternatives for disposal of the tailings, and that these arguments influenced the circuit court to stay an immediate shutdown as well. Cases of this type are fascinating for the very human element that they introduce into statutory interpretation. Psychologists tell us that factors as diverse as age, gender, and socioeconomic status influence our willingness to take risks, yet courts must come to determinations for all of us as to what risks society may accept from industries in our communities. Together with the next case, *Ethyl Corp.*

v. EPA, Reserve has been very influential in toxic substances cases where harms are difficult to ascertain.

■ CASE VOCABULARY

EN BANC: All of the judges of a court (usually a federal circuit) sitting together to hear an appeal on a novel or controversial issue where it is felt that the entire court must come to one ruling to cover all cases.

LEGALLY COGNIZABLE: Having the level or quality that the law takes into account; conversely, not being so insignificant or different in kind that it falls outside of the law in question.

Ethyl Corp. v. EPA

(Lead Additive Producer) v. *(Federal Agency)*

541 F.2d 1 (D.C. Cir. 1976) (en banc)

AGENCIES MAY USE TRENDS AND PROJECTIONS TO JUSTIFY REGULATIONS UNDER LAWS INTENDED TO PREVENT HARM AND WHERE EMPIRICAL DATA ON HARM IS INCOMPLETE

■ **INSTANT FACTS** EPA determined that lead additives in gasoline caused a "substantial risk of harm" to health and ordered reductions in the amount of lead allowed in gasoline.

■ **BLACK LETTER RULE** When the purpose of a statute is to prevent harm, agency administrators are rationally justified in taking into account imperfect trends and projections if evidence is difficult to come by.

■ **PROCEDURAL BASIS**

En banc review of circuit court panel's decision to strike down an EPA regulation.

■ **FACTS**

The Clean Air Act authorized the Environmental Protection Agency [EPA] to regulate gasoline additives if EPA found that the additives, when present in automobile exhaust "will endanger the public health or welfare" (Clean Air Act § 211(c)(1)(A)). In considering a regulation for lead additives in gasoline, the EPA found that it could not determine precisely what levels of lead caused harm, and could not determine exactly what harms were caused by different levels of lead. The EPA administrator, however, determined that lead in gasoline presented "a substantial risk of harm" and ordered reductions in lead additives. The EPA based the reduction on three factors: (1) many Americans, especially children, already had dangerously high levels of lead in their blood, (2) airborne lead, like that in automobile exhaust, was absorbed through respiration, and (3) airborne lead fell to the ground and mixed with dust creating further harm to children. Lead additive manufacturers, who opposed the regulation, argued that the Clean Air Act should be read to require the EPA administrator to have "proof of actual harm" based on evidence that could be considered scientifically certain.

■ **ISSUE**

Does a precautionary statute authorize an agency's expert administrator to issue a regulation to protect the public health based on trends and projections when scientific evidence is difficult to obtain and incomplete?

■ **DECISION AND RATIONALE**

(Wright, Circuit Judge) Yes. "Where a statute is precautionary in nature, the evidence difficult to come by, uncertain, or conflicting because it is on the frontiers of scientific knowledge, the regulations designed to protect the public health, and the decision is that of an expert administrator, we will not demand rigorous step-by-step proof of cause and effect." The EPA administrator correctly interprets the language of the Clean Air Act that states "will endanger the public health or welfare" to mean, "presents a significant risk of harm." The agency administrator must assess both the probability and severity of the risks of harm. The administrator cannot, of course, just guess or go with a hunch, but also does not need a scientific certainty of 95%. The agency is more like a fact-finder in civil litigation who need only reach a "preponderance of the evidence" standard. If the administrator's conclusion that lead in automobile exhaust "will endanger" the public health has been rationally justified, the appellate courts will treat that as they would a finding-of-fact, and that conclusion supports the regulation. The panel's decision is reversed.

Analysis:

To understand this case, and the ways in which it differs from *Reserve Mining Company v. EPA*, one has to know a little bit about administrative law. Under the Administrative Procedures Act, federal agencies have many rules, the details of which don't matter too much here, about how they must go about issuing regulations. Once a regulation has been issued using the proper procedures, the rule-making process is treated like a trial court case, and review of regulations usually skips over the district court level and goes right up to the circuit court. That explains why, in *Ethyl*, there is no plaintiff or defendant in the usual sense. It also explains why the court is willing to be deferential to the EPA administrator's findings. Some of the differences between *Reserve* and *Ethyl*, then, are explained by the differences in the Clean Water Act and the Clean Air Act. The Clean Water Act (*Reserve*) says, in effect, that the EPA is authorized to be a plaintiff against polluters who "endanger . . . the health or welfare of persons"; the Clean Air Act (*Ethyl*) says that the EPA is authorized to issue regulations limiting additives that "will endanger the public health or welfare." Those differences aside, both cases require the evaluation of risks based on both the probability and severity of the harm. In *Ethyl*, however, we do not find much, if any, discussion of the impact of the EPA regulation on the economics of the lead additives industry such as the Eighth Circuit gave to the closure of the *Reserve* operation. This is partly explained by the procedural differences in the cases: in *Reserve*, the court must decide whether to close a particular business operation, while in *Ethyl* it must decide the viability of a rule that the industry may respond to as it sees fit. Also important are the differences in evidence: in *Reserve*, the court questions whether the taconite tailings have been shown to be harmful, in *Ethyl*, it is the level of lead in automobile emissions, not whether lead is harmful, that is at issue. Taken together, *Reserve* and *Ethyl* have proven to be very influential on questions of uncertainty in the amount of harm caused or threatened by toxic substances.

Industrial Union Dept., AFL-CIO v. American Petroleum Institute

(*Workers Representatives*) v. (*Industry Council*)
448 U.S. 607 (1980)

A THRESHOLD DECISION THAT A STANDARD IS REASONABLY NECESSARY AND APPROPRIATE TO REMEDY A SIGNIFICANT HEALTH RISK IS REQUIRED BEFORE OSHA MAY PROMULGATE TOXIC SUBSTANCE STANDARDS

■ **INSTANT FACTS** The Fifth Circuit struck down an OSHA permissible exposure limit for benzene of 1 ppm because the Fifth Circuit found that OSHA had not established that the benefits of the limit were reasonably related to its costs.

■ **BLACK LETTER RULE** Prior to promulgating any toxic substance standards, OSHA must make a threshold determination that such a standard is reasonably necessary and appropriate to remedy a significant material health risk.

■ **PROCEDURAL BASIS**

Appeal to the Supreme Court of the United States from a Fifth Circuit decision striking down a standard promulgated by the Occupational Safety and Health Administration.

■ **FACTS**

The Occupational Safety and Health Act (OSH Act) empowered the Occupational Safety and Health Administration (OSHA) to set standards for exposure to toxic substances in the workplace. Section 3(8) of the OSH Act defined a "occupational safety and health standard" as a standard which required conditions or practices "reasonably necessary or appropriate" to create "safe or healthful employment or places of employment." Section 6(b)(5) told the OSHA Secretary what to consider when promulgating standards on toxic substances in the workplace. The Secretary was to set the standard that "most adequately assures, to the extent feasible" that no employee would "suffer material impairment of health or functional capacity" even if the employee was regularly exposed to the toxic substance. Furthermore, the statute directed the Secretary to consider the latest scientific evidence, feasibility, and experience in the regulatory field. In May 1977 OSHA, acting at the urging of the National Institute for Occupational Safety and Health, issued an emergency temporary standard limiting workers' exposure to benzene to 1 ppm. The Fifth Circuit invalidated the emergency standard. OSHA then held a rulemaking session and announced a permanent exposure limit of 1 ppm. Studies showed that exposure to benzene contributed to leukemia, nonmalignant blood disorders, and chromosome damage. All the studies were based on exposure levels above 10 ppm. OSHA determined that benzene is a human carcinogen, that the industry could not show that there was any safe level for benzene exposure, and that the lowest feasible level for benzene exposure was 1 ppm. OSHA determined that the 1ppm standard would benefit 35,000 employees at an initial cost of over $450 million and an on-going annual cost of around $34 million. The Fifth Circuit struck down the permanent standard as well, finding that OSHA had not shown that the benefits of the 1 ppm limit were reasonably related to the costs of imposing such a standard. OSHA appealed to the Supreme Court on the question of whether OSHA was required to do cost-benefit balancing under the OSH Act. OSHA argued that § 6(b)(5) of the OSH Act required it to make rules that assured a safe working environment or at least reduced exposure to toxic substances as much as feasible, i.e., without driving the industry out of business. The industry argued that the "reasonably necessary and appropriate" language of § 3(8) and the "feasible" standard of § 6(b)(5) required at least rough cost-benefit balancing.

■ ISSUE

Did OSHA make a threshold decision prior to promulgating its benzene standard that such a standard was reasonably necessary and appropriate to remedy a significant material health risk?

■ DECISION AND RATIONALE

(Stevens, J.) No. Because the OSHA Secretary did not make a threshold finding we will not answer the question of whether OSHA is required to balance costs and benefits when promulgating standards. OSHA's contention that the statute requires it to insure risk-free workplaces so long as the standards do not entirely destroy an industry is incorrect. The language, structure and legislative history of the OSH Act show that it intends to eliminate significant risks of harm. Section 3(8) does empower OSHA to set standards that are "reasonably necessary or appropriate to provide safe or healthful" work and workplaces, "safe" doesn't mean totally "risk-free." Moreover, it is this language that requires OSHA to make the threshold decision that work or workplaces are "unsafe" before setting any standards. Other parts of the OSH Act require OSHA to do some cost-benefit analysis in order to prioritize the needs for various standards (§ 6(g)) and to justify substantial departures from existing consensus standards (§ 6(b)(8)). These sections suggest that Congress meant for the OSH Act to apply to significant risks and not to be as broad as OSHA claims. In fact, if OSHA's interpretation was correct, the OSH Act might be an unconstitutional delegation of Congress' legislative power, and unconstitutional interpretations should always be avoided if possible. In the legislative history, all of the examples that Congress talked about in debating the bill, were examples of significant risk to health. Congress intended OSHA to have the burden of proof of showing, in this case, that it is more likely than not that the current 10 ppm exposure limit for benzene presents a significant material health risk. The record of this case shows that OSHA improperly rejected consideration of industry's testimony concerning a dose-response curve that indicated that, even at the present level of exposure, benzene would cause a maximum of two deaths among 30,000 workers every six years. It is usual in Administrative Law for the proponent of a rule to have the burden of proof, and Congress will explicitly shift that burden when it intends otherwise. In this case, OSHA did not meet its burden. All OSHA could conclude was that the benefits of the new 1 ppm standard were "likely" to be "appreciable." The burden of proof will not handcuff OSHA into waiting for deaths to occur before it can regulate. First, OSHA does not have to make hard mathematical calculations. Second, OSHA is statutorily allowed to use the "best available evidence," a standard below scientific certainty. Finally, OSHA can rationally judge the significance of risks brought about by exposure to toxic substances in a variety of ways. OSHA cannot, however, avoid determining what constitutes a "significant risk" and showing that such a risk is present in making its threshold determination that an exposure standard is needed. Affirmed.

■ CONCURRENCE

(Powell, J.) OSHA might have been able to support its benzene standard as part of a comprehensive cancer policy, but OSHA did not have such a policy in place when it promulgated the benzene standard of 1 ppm. The Fifth Circuit was correct in holding that the language of the OSH Act § 3(8) requires that when promulgating standards, OSHA must show that costs are not disproportionate to benefits.

■ CONCURRENCE

(Rehnquist, J.) The OSH Act should be declared an unconstitutional delegation of Congress' legislative authority. This is a case of Congress attempting to avoid difficult legislative issues by passing the buck to an agency. The language of § 6(b)(5) does not really give any guidance to the Secretary of OSHA as to where along the continuum of safety the Agency should draw the line in promulgating rules.

■ DISSENT

(Marshall, J.) Congress intended OSHA to regulate toxic substance levels in the workplace very stringently despite cases where uncertainty would exist as to exposure risks. There is nothing in the statute requiring OSHA to identify "significant" risks. In setting the standard for benzene at 1 ppm, OSHA considered costs and the benefits. At this time, there is no way to quantify risk of benzene exposure at low levels. OSHA made a threshold determination by finding that the new 1 ppm standard was necessary "to adequately protect employees from the hazards of exposure to benzene." Requiring a dose-response risk assessment at this time would be arbitrary since too little research exists for low exposure levels.

Analysis:

For the litigants, the "Benzene decision" (as it has come to be known) must have felt a little like playing a whole football game only to have it nullified by an irregularity in the coin toss. By basing its decision on the threshold finding, the Court surprised the parties, who argued the merits of the cost-benefit analysis scheme. The Supreme Court does not often agree to hear regulatory cases, so this case had to be considered very influential for the future of toxic substance regulations. Because there were two separate concurrences and a dissenting opinion (joined by three other justices, by the way), it is clear that the plurality decision was controversial. The decision has worn well over time, however, and influenced risk assessment in many federal agencies. The requirement that agencies determine a threshold of unacceptable or unreasonable risk became an accepted part of the regulatory scheme. Perhaps the most controversial aspect of the plurality decision was its use of the term "significant." As the dissent noted, the word "significant" doesn't appear in the sections of the OSH Act (§§ 3(8) and 6(b)(5)) being examined by the Court. The plurality argues that "safe" is not equivalent to "risk-free," and many things that we consider safe entail risks (here, they cite everyone's favorite examples: driving a car and breathing city air). Therefore, the plurality states, "a workplace can hardly be considered 'unsafe' unless it threatens the workers with a significant risk of harm." This is what triggers the threshold finding requirement; the agency must make a finding that the work environment is unsafe before it can regulate.

■ CASE VOCABULARY

DOSE-RESPONSE CURVE: This is a technique of risk assessment that attempts to relate the level of exposure to a hazard to the amount of harm that exposure causes; this may be complicated by the differences in the amount of exposure at one time versus the length of exposure over time. The terminology comes from drug testing, thus the word "dose."

Chlorine Chemistry Council v. EPA

(Trade Association) v. *(Environmental Protection Agency)*
206 F.3d 1286 (D.C. Cir. 2000)

THE EPA CANNOT SET A STANDARD WHEN THE BEST EVIDENCE SUPPORTS A DIFFERENT ONE

■ **INSTANT FACTS** Despite publishing a scientific advisory committee finding that the presence of chloroform in drinking water was unlikely to be carcinogenic below a certain dose range, the Environmental Protection Agency (EPA) (D) promulgated a final rule setting the MCLG (maximum contaminate level goal) for chloroform at zero.

■ **BLACK LETTER RULE** The "best available evidence" rule cannot be rejected because of the possibility of contradiction in the future by evidence unavailable at the time of the action.

■ PROCEDURAL BASIS

The Chlorine Chemistry Council (Council) (P) brought an action to vacate the EPA's (D) final rule setting the zero MCLG for chloroform and require the EPA (D) to promulgate a final rule setting a nonzero MCLG for chloroform.

■ FACTS

The EPA (D) originally proposed a rule on disinfectants and disinfectant byproducts in water that included a zero MCLG for chloroform based on an absence of data to suggest a threshold level below which there would be no potential carcinogenic effects. Subsequently, the EPA (D) published a Notice of Data of Availability (NODA) that included a scientific advisory committee's findings that chloroform was an unlikely carcinogenic below a certain dose range. The EPA (D) then proposed a nonzero MCLG for chloroform. However, when the EPA (D) promulgated its final rule, it set the MCLG for chloroform at zero. The EPA (D) justified its action on the basis that additional deliberations with their science advisory board (SAB) were needed prior to departing from a long-held EPA policy. The Council (P) brought an action to vacate the EPA's (D) final rule and to promulgate a final rule setting a nonzero MCLG. The EPA (D), after considering an SAB draft report, moved to vacate the MCLG. The court denied the motion because it did not contain a commitment to promulgate a nonzero MCLG for chloroform.

■ ISSUE

Was the EPA (D) justified in promulgating a zero MCLG for chloroform when the best available evidence indicated that a different standard would be acceptable?

■ DECISION AND RATIONALE

(Williams, J.) No. In promulgating a zero MCLG for chloroform, the EPA (D) openly overrode the "best available" scientific evidence, which suggested that chloroform was an unlikely carcinogenic below a certain dose level. Although it may be desirable for the EPA (D) to consult with its SAB in the future regarding the appropriate MCLG for chloroform, the EPA (D) is bound by statute to consider the "best available" scientific evidence at the time. Even though the EPA (D) argued that publishing the scientific advisory committees' findings in a NODA did not represent an "ultimate conclusion" with respect to chloroform, that did not change the fact that those findings were the "best evidence" available. EPA final rule vacated.

Analysis:

The court in *Chlorine Chemistry Council, Inc.* differentiates between a change in an agency policy and a change in an agency result, and notes that adopting a nonzero MCLG, while a significant step, simply represents a change in result. The EPA is free to amend its standards in the future, but only after the best available evidence supports such an amendment.

■ CASE VOCABULARY

BEST EVIDENCE: Evidence of the highest quality available, as measured by the nature of the case rather than the thing being offered as evidence. The term is usually applied to writings and recordings.

ENVIRONMENTAL PROTECTION AGENCY: A federal agency created in 1970 to coordinate governmental action to protect the environment.

Corrosion Proof Fittings v. EPA

(Industry Council) v. *(Regulatory Agency)*

947 F.2d 1201 (5th Cir. 1991)

EPA MUST CONSIDER INTERMEDIATE LEVEL CONTROLS, AVAILABILITY OF SUBSTITUTES, AND CALCULATE COSTS AND BENEFITS OVER A SUFFICIENT TIME PERIOD TO SHOW REASONABLE BASIS FOR A TOXIC SUBSTANCE BAN UNDER TSCA

■ **INSTANT FACTS** Corrosion Proof Fittings challenged an Environmental Protection Agency's rule, made under the Toxic Substances Control Act, that prohibited future manufacture, processing, importation and sale of asbestos.

■ **BLACK LETTER RULE** To meet its statutory burden under TSCA of showing a reasonable basis for the least burdensome adequate protection from an unreasonable risk, the EPA must consider intermediate level standards, calculate costs and benefits equitable for a sufficient period of time, and analyze the availability and risk of substitutes to toxic substances.

■ **PROCEDURAL BASIS**

Circuit Court review of a proposed Environmental Protection Agency regulation.

■ **FACTS**

The Toxic Substances Control Act (TSCA) required that, if the Environmental Protection Agency (EPA) (D) concluded on a "reasonable basis" that a toxic substance presented an "unreasonable risk," EPA (D) should issue the "least burdensome" regulations adequate to protect the public against that risk (§ 6(a)). TSCA also required EPA (D) to consider the benefits of the substances in question, the availability of substitutes for those substances, and the economic consequences of any proposed regulation. Relying on TSCA, the EPA (D) issued a regulation of asbestos that banned its manufacture, distribution, importation and processing in almost all products. EPA (D) presented calculations for the costs and benefits of the total ban regulation, and for the status quo with no further restrictions. EPA (D) rejected intermediate alternatives (e.g., labeling, controlled asbestos use under the auspices of other agencies) without presenting detailed calculations of them. There was dispute about whether EPA (D) should discount the benefit of lives saved to correspond with its discounting of economic costs. EPA (D) estimated costs and benefits for the next thirteen years, and claimed lives saved after the thirteen year period as "unquantified benefits." EPA (D) rejected considering the harms created by asbestos substitutes because analysis of all the substitutes might delay the phase-out of asbestos, which was known to cause harm. EPA (D) also argued that the ban would force industry to innovate other substitutes for asbestos. EPA (D) provided a waiver provision, so that industries that could find no substitutes could lengthen the asbestos phase-out period. The EPA's (D) analysis yielded economic costs as high as $74 million per life saved over the next thirteen years. Industries including Corrosion Proof Fittings (P) challenged the EPA's (D) total ban regulation.

■ **ISSUE**

Should the EPA (D) have a reasonable basis to show that a ban is the least burdensome regulation to protect against an unreasonable risk?

■ DECISION AND RATIONALE

(Smith) Yes. EPA (D) failed to meet its burden of showing that the risk of asbestos was unreasonable, and that the regulation had a reasonable basis and was the least burdensome alternative to adequately protect the public. EPA (D) correctly interpreted TSCA as a comprehensive statute designed to regulate toxic substances that are found in many different industries and applications. By choosing an overall ban on asbestos, the most burdensome alternative available, EPA (D) set the bar very high for what it must show under TSCA. By comparing in detail only the costs and benefits of a total ban and the costs and benefits of taking no action, however, EPA (D) failed to meet its burden of proof in justify its regulation. EPA (D) should have begun by calculating the costs and benefits of the least burdensome regulatory alternative. If EPA (D) found this alternative inadequate to protect the public against the risks of asbestos, it should have then analyzed the next least burdensome alternative and so on. As it is, EPA (D) just alluded to the intermediate level alternatives that it skipped over, and this does not meet the statutory burden of proof. To properly calculate the costs of regulations, EPA (D) must discount costs; thus, for the sake of accuracy, EPA (D) should discount benefits as well, even if those benefits are in terms of human lives. By choosing to calculate costs and benefits for only thirteen years, EPA (D) made the unquantified period unreasonably long and thus has over-valued "unquantified benefits." EPA (D) mishandled the analysis of asbestos substitutes in two ways. First, the EPA (D) cannot choose to ignore the absence of adequate substitutes when it calculates the costs of its regulations. The availability of a waiver, the burden of which lies on the industry seeking a phase-out extension, is not adequate to avoid such calculations. Second, EPA (D) cannot ignore the potential dangers of known substitutes. If the substitutes are themselves dangerous, those dangers necessarily offset the supposed advantages of an asbestos ban. EPA (D) does not have to affirmatively test every potential substitute, but it must consider credible evidence offered in the rulemaking process about substitutes. By not addressing the toxicity of substitute substances, the EPA (D) fails to establish the reasonable basis for its regulation. Finally, the figures presented by EPA (D) show that the benefits of the asbestos ban are not reasonably related to its benefits. "The EPA's willingness to argue that spending $23.7 million to save less than one-third of a life reveals that its economic review of its regulations, as required by TSCA, was meaningless." The regulation is vacated and remanded to EPA.

Analysis:

Although this is a pretty technical decision to read, it is a good introduction to several key toxic substance topics since it addresses the adequacy of the agency's evidence, the "least burdensome" language in the statute, cost-benefit analysis, and the notion of discounting projected costs and benefits. Nothing is so striking to someone encountering it for the first time as the last of these propositions. The principle of discounting comes from accounting and economics and is a tool for adjusting probabilities up or down according to the likelihood that outside conditions will change. For example, figuring out how much a dollar you spend today could earn for you over the next five years is pretty tricky, but economists can do a reasonable job with that kind of projection. The practical issue surrounding discounting in this case is whether EPA (D) must discount the probability of future benefits at the same rate that it discounts the probability of future costs. It seems obvious that the agency should do this as the court says, to preserve an "apples-to-apples comparison." That's all well and good until you realize that the future benefits being discounted are human lives. Now, a number of issues arise: can we put a price tag on human life? Are lives worth more or less as people age? Are some lives worth more than others?

■ CASE VOCABULARY

VACATE: This administrative law term is given to a court's holding that an agency regulation or rule is unenforceable; when a vacated rule is remanded to an agency, the agency can hold another rulemaking session to either change the regulation or find better support for the vacated regulation.

CHAPTER FOUR

Waste Management and Pollution Prevention

American Mining Congress v. EPA

Instant Facts: Trade associations challenged the EPA's authority under the Resource Conservation and Recovery Act ("RCRA") [federal statute dealing with the disposal of solid and hazardous wastes] to regulate materials that were intended for immediate reuse into ongoing operations, and that were not discarded or otherwise disposed of.

Black Letter Rule: Under RCRA, the EPA does not have the authority to regulate materials intended for immediate reuse into ongoing manufacturing operations, that were not discarded or otherwise disposed of, as "solid waste."

City of Chicago v. Environmental Defense Fund

Instant Facts: A private environmental group sued an incineration facility claiming the facility was not managing its ash in accordance with the Resource Conservation and Recovery Act ("RCRA") [federal statute dealing with the disposal of solid and hazardous wastes].

Black Letter Rule: Under RCRA, the EPA may regulate ash generated by the incineration of household waste.

United States v. Olin Corporation

Instant Facts: The court asked the parties to address whether the CERCLA [federal statute addressing cleanup of hazardous substances] was constitutionally applicable to their consent decree under the Commerce Clause and whether CERCLA could be applied to activity that occurred prior to its enactment.

Black Letter Rule: Congress has the power to regulate the disposal of hazardous waste under the Commerce Clause, and CERCLA may be applied retroactively.

New York v. Shore Realty Corporation

Instant Facts: New York sued a landowner for cleanup of hazardous substances that were on the land before the landowner purchased it.

Black Letter Rule: Current owners of contaminated land are liable under CERCLA, even if they did not own the land at the time of the disposal or cause the presence or release of the waste.

United States v. Bestfoods

Instant Facts: The federal government sued a parent corporation that actively participated in and exercised control over the operation of a polluting facility owned by a subsidiary.

Black Letter Rule: A parent corporation that actively participated in and exercised control over the operation of a polluting facility owned by a subsidiary is directly liable as an "operator" under CERCLA.

United States v. Aceto Agricultural Chemicals Corp.

Instant Facts: The EPA sued pesticide manufacturers who provided pesticides to a pesticide formulation facility for cleanup costs.

Black Letter Rule: Under the Comprehensive Environmental Response, Compensation, and Liability Act of 1980 ("CERCLA") [federal statute addressing cleanup of hazardous substances], a company that provides a hazardous substance to a formulation facility and who has no control over the facility may be liable as a "generator."

O'Neil v. Picillo

Instant Facts: Two generators of hazardous waste were found jointly and severally liable for the government's cleanup costs.

Black Letter Rule: Under the Comprehensive Environmental Response, Compensation, and Liability Act of 1980 ("CERCLA") [federal statute addressing cleanup of hazardous substances], defendants are jointly and severally liable unless they can prove the damage is divisible.

Cooper Industries, Inc. v. Aviall Services, Inc.

Instant Facts: Aviall (P) sued Cooper (D) for contribution to cleanup costs Aviall (P) incurred for properties that were previously owned and contaminated by Cooper (D), and a dispute arose as to whether Aviall (P) had to first be sued under CERCLA in order to sue Cooper (D) for contribution.

Black Letter Rule: CERCLA authorizes contribution for environmental cleanup costs from other responsible parties only when the party seeking contribution has been sued under CERCLA § 106 or 107(a).

United States v. Vertac Chemical Corp.

Instant Facts: Hercules (D) and Uniroyal (D) were the two remaining defendants in an action by the government to recover the Environmental Protection Agency's (EPA) costs in cleaning up a hazardous-waste site.

Black Letter Rule: In resolving contribution claims, the court may allocate response costs among liable parties using whatever equitable factors the court determines are appropriate.

Akzo Nobel Coatings Inc. v. Aigner Corp.

Instant Facts: Akzo (P) and Aigner (D) each sought a contribution from the other for the expenses each of them incurred in performing hazardous-waste clean-up at a site to which they had shipped solvents for reprocessing,

Black Letter Rule: The Uniform Comparative Fault Act (UFCA) is not appropriate for determining the contribution costs between two parties if there are other financially sound PRPs.

Philadelphia v. New Jersey

Instant Facts: Several out-of-state cities and New Jersey private landfill owners challenged under the Commerce Clause a New Jersey law prohibiting the importation of wastes collected outside of New Jersey.

Black Letter Rule: Under the Commerce Clause, a state may not prohibit the importation of hazardous wastes from outside the state.

C & A Carbone, Inc. v. Town of Clarkstown

Instant Facts: A Clarkstown (D) ordinance requiring all waste within the town to be deposited at a certain transfer station was challenged under the Commerce Clause.

Black Letter Rule: Under the Commerce Clause, a town may not require that all waste within the town be transferred to a certain transfer station.

In the Matter of Louisiana Energy Services, L.P.

Instant Facts: The applicant sought to build a nuclear processing plant adjacent to two predominantly African–American communities.

Black Letter Rule: The site of an undesirable land use may not be selected based on racial considerations.

American Mining Congress v. EPA

(Trade Association) v. *(Government Agency)*

824 F.2d 1177 (D.C. Cir. 1987)

UNDER RCRA, EPA MAY NOT REGULATE MATERIALS INTENDED FOR IMMEDIATE REUSE INTO ONGOING OPERATIONS.

■ **INSTANT FACTS** Trade associations challenged the EPA's authority under the Resource Conservation and Recovery Act ("RCRA") [federal statute dealing with the disposal of solid and hazardous wastes] to regulate materials that were intended for immediate reuse into ongoing operations, and that were not discarded or otherwise disposed of.

■ **BLACK LETTER RULE** Under RCRA, the EPA does not have the authority to regulate materials intended for immediate reuse into ongoing manufacturing operations, that were not discarded or otherwise disposed of, as "solid waste."

■ PROCEDURAL BASIS

Petition for review in administrative law action to D.C. Circuit Court of Appeals.

■ FACTS

Under RCRA, Congress granted the EPA (R) authority to regulate solid waste. RCRA defines "solid waste" as "discarded material." In its final rule, the EPA (R) defined "discarded material" to include not only materials being abandoned or disposed of, but also materials used in certain recycling and reuse activities. The American Mining Congress ("AMC") (P) and other trade associations representing mining and oil refining interests challenged the scope of the EPA's (R) final rule. AMC (P) argues that the EPA's (R) authority under RCRA is limited to controlling materials that are discarded or abandoned, and not materials that are to be reused in ongoing manufacturing operations.

■ ISSUE

Under RCRA, does the EPA have the authority to regulate materials that are to be immediately reused in ongoing manufacturing operations?

■ DECISION AND RATIONALE

(Starr, J.) No. In RCRA, Congress specifically defined "solid waste" as "discarded material." To interpret Congress's intent under the statute, we first look at the ordinary meaning of Congress's words. The ordinary meaning of "discarded" is "disposed of," "thrown away," or "abandoned." Including materials intended to be reused strains this meaning. We next look at the purpose of the statute. Through RCRA, Congress intended to address the growing problem of solid waste disposal. Materials that are intended for reuse are not part of this problem and are not covered by the statute. Petition for review granted.

■ DISSENT

(Mikva, J.) RCRA does not cover only solid waste that is discarded or thrown away. Unlike the majority, I believe the definition of "disposal" should be interpreted functionally. In other words, waste is "disposed of" if it poses a risk to health or the environment, the problem Congress intended to address in RCRA. Whether a manufacturer will reuse the material is irrelevant to the risks the material presents while it is being stored or transported.

Analysis:

In this case, the court attempts to define "solid waste," a very broad term. In its attempt, the court foregoes paying deference to the EPA's determination that even materials that will be reused are part of the waste disposal problem. Instead, the court uses a more conservative approach and looks at the language of the statute, rather than at the big picture. Indeed, the court's definition paves the way for additional environmental damage and creates a loophole for regulated industries to exploit. In a subsequent case, *American Mining Congress v. EPA (AMC II)*, the D.C. Circuit held that *AMC I* was limited only to materials destined for immediate reuse. But, who's to say how long a manufacturer may store a material before reusing it?

City of Chicago v. Environmental Defense Fund

(*City*) v. (*Private Environmental Group*)

511 U.S. 328 (1994)

UNDER RCRA, EPA MAY REGULATE HOUSEHOLD WASTE ASH

■ **INSTANT FACTS** A private environmental group sued an incineration facility claiming the facility was not managing its ash in accordance with the Resource Conservation and Recovery Act ("RCRA") [federal statute dealing with the disposal of solid and hazardous wastes].

■ **BLACK LETTER RULE** Under RCRA, the EPA may regulate ash generated by the incineration of household waste.

■ **PROCEDURAL BASIS**

Certification by U.S. Supreme Court of Seventh Circuit decision.

■ **FACTS**

Section 3001(i) of RCRA exempts from regulation facilities burning household waste. The Environmental Defense Fund ("EDF") (P) sued municipal incineration facilities (R) whose ash from burning household waste exceeded EPA toxicity tests. EDF (P) claimed that the facilities' (R) failure to manage their ash violated RCRA, as amended in 1984. The facilities (R) claimed that because household waste was exempt from regulation, so was the ash it generated. The district court found for the facilities (R). The Seventh Circuit reversed.

■ **ISSUE**

Under RCRA, does the EPA have the power to regulate the ash generated by a facility burning household waste?

■ **DECISION AND RATIONALE**

(Scalia, J.) Yes. RCRA's definition of "hazardous waste" excludes household waste and the disposal of ash generated from burning household waste. However, RCRA was amended in 1984. Section 3001(i) of the amended RCRA exempts facilities from regulation. However, it does not exempt the ash itself. Unlike the original RCRA, § 3001(i) does not specifically exempt the ash from regulation. In addition, in the statute, Congress expressly declares that its underlying policy is to treat, store, and dispose of waste to minimize health and environmental threats. Thus, toxic ash should not be permitted to be disposed of in ordinary landfills. Moreover, while RCRA may exempt a facility's management activities, it does not exempt the facility in its capacity as a generator of hazardous waste. Despite the facilities' (P) contention, our interpretation does not make the amended § 3001(i) an "empty gesture." The amendment restricts a previous exemption. In addition, our decision does not render § 3001(i) ineffective for promoting household and nonhazardous resource recovery by subjecting such facilities to enormous expense. RCRA's goals of encouraging resource recovery and protecting against contamination must sometimes conflict. Judgment affirmed.

■ **DISSENT**

(Stevens, J.) In the EPA's 1980 RCRA regulations, household waste and the residue remaining after incineration were not considered hazardous waste. The purpose of the 1984 amendments was to clarify that if a facility treats a mixture of household waste and nonhazardous waste, the facility is not deemed to be treating hazardous waste. Even though the statute refers only to the exemption of the facility that burns the waste, the title of the section, "Clarification of Household Waste Exclusion," makes clear that the waste is excluded. While the majority's decision will provide additional environmental protections, whether these environmental benefits justify the costs of the additional regulation is a question of policy that the EPA, not the courts, should resolve.

Analysis:

Wastes that the EPA lists as hazardous are regulated under subtitle C of RCRA. Wastes that are not listed are regulated under subtitle C if they have certain characteristics of hazardous waste, such as ignitability, corrosivity, reactivity, or toxicity. Household waste is not considered hazardous because it presumably consists of household garbage, such as food, papers, and containers. However, in tests leading up to this case, the ash generated by burning household waste flunked the EPA's toxicity tests. In this case, the Court takes a somewhat convoluted route to reach a pro-environment decision. Even the EPA, in a 1992 memorandum, came out the other way and determined that § 3001 exempts the ash from regulation.

United States v. Olin Corporation

(Federal government) v. *(Owner or Operator of Hazardous Waste Site)*
107 F.3d 1506 (11th Cir. 1997)

CERCLA IS CONSTITUTIONAL UNDER THE COMMERCE CLAUSE AND IT CAN BE APPLIED RETRO-
ACTIVELY

■ **INSTANT FACTS** The court asked the parties to address whether the CERCLA [federal statute addressing cleanup of hazardous substances] was constitutionally applicable to their consent decree under the Commerce Clause and whether CERCLA could be applied to activity that occurred prior to its enactment.

■ **BLACK LETTER RULE** Congress has the power to regulate the disposal of hazardous waste under the Commerce Clause, and CERCLA may be applied retroactively.

■ **PROCEDURAL BASIS**

Appeal of district court's denial of motion to enter consent decree and dismissal of government's complaint.

■ **FACTS**

Olin Corporation ("Olin") (R) and the federal government (P) entered into a consent decree in which Olin (R) agreed to pay for cleanup from disposal activity that occurred prior to the effective date of December 11, 1980 of the Comprehensive Environmental Response, Compensation and Liability Act of 1980 ("CERCLA") [federal statute addressing cleanup of hazardous substances]. When the parties presented the consent decree to the district court for approval, the court asked them to address the impact of two U.S. Supreme Court cases. In *United States v. Lopez*, the Court discussed the scope of the federal government's powers under the Commerce Clause and in *Landgraf v. USI Film Products*, the Court rendered a decision on the analytical framework for determining retroactivity. The district court held that Congress did not have the power to regulate the conduct at issue in this case under the Commerce Clause and that CERCLA did not impose liability for conduct predating its enactment.

■ **ISSUE**

Does Congress have the power to regulate hazardous waste disposal under the Commerce Clause, and does CERCLA apply retroactively to conduct predating its enactment?

■ **DECISION AND RATIONALE**

(Kravitch, J.) Yes on both issues. With respect to the Commerce Clause issue, here Congress is regulating an intrastate activity that substantially affects interstate commerce. Contrary to the district court's ruling, under the Commerce Clause, the regulated activity need not be economic. Under *Lopez*, a statute is valid under the Commerce Clause if it arises out of a commercial transaction which substantially affects interstate commerce. Here, waste disposal, whether on-site or off-site, substantially affects interstate commerce. It is connected to the recent growth of the chemical industry and the costs of handling its waste. Chemical contamination has also caused increased agricultural losses. Even on-site disposal that causes no off-site damage affects interstate commerce because it is part of

Congress's broader scheme to protect interstate commerce from pollution. With respect to the retroactivity issue, while *Landgraf* reaffirms the presumption against retroactivity, we must look at Congress's actual intent. Although the statute contains no explicit statement regarding retroactivity, Congress's intent is clear. By imposing liability against former owners and operators, Congress manifested its intent to reach conduct preceding CERCLA's enactment. In addition, its requirement that former owners and operators notify the EPA of the existence of any facility where hazardous substances are or have been stored addresses conduct that occurred before CERCLA's effective date. In addition, the fact that an essential purpose of CERCLA is to impose liability for cleanup on those responsible for the problems, and not on taxpayers in general, indicates Congress's intent that CERCLA apply retroactively to address contamination that occurred prior to its effective date. Finally, congresspersons commenting on the chief predecessor bill to CERCLA expressed the belief that it would be applied retroactively.

Analysis:

This decision makes applying CERCLA much easier. If the court had affirmed the district court's decision on the Commerce Clause issue, the EPA would have to limit CERCLA to cleanups that actually affect interstate commerce, such as off-site disposals that cause off-site damage. Not only would this have been more difficult to apply, but it would have greatly reduced CERCLA's power. To reach its decision on the Commerce Clause issue, the court determined that Congress's purpose in enacting CERCLA was very broad, i.e., protecting interstate commerce from pollution, as opposed to a more limited purpose, i.e., supporting Olin's (R) claim that its on-site disposal did not cause any off-site damage. Similarly, if the court had affirmed the district court's decision on the retroactivity issue, much time and litigation would have been spent determining when hazardous substances were actually released and whether they were released after or before CERCLA's effective date.

■ CASE VOCABULARY

CONSENT DECREE: A court order entered in accordance with the parties' agreement, punishable by the court's contempt power.

New York v. Shore Realty Corporation

(State) v. *(Land Owner)*
759 F.2d 1032 (2nd Cir. 1985)

CURRENT OWNERS OF LAND CONTAINING HAZARDOUS SUBSTANCES, EVEN IF NOT OWNER AT TIME OF DISPOSAL, ARE LIABLE UNDER CERCLA

■ **INSTANT FACTS** New York sued a landowner for cleanup of hazardous substances that were on the land before the landowner purchased it.

■ **BLACK LETTER RULE** Current owners of contaminated land are liable under CERCLA, even if they did not own the land at the time of the disposal or cause the presence or release of the waste.

■ **PROCEDURAL BASIS**

Not stated.

■ **FACTS**

New York (P) sued Shore Realty Corp. ("Shore") (D) and Donald LeoGrande (D), its officer and shareholder, to cleanup hazardous substances on land Shore owned. At the time of the purchase, LeoGrande (D) knew about the existence of the hazardous substances. Neither Shore (D) nor LeoGrande (D) generated or transported the hazardous waste to the property. Shore (D) argued that it was not liable under the Comprehensive Environmental Response, Compensation, and Liability Act of 1980 ("CERCLA") [federal statute addressing cleanup of hazardous substances] because CERCLA should apply only to owners at the time of the disposal of the hazardous substances or to parties who caused the release of the hazardous substances. Shore (D) also argued that it could assert the affirmative defense under § 9607(b). Under that affirmative defense, a defendant is not liable when a third party's act or omission caused the contamination and the defendant establishes that he exercised due care with respect to the waste and took precautions against the third party's foreseeable acts or omissions.

■ **ISSUE**

Are current owners of contaminated property liable under CERCLA if they did not own the property when it became contaminated?

■ **DECISION AND RATIONALE**

(Oakes, J.) Yes. Under 42 U.S.C. § 9607(a)(1), CERCLA applies to all current owners and operators of contaminated land. Unlike § 9607(a)(2), which applies to prior owners, § 9607(a)(1) does not limit liability to owners who owned or operated the facility at the time of the contamination. Section 9607(a)(1) does not require that the liable party cause the contamination. If it did, the affirmative defenses in § 9607(b) would be superfluous. In addition, if Shore's (D) argument were correct, CERCLA would be stripped of its power because owners of hazardous waste sites could sell their land to new owners who would not be liable under CERCLA, and then disappear. Finally, Shore (D) may not assert the affirmative defense under § 9607(b)(3). The "third party" described in the statute cannot be the prior owner because the acts or omissions referred to in the statute must be those occurring during Shore's (D) ownership of the property. If the "third party" is the tenant on the property after

Shore (D) owned it, the affirmative defense does not apply because Shore (D) did not take any precautions against any foreseeable acts or omissions by the tenants.

Analysis:

This case upholds CERCLA's very broad reach. It is fair to hold current owners of contaminated land liable because they can conduct environmental tests before they purchase the property to determine whether the property is contaminated and, if so, whether it makes economic sense to follow through with the purchase. Prior owners may be difficult, if not impossible, to find. In addition, the affirmative defense in § 9607(b)(3) which Shore (D) attempted to assert is rarely successful. It applies to situations where third parties sneak on the land in the middle of the night and dump hazardous waste without the owner's knowledge.

■ CASE VOCABULARY

FACILITY: Under CERCLA, a building, pipe, storage container, or area where a hazardous substance has been deposited, stored, disposed of, or placed, or otherwise come to be located.

United States v. Bestfoods

(Federal government) v. *(Not Stated)*
524 U.S. 51 (1998)

PARENT CORPORATION THAT EXERCISED CONTROL OVER POLLUTING FACILITY OWNED BY SUBSIDIARY IS DIRECTLY LIABLE AS AN OPERATOR UNDER CERCLA

■ **INSTANT FACTS** The federal government sued a parent corporation that actively participated in and exercised control over the operation of a polluting facility owned by a subsidiary.

■ **BLACK LETTER RULE** A parent corporation that actively participated in and exercised control over the operation of a polluting facility owned by a subsidiary is directly liable as an "operator" under CERCLA.

■ **PROCEDURAL BASIS**

Certification to U.S. Supreme Court of Sixth Circuit Court of Appeals decision for CERCLA cleanup costs.

■ **FACTS**

The federal government (P) sued CPC (D) for the costs of cleaning up industrial waste generated by a chemical plant. CPC (D) was the parent corporation of Ott II (D), the owner of the property. CPC (D) actively participated in and exercised control over the facility. The district court applied the "actual control" test to determine whether CPC (D) actually operated OTT II's (D) business and found CPC (D) liable under the Comprehensive Environmental Response, Compensation, and Liability Act of 1980 ("CERCLA") [federal statute addressing cleanup of hazardous substances]. The Sixth Circuit disagreed with the application of that test and held that a parent corporation can be liable under CERCLA only in joint ventures with a subsidiary.

■ **ISSUE**

Is a parent corporation that actively participated in and exercised control over the operation of a polluting facility owned by a subsidiary directly liable as an "operator" under CERCLA?

■ **DECISION AND RATIONALE**

(Souter, J.) Yes. CPC (D) may be liable under two different theories here: derivative liability as a parent corporation and direct liability as an operator of a polluting facility. CERCLA incorporates basic corporate law. Under corporate law, a parent corporation is not directly liable for its subsidiary's acts. However, the parent may be derivatively liable if the corporate veil could be pierced. Thus, if CPC (D) exercised control over OTT II (D), it would not be directly liable under CERCLA. However, here, CPC (D) may be directly liable as an "operator" of a polluting facility. Under CERCLA, an "operator" is someone who directs the workings of, manages, or conducts the affairs of a facility directly related to pollution. Contrary to the district court's analysis, we should look at the relationship between CPC (D) and the facility, not at the relationship between CPC (D) and OTT II (D). Thus, the evidence shows that CPC (D) operated the facility; whether CPC (D) operated OTT II (D) is not relevant. The fact that directors of CPC (D) also acted as directors of OTT II (D) is not relevant. What is relevant is whether

CPC's (D) officers merely oversaw OTT II's (D) operation of the facility, or whether CPC (D) officers directly operated the facility. Remanded for a determination of whether CPC (D) is an operator.

Analysis:

The distinction the Court makes here between a parent corporation's derivative liability and its direct liability as an operator may be difficult to apply. It may be difficult to determine whether the parent is overseeing the subsidiary's operation of a facility or directly operating it itself. This is particularly true when employees of the parent corporation are also employees of the subsidiary. If a parent corporation wants to continue overseeing a subsidiary's activities, but wishes to avoid direct operator liability, under the Court's ruling, the parent should have employees who do not also work for the subsidiary do the overseeing, stay as uninvolved as possible in the day-to-day operations of the facility, and keep very separate books and records.

United States v. Aceto Agricultural Chemicals Corp.

(Federal Government) v. *(Pesticide Manufacturer)*

872 F.2d 1373 (8th Cir. 1989)

PARTY WHO PROVIDES HAZARDOUS SUBSTANCE TO OPERATOR OF FACILITY MAY BE LIABLE AS A "GENERATOR" UNDER CERCLA

■ **INSTANT FACTS** The EPA sued pesticide manufacturers who provided pesticides to a pesticide formulation facility for cleanup costs.

■ **BLACK LETTER RULE** Under the Comprehensive Environmental Response, Compensation, and Liability Act of 1980 ("CERCLA") [federal statute addressing cleanup of hazardous substances], a company that provides a hazardous substance to a formulation facility and who has no control over the facility may be liable as a "generator."

■ **PROCEDURAL BASIS**

Interlocutory appeal of district court's denial of Fed. R. Civ. P. 12(b)(6) motion.

■ **FACTS**

Aidex Corporation ("Aidex") operated a pesticide formulation facility. Aceto Agricultural Chemicals Corp. ("Aceto") (D) hired Aidex to formulate its technical grade pesticides into commercial grade products. During the formulation process, Aceto (D) retained ownership of the pesticide. Contamination was an "inherent" part of the formulation process, the site was highly contaminated. Aidex was declared bankrupt. The EPA (P) and the State of Iowa (P) sued Aceto (D) and other pesticide manufacturers under CERCLA for the cleanup costs. In the district court, Aceto (D) moved to dismiss the complaint under Fed. R. Civ. Pro. 12(b)(6), arguing that it contracted with Aidex for the formulation of a product, not the disposal of a waste, and that Aidex controlled the formulation and the waste disposal. The district court denied the motion on the grounds that CERCLA should be interpreted very broadly and that common law principles of vicarious liability apply.

■ **ISSUE**

Is a party who provides a hazardous substance to the operator of a facility liable as a "generator" under CERCLA, even if it had no control over operations at the site?

■ **DECISION AND RATIONALE**

(Larson, J.) Yes. Under CERCLA, 42 U.S.C. § 9607(a), any person who "arranged for" the treatment or disposal of a hazardous substance at a facility may be liable as a "generator." This language must be interpreted very broadly in light of CERCLA's broad remedial statutory scheme. CERCLA's goal is to impose responsibility for cleanup costs on all responsible parties. This goal would be thwarted if we accepted Aceto's (D) characterization of its relationship with Aidex as merely one to formulate a useful product. While courts have refused to impose liability where a substance is sold to another party who then incorporates it into a product which is later disposed of, this is not the case here. Aceto (D) retained ownership of the hazardous substance and directed Aidex's formulation. In addition, common law rules regarding vicarious liability apply here. Affirmed.

Analysis:

When drafting CERCLA, Congress did not define the term "arranger" and legislative history does not provide any guidance. The court here defines it very broadly, in keeping with CERCLA's broad remedial purpose. Several points here may have tipped the scale against Aceto (D). First, Aceto (D) retained ownership of the pesticide while Aidex processed it. Aceto (D) also controlled the formulation process. In addition, it was well known in the pesticide industry that contamination was "inherent" in the formulation process. However, if in fact contamination is inherent, it is difficult to know what a responsible pesticide manufacturer could do to control the risks of contamination and escape CERCLA liability.

O'Neil v. Picillo

(Not stated) v. *(Pig Farmers)*
883 F.2d 176 (1st Cir. 1989)

UNDER CERCLA, DEFENDANTS ARE JOINTLY AND SEVERALLY LIABLE UNLESS THEY CAN PROVE THE DAMAGE IS DIVISIBLE

■ **INSTANT FACTS** Two generators of hazardous waste were found jointly and severally liable for the government's cleanup costs.

■ **BLACK LETTER RULE** Under the Comprehensive Environmental Response, Compensation, and Liability Act of 1980 ("CERCLA") [federal statute addressing cleanup of hazardous substances], defendants are jointly and severally liable unless they can prove the damage is divisible.

■ **PROCEDURAL BASIS**

Appeal of district court bench decision for environmental cleanup costs.

■ **FACTS**

The Picillos (D) allowed part of their pig farm to be used as a waste disposal site. Thousands of barrels of hazardous substances were dumped on the site, resulting in a fire and massive contamination. The EPA and the State of Rhode Island (P) paid to clean up the site. The State (P) sued 35 defendants to recover its cleanup costs. Thirty defendants entered into settlements. The district court found three of the remaining defendants jointly and severally liable under CERCLA for the State's past cleanup costs not covered by the settlement agreements and for all future costs. Two defendants held liable as generators, American Cyanamid (D) and Rohm and Haas (D) appealed, arguing that their contribution to the contamination was insubstantial and, therefore, it was unfair to hold them jointly and severally liable for all the State's (P) past expenses. They contended that the costs were divisible among the defendants. They also contended that they should not be liable for future costs because the State (P) had not demonstrated that such work would be necessary.

■ **ISSUE**

Under CERCLA, are defendants jointly and severally liable for cleanup costs?

■ **DECISION AND RATIONALE**

(Coffin, J.) Yes, unless the defendants can prove that the damage is divisible. CERCLA does not expressly provide for joint and several liability. However, the majority of courts hold that joint and several liability applies unless the defendant can demonstrate that the harm is divisible. Practically speaking, it is nearly impossible for defendants to show divisible environmental harm. This may result in defendants paying for more than their share of harm. When Congress enacted the Superfund Amendments and Reauthorization Act of 1986 ("SARA") [CERCLA reauthorization and amendments], it did not address joint and several liability, but it added provisions softening the blow. It added provisions directing the EPA to offer early settlements to parties with minimal responsibility and allowing defendants to sue other responsible parties for contribution. With respect to American Cyanamid's (D) and Rohm and Haas's (D) claim that the damages here were divisible, we agree that we should apportion the costs of removing the toxic barrels if those costs are divisible. We agree with the EPA that remedial action to clean contaminated groundwater may not be divisible. However, because American Cyanamid (D) and Rohm and Haas (D) have not met their burden that the damage was divisible, we decline to rule on the EPA's argument that we should look at the damage that was averted to determine whether it is divisible. The district court's statements quantifying the number of barrels of hazardous material contributed by American Cyanamid (D) and Rohm and Haas (D) are inconclusive. These are the number of barrels that could be positively attributed to each of them; however, most of the waste could not be identified. With respect to American Cyanamid's (D) and Rohm and Haas's (D) claim that they should not be held liable for future costs because the State (P) has not shown that such work will ever be needed, first, the State (P) may take only cost-efficient measures. American Cyanamid (D) and Rohm and Haas (D) will have an opportunity to challenge the State's (P) remedial efforts in the future. Further, the State (P) may conclude that future measures are not necessary. Affirmed.

Analysis:

Here, the court follows the precedent of *United States v. Chem-Dyne Corp.* [polluter has burden to prove divisible damage]. Meeting the burden to prove that damage from contamination is divisible if theoretically possible, but very unlikely in the real world where hazardous materials mix and interact in infinite ways. While defendants' ability to sue other responsible parties for contribution alleviates the hardship of joint and several liability, parties who settled with the EPA or a state may not be liable for contribution. It is unclear whether joint and several liability makes parties more or less likely to take precautions to prevent contamination. On the one hand, joint and several liability may make parties more likely to take precautions because they fear liability for all the likely damage that may occur at a site, not just the damage they caused. However, on the other hand, parties may take fewer precautions because they know that liability for cleanup will be spread among many other responsible parties.

Cooper Industries, Inc. v. Aviall Services, Inc.

(Property Contaminator) v. *(Co-contaminator Seeking Contribution)*

543 U.S. 157 (2004)

CERCLA LIABILITY IS A CONDITION PRECEDENT TO A CONTRIBUTION ACTION

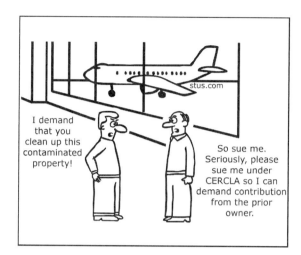

■ **INSTANT FACTS** Aviall (P) sued Cooper (D) for contribution to cleanup costs Aviall (P) incurred for properties that were previously owned and contaminated by Cooper (D), and a dispute arose as to whether Aviall (P) had to first be sued under CERCLA in order to sue Cooper (D) for contribution.

■ **BLACK LETTER RULE** CERCLA authorizes contribution for environmental cleanup costs from other responsible parties only when the party seeking contribution has been sued under CERCLA § 106 or 107(a).

■ **PROCEDURAL BASIS**

Supreme Court review of a finding in favor of the plaintiff, which reversed a district court ruling in the defendant's favor.

■ **FACTS**

Cooper Industries (D) owned and operated four contaminated aircraft engine maintenance sites in Texas until 1981, when it sold them to Aviall Services (P). Aviall (P) operated the sites for a number of years until it discovered that both Cooper (P) and Aviall (P) had contaminated the facilities when hazardous substances leaked into the ground and ground water through underground storage tanks and spills. Aviall (P) notified the appropriate Texas authority, which ordered Aviall (P) to clean up the site or face penalties. Aviall (P) cleaned up the properties under state supervision, then sold the properties to a third party, but Aviall (P) remained contractually obligated for the cleanup. Aviall (P) then sued Cooper (D) under the Comprehensive Environmental Response, Compensation and Liability Act (CERCLA), seeking contribution for clean-up costs. The trial court held that Aviall (P) was not entitled to contribution because Aviall (P) had not been sued under § 106 or 107(a) of the Act, as required by CERCLA § 113(f). The circuit court of appeals reversed, and Cooper (D) sought review in the Supreme Court.

■ **ISSUE**

May a private party who has not been sued under CERCLA obtain contribution thereunder for environmental cleanup costs from other responsible parties?

■ **DECISION AND RATIONALE**

(Thomas, J.) No. CERCLA authorizes contribution for environmental clean-up costs from other responsible parties under § 113(f) only when the party seeking contribution has been sued under CERCLA § 106 or 107(a). The clear language of the statute mandates this result. The right to seek contribution under § 113(f) simply does not apply to voluntary cleanups.

Under CERCLA, the federal government may clean up a contaminated area itself, or it may compel responsible parties to perform the cleanup. In either case, the government may recover its costs from

---

the responsible party. CERCLA includes an express provision for contribution, providing some relief to parties held responsible for cleanup costs: "[a]ny person may seek contribution from any other person who is liable or potentially liable ... during or following any civil action under [§ 106 or 107(a)] of this title." This "during or following" language cannot be read in any other way but to require a civil action under CERCLA as a condition precedent to a contribution action. Accordingly, persons who have not been sued under § 106 or 107 may not seek contribution under CERCLA § 113(f). Reversed.

Analysis:

The *Aviall* court declined to address the issue of whether contribution was available under § 107(a) as a "stand-alone" claim, directing the court below to consider that issue. Since the *Aviall decision*, many courts have wrestled with rights of action under CERCLA. Most courts continue to restrict contribution remedies to those authorized by § 113(f)(1). Others have looked to § 107(a) to provide an alternate form of relief, either through cost-recovery actions against other responsible parties, or through "an implied right of contribution." In *Consolidated Edison Company of New York, Inc. v. UGI Utilities, Inc.*, for instance, the Second Circuit Court of Appeals stated that CERCLA "section 107(a) permits a party that has not been sued or made to participate in an administrative proceeding, but that, if sued, would be held liable under section 107(a), to recover necessary response costs incurred voluntarily."

■ CASE VOCABULARY

CERCLA: Comprehensive Environmental Response, Compensation, and Liability Act of 1980. This statute holds responsible parties liable for the cost of cleaning up hazardous-waste sites.

CONDITION PRECEDENT: An act or event, other than a lapse of time, that must exist or occur before a duty to perform something promised arises. If the condition does not occur and is not excused, the promised performance need not be rendered. The most common condition contemplated by this phrase is the immediate or unconditional duty of performance by a promisor.

United States v. Vertac Chemical Corp.

(*Government*) v. (*Chemical Corporation*)

79 F.Supp.2d 1034 (E.D. Ark. 1999)

A GREATER ALLOCATION OF CLEAN-UP LIABILITY IS JUSTIFIED IN THE ABSENCE OF COOPERATION TO PREVENT HARM

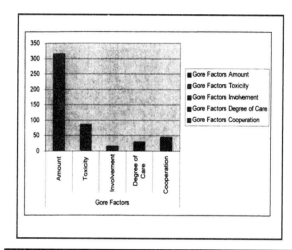

■ **INSTANT FACTS** Hercules (D) and Uniroyal (D) were the two remaining defendants in an action by the government to recover the Environmental Protection Agency's (EPA) costs in cleaning up a hazardous-waste site.

■ **BLACK LETTER RULE** In resolving contribution claims, the court may allocate response costs among liable parties using whatever equitable factors the court determines are appropriate.

■ **PROCEDURAL BASIS**

Trial-court hearing seeking an allocation of costs between Hercules (D) and Uniroyal (D) after they had been liable for the EPA costs in cleaning up a hazardous-waste site.

■ **FACTS**

For several years, Hercules (D) owned and operated a chemical plant site and maintained safety and environmental programs in its operation of the plant. The subsequent owner, Vertac Chemical Corp., did not operate the plant site with the same attention to safety and environmental concerns. Uniroyal (D) never owned or operated the plant but, during the time the plant was in operation, arranged for the disposal of hazardous wastes at the plant. The plant was subsequently shut down due to hazardous-waste contamination. The EPA cleaned up the site and sought reimbursement under CERCLA for the clean-up costs. The owner/operator of the plant, Vertac, and other defendant-arrangers reached settlements with the government. Hercules (D) and Uniroyal (D) were subsequently found liable for the balance of the costs incurred in cleaning up the plant site.

■ **ISSUE**

Should the allocation of hazardous-waste clean-up costs be determined exclusively under the volumetric approach?

■ **DECISION AND RATIONALE**

(Howard, J.) No. The volumetric approach is an appropriate starting point in allocating hazardous-waste clean-up costs because it takes into account the relative involvement of Hercules (D) and Uniroyal (D) at the site and their level of contribution in the contamination of the site. However, the resolution of CERCLA claims is governed under 42 U.S.C. § 9613, which provides that "the court may allocate response costs among liable parties using such equitable factors as the court determines are appropriate." The "Gore factors" are often used to arrive at what would be an equitable resolution. The sixth of these factors is the degree of cooperation by the parties with federal, state, or local officials to prevent any harm to the public health or the environment. Under the volumetric approach, Uniroyal's (D) liability for the clean-up costs should be 1.76% of the balance of the clean-up costs incurred by the EPA. However, the application of the sixth "Gore factor" warranted an upward departure for Uniroyal's (D) percentage of liability because, while Hercules (D) responded immediately to the EPA's orders under § 106 of CERCLA and undertook extensive remediation, Uniroyal (D) took the position that it had cause to disregard those same orders. Consequently, Uniroyal's (D) percentage of liability was properly increased to 2.6% and the percentage of liability assigned to Hercules (D) was decreased to 97.4 %.

Analysis:

The allocation of costs under CERCLA is a highly equitable procedure. Because of the broad discretion of the court under 42 U.S.C. § 9613 to consider whatever factors it considers equitable, the court is empowered to make a very subjective decision as to the allocation of liability, which can, as in this case, lead to bitter disputes as to financial responsibility for clean-up costs.

■ CASE VOCABULARY

CERCLA: Comprehensive Environmental Response, Compensation, and Liability Act of 1980. This statute holds responsible parties liable for the cost of cleaning up hazardous-waste sites.

DEPARTURE: A deviation or divergence from a standard rule, regulations, measurement, or course of conduct.

DOWNWARD DEPARTURE: In the federal sentencing guidelines, a court's imposition of a sentence more lenient than the standard guidelines propose, as when the court concludes that a criminal's history is less serious than it appears.

ENVIRONMENTAL PROTECTION AGENCY: A federal agency created in 1970 to coordinate governmental action to protect the environment.

PRP: Potential responsible party.

SUPERFUND: The program that funds and administers the cleanup of hazardous-waste sites through a trust fund (financed by taxes on petroleum and chemicals and a new tax on corporations) created to pay for cleanup pending reimbursement from the liable parties. The popular name for the act that established this program—the Comprehensive Environmental Response, Compensation, and Liability Act of 1980 (CERCLA).

UPWARD DEPARTURE: In the federal sentencing guidelines, a court's imposition of a sentence harsher than the standard guidelines propose, as when the court concludes that a criminal's history did not take into account additional offenses committed while the prisoner was out on bail.

Akzo Nobel Coatings, Inc. v. Aigner Corp.

(Shipper of Solvents for Reprocessing) v. *(Another Shipper of Solvents for Reprocessing)*

197 F.3d 302 (7th Cir. 1999)

A *PRO TANTO* APPROACH IS PROPER WHEN DETERMINING CONTRIBUTION COSTS FOR HAZARD-OUS–WASTE CLEAN–UP

■ **INSTANT FACTS** Akzo (P) and Aigner (D) each sought a contribution from the other for the expenses each of them incurred in performing hazardous-waste clean-up at a site to which they had shipped solvents for reprocessing,

■ **BLACK LETTER RULE** The Uniform Comparative Fault Act (UFCA) is not appropriate for determining the contribution costs between two parties if there are other financially sound PRPs.

■ **PROCEDURAL BASIS**

Appeal from a contribution action brought by Akzo (P) against a consortium of other PRPs, including Aigner (D), after a district court ordered Akzo (P) to reimburse Aigner (D) for a percentage of the hazardous-waste clean-up costs that Aigner (D) would incur.

■ **FACTS**

Akzo (P) and Aigner (D) each shipped solvents to a reprocessing site. The company that operated the reprocessing site mishandled the solvents that it received from its customers. When the company went out of business, its customers were forced to become responsible under CERCLA for the hazardous waste clean up. After hearing arguments on the equitable allocation formulas, a district court divided liability between Akzo (P) and Aigner (D) on the basis of the volume of hazardous waste disposed of on the site. The district court determined that, although Akzo (P) only generated nine percent by volume of all the solvents processed at the site, the Uniform Comparative Fault Act (UCFA) required that Akzo's (P) liability should be based on its percentage by volume of all the solvents that were shipped by Akzo (P) and Aigner (D). As a result, Akzo's (P) liability was determined to be thirteen percent and Akzo (P) appealed the decision.

■ **ISSUE**

Should contribution to hazardous-waste clean-up costs be determined under the Uniform Comparative Fault Act (UCFA)?

■ **DECISION AND RATIONALE**

(Easterbrook, J.) No. Applying the Uniform Comparative Fault Act (UCFA) would be appropriate if Akzo (P) and Aigner (D) were the only two financially sound parties. However, Aigner (D) has settled contribution claims with other firms that shipped solvents for reprocessing and it has outstanding claims against other PRPs. Applying the UCFA is, therefore, not the proper method for determining Akzo's (P) contribution costs because it ignores the contributions that have been, and will be, made to Aigner (D). The *pro tanto* approach (where anything collected by the parties in the contribution action is deducted from the total clean-up costs and each party's contribution cost is based on the its percentage of liability, multiplied by the remaining clean-up cost amounts) is proper because it more accurately determines contribution liability and enables a court to avoid a potentially complex and unproductive inquiry into the responsibility of missing parties. Accordingly, the district court judgment is vacated, to the extent that it quantifies Akzo's (P) contribution liability and the case is remanded for a determination of how much Aigner (D) has collected from third parties in settlement, and to then require Akzo (P) to pay a percentage of the clean-up costs net of those recoveries.

Analysis:

Since the contribution costs that a party is liable for under a *pro tanto* approach is net of any payments collected from PRPs, the potential exists for side agreements with PRPs in which lesser settlements are agreed upon, the effect of which is to increase the contribution cost as between the parties. The court addressed this ISSUE by noting that Akzo (P) could not bring its own contribution actions against parties with which it believed Aigner (D) had settled for too little. According to the court, the only ways to guard against inadequate collections from third parties are to either intervene in suits against them or challenge the settlements immediately after they are reached.

■ CASE VOCABULARY

CERCLA: Comprehensive Environmental Response, Compensation, and Liability Act of 1980. This statute holds responsible parties liable for the cost of cleaning up hazardous-waste sites.

ENVIRONMENTAL PROTECTION AGENCY: A federal agency created in 1970 to coordinate governmental action to protect the environment.

PRP: Potential responsible party.

PRO TANTO: To that extent; for so much; as far as it goes; the debt is *pro tanto* discharged.

SUPERFUND: The program that funds and administers the cleanup of hazardous-waste sites through a trust fund (financed by taxes on petroleum and chemicals and a new tax on corporations) created to pay for cleanup pending reimbursement from the liable parties. The popular name for the act that established this program—the Comprehensive Environmental Response, Compensation, and Liability Act of 1980 (CERCLA).

Philadelphia v. New Jersey

(City Seeking to Dump Waste) v. *(State)*
437 U.S. 617 (1978)

UNDER THE COMMERCE CLAUSE, STATE MAY NOT PROHIBIT IMPORTATION OF OUT-OF-STATE WASTE WITHIN ITS BORDERS

■ **INSTANT FACTS** Several out-of-state cities and New Jersey private landfill owners challenged under the Commerce Clause a New Jersey law prohibiting the importation of wastes collected outside of New Jersey.

■ **BLACK LETTER RULE** Under the Commerce Clause, a state may not prohibit the importation of hazardous wastes from outside the state.

■ **PROCEDURAL BASIS**

Certification to U.S. Supreme Court from New Jersey Supreme Court.

■ **FACTS**

In 1973, New Jersey enacted a law prohibiting the importation of most solid and liquid wastes collected outside of New Jersey. The wastes would only be allowed in New Jersey after the commissioner of the State Department of Environmental Protection determined that the importation would not endanger public health and promulgated regulations regarding the treatment and disposal of the waste. Several out-of-state cities, including Philadelphia (P), and private landfill owners in New Jersey challenged the law under the Commerce Clause. The New Jersey Supreme Court upheld the statute. The U.S. Supreme Court first remanded the case to determine whether the Resource Conservation and Recovery Act ("RCRA") [federal statute dealing with the disposal of solid and hazardous wastes] preempted the New Jersey law. The New Jersey court found no preemption. Philadelphia (P) appealed again to the U.S. Supreme Court.

■ **ISSUE**

Does a state law prohibiting the importation of wastes violate the Commerce Clause?

■ **DECISION AND RATIONALE**

(Stewart, J.) Yes. First, out-of-state wastes are "commerce" within the meaning of the Commerce Clause. Ordinarily, the Commerce Clause strictly bars state legislation that promotes "economic isolation" and protectionism because the legislation prevents interstate commerce. However, when the purpose of the legislation is to safeguard citizens' health and safety, we must be more flexible. New Jersey (D) claims that its purpose in passing the law was to protect its environment and slow down the depletion of its existing landfills. Philadelphia (P) claimed that the purpose of the law was to suppress competition and stabilize the cost of solid waste disposal for New Jersey residents. However, New Jersey's (D) actual purpose is not relevant; whatever its actual purpose, New Jersey (D) may not accomplish this purpose by discriminating against out-of-state parties, which this law clearly does. New Jersey's (D) argument that this law is similar to quarantine laws, barring the importation of diseased livestock and other noxious articles, that have been upheld under the Commerce Clause is without merit. Unlike in the quarantine cases, there is no claim here that just moving the waste through

New Jersey (D) endangers health. The harm here occurs after the waste is disposed of in landfill sites, and is no different from the harm caused by in-state waste. Reversed.

■ **DISSENT**

(Rehnquist, J.) Under the majority's decision, New Jersey (D) must either prohibit all landfill operations or it must accept waste from all over the United States. I dissent because I do not believe the Commerce Clause requires such a Hobson's choice. I believe the quarantine cases apply to the present one. I cannot distinguish between waste products and diseased meat.

Analysis:

As Justice Rehnquist states, it is hard to distinguish between the quarantine cases that were upheld under the Commerce Clause and the hazardous waste at issue here. If, as the Court states, burdens on interstate commerce may be unavoidable when state legislation is meant to safeguard the health and safety of its citizens, it is hard to imagine what kind of law may pass constitutional muster if the New Jersey law did not.

C & A Carbone, Inc. v. Town of Clarkstown

(Solid Waste Processor) v. *(Municipality)*

511 U.S. 383 (1994)

UNDER COMMERCE CLAUSE, TOWN MAY NOT REQUIRE THAT ALL WASTE WITHIN THE TOWN BE DEPOSITED AT A CERTAIN TRANSFER STATION

■ **INSTANT FACTS** A Clarkstown (D) ordinance requiring all waste within the town to be deposited at a certain transfer station was challenged under the Commerce Clause.

■ **BLACK LETTER RULE** Under the Commerce Clause, a town may not require that all waste within the town be transferred to a certain transfer station.

■ **PROCEDURAL BASIS**

Certification to U.S. Supreme Court.

■ **FACTS**

Through a consent decree with the State of New York, Clarkstown (D) agreed to build a solid waste transfer station. A private contractor agreed to build the station and operate it for five years, after which Clarkstown (D) would buy it for one dollar. Clarkstown (D) guaranteed the contractor a minimum revenue each year. To meet this guarantee, Clarkstown (D) passed an ordinance requiring all nonhazardous waste within the town to be deposited at the transfer station. C & A Carbone, Inc. ("Carbone") (P), a competing company, was permitted to continue receiving solid waste but was required to bring the waste to the transfer station and pay a fee. Carbone (P) challenged the ordinance under the Commerce Clause.

■ **ISSUE**

Under the Commerce Clause, may a town require that all waste within the town be transferred to a certain transfer station?

■ **DECISION AND RATIONALE**

(Kennedy, J.) No. The ordinance at issue regulates interstate commerce. It increases the cost for out-of-state companies to dispose of their solid waste in Clarkstown (D). It also bars out-of-state businesses from importing the processing service. Clarkstown (D) argues that the ordinance does not discriminate because all waste, local and out-of-town, must be brought to the transfer station. However, the article of commerce here is not the waste, but the right to process and dispose of it. The ordinance allows only a certain operator to process the waste. Thus, the ordinance discriminates against interstate commerce and squelches competition. Clarkstown (D) argues that this discrimination is permissible because it ensures the safe handling and treatment of solid waste. But Clarkstown (D) has other nondiscriminatory ways to accomplish this objective, such as enacting uniform safety regulations. Clarkstown (D) may not justify the ordinance as a way to steer solid waste away from unsafe out-of-town disposal sites. This would improperly extend the town's police power beyond its jurisdiction. Ultimately, the ordinance is a finance measure to ensure that the local facility will be profitable and that Clarkstown (D) will be able to buy it back cheaply. Clarkstown (D) could have used taxes or municipal bonds to achieve this end. Reversed.

■ CONCURRENCE

(O'Connor, J.) I agree that the ordinance is invalid under the Commerce Clause, but not because it discriminates against interstate commerce. It is invalid because it imposes an excessive burden on interstate commerce. The ordinance does not discriminate against out-of-town interests in favor of in-town interests. Rather, it gives a monopoly to one interest at the expense of all competitors. This burden on interstate commerce is excessive in relation to Clarkstown's (D) interest in ensuring a fixed supply of waste for its station.

■ DISSENT

(Souter, J.) The ordinance does not give a benefit to any private interest, but instead aids the government in satisfying a traditional governmental responsibility. Therefore, the ordinance is not the type of measure the Commerce Clause was meant to prevent.

Analysis:

Although the ordinance at issue here did not discriminate against local and non-local interests like those in *Philadelphia v. New Jersey* [state may not prohibit importation of out-of-state waste within its borders] and *Oregon Waste Systems, Inc. v. Department of Environmental Quality* [state may not recoup disposal costs by charging higher surcharge for disposal of out-of-state waste], the Court struck it down as discriminatory. The Court seems to have stretched to reach this conclusion. While it is true that out-of-town competitors were required to pay more to dispose of their solid waste in Clarkstown (D) and were barred from conducting processing services on Clarkstown (D) waste, the same was true for local Clarkstown (D) competitors. It is interesting to note that if Clarkstown (D) had hired a single company to collect the town's garbage and have that garbage incinerated by a single incinerator, this may not violate the Commerce Clause. In *USA Recycling v. Town of Babylon*, the Second Circuit held that a local government can take over the collection and disposal of garbage and finance it through taxes without violating the Commerce Clause. The court held that this arrangement did not force local businesses to buy services from anyone. In addition, a law banning all disposal of hazardous waste within its borders, regardless of the waste's point of origin, may not violate the Commerce Clause.

In the Matter of Louisiana Energy Services, L.P.

(Nuclear License Applicant)

Nuclear Regulatory Commission Atomic Safety and Licensing Board (1997)

SITE OF UNDESIRABLE LAND USE MAY NOT BE SELECTED BASED ON RACIAL CONSIDERATIONS

■ **INSTANT FACTS** The applicant sought to build a nuclear processing plant adjacent to two predominantly African-American communities.

■ **BLACK LETTER RULE** The site of a undesirable land use may not be selected based on racial considerations.

■ PROCEDURAL BASIS

Administrative law decision based on nuclear license application.

■ FACTS

Louisiana Energy Services, L.P. ("LEP") (A) sought a license to process nuclear material on a site adjacent to two impoverished, predominantly African-American communities. Citizens Against Nuclear Trash ("CANT") (I) intervened in the proceeding to object to the proposed site. CANT (I) claimed the site was selected based on racial discrimination. CANT (I) presented statistical evidence that as proposed sites were narrowed down, the level of poverty and African Americans in the proposed sites rose dramatically. CANT (I) claimed the criteria used to select the site were biased in that they looked at proximity to lakes and to institutions such as schools, hospitals, and nursing homes, which all tend to be in wealthier communities. LEP ("A") claimed that racial factors were not considered in the site selection. The Nuclear Regulatory Commission ("NRC") staff concluded that the site selection was not based on race. While the application was pending, in 1994, President Clinton issued Executive Order 12,898 ordering all federal agencies to ensure that their health and environmental programs do not discriminate based on race.

■ ISSUE

May the site of an undesirable land use be selected based on racial criteria?

■ DECISION AND RATIONALE

(Moore, Cole, Shon, J.) No. The NRC staff failed to comply with Executive Order 12,898 in that in conducted only a facial review of LEP's (A) application. Racial discrimination is rarely, if ever, admitted, and direct evidence of it is seldom found. We realize the NRC staff is more skilled at dealing with technical issues than with unearthing discrimination; nonetheless, they are still required to conduct a thorough investigation, hiring any outside experts that may be necessary. CANT's (I) evidence, particularly its statistical evidence, presents a reasonable inference that racial considerations played some role in the site selection process.

Analysis:

This "environmental justice" case requires the NRC to conduct a more thorough investigation into whether racial factors were considered in selecting the site for LEP's (A) plant. The Board seemed particularly impressed by the statistical evidence CANT (I) presented that as proposed sites were narrowed down, the level of poverty and African Americans in the proposed sites rose dramatically. Presumably, a license applicant could get around this by keeping a few non-minority communities in its short list of proposed sites, but ultimately select a minority community. The Board also noted that the selected site was far from any schools, hospitals, and nursing homes, indicating that it was in a poor, undesirable community. But, isn't it a good idea to keep a nuclear plant far from these institutions, so that any harm caused by the plant will be minimal? It seems difficult to balance the need for environmental justice with the need to protect as many people as possible.

CHAPTER FIVE

Air Pollution Control

Lead Industries Association v. EPA

Instant Facts: Lead manufacturers and users sued EPA for setting the NAAQS for lead at too low a level.

Black Letter Rule: (1) Section 109 of the Clean Air Act precludes EPA from considering costs when formulating NAAQSs. (2) Statutory command that EPA set primary standards at a level protecting public from "adverse health effects" is not limited to effects known to be clearly harmful.

Whitman v. American Trucking Associations

Instant Facts: As required by statute, the EPA Administrator (D) reviewed certain national ambient air quality standards (NAAQS) that had it had promulgated and revised the NAAQS for particular matter and ozone.

Black Letter Rule: The Administrator of the EPA cannot consider implementation costs in setting national ambient air quality standards under § 109(b) of the Clean Air Act (CAA).

Union Electric Company v. EPA

Instant Facts: Utility company challenged EPA approval of Missouri's state implementation plan because utility claimed the plan was economically and technologically impossible.

Black Letter Rule: Under Clean Air Act § 110, EPA may not consider economic impacts or technological feasibility when evaluating a state implementation plan.

Virginia v. EPA

Instant Facts: Virginia challenged EPA's SIP call, which effectively ordered Virginia to adopt California's ozone emissions standards.

Black Letter Rule: Clean Air Act § 110 does not permit EPA to condition approval of a state implementation plan on the state's adoption of EPA's preferred control measure.

Alaska Department of Environmental Conservation v. Environmental Protection Agency

Instant Facts: The Alaska Department of Environmental Conservation (P) approved the construction of a new generator at the Red Dog Mine, but the EPA (D) blocked the construction based on the failure to comply with the Clean Air Act.

Black Letter Rule: The EPA's (D) authority under the Clean Air Act includes not only the power to mandate the inclusion of emissions-control designations in pre-construction permits, but also the power to determine whether the designations are in accord with the provisions of the Act.

United States v. Duke Energy Corp.

Instant Facts: The EPA (P) sued Duke Energy Corp. (D) for making modifications to its energy plants without obtaining prior approval under the Clean Air Act, but the trial court granted summary judgment to Duke (D) and the EPA (P) appealed.

Black Letter Rule: When Congress mandates a specific definition of a statutory term, an agency cannot interpret the meaning of the term differently under its regulations.

New York v. EPA

Instant Facts: Various groups (P) challenged the definition of "modification" in a new EPA (D) regulation, which differed from earlier definitions of the term.

Black Letter Rule: When an issue of environmental concern requires a high degree of technical expertise, the court will defer to the informed discretion of the responsible federal agency, upholding the agency's decision unless it is unsupported by substantial evidence.

Michigan v. EPA

Instant Facts: Various states petitioned for review of an EPA (D) ruling that called for changes in SIPs deemed ''cost-effective'' by the EPA (D).

Black Letter Rule: The EPA (D) may consider both the health effects of pollution and the cost of abating it when determining whether a state's SIP fails to comply with the Clean Air Act.

Appalachian Power Co. v. EPA

Instant Facts: States affected by other states' emissions sought relief from the EPA (D), which issued a ruling requiring the polluting states to reduce their emissions, and the polluters petitioned for review.

Black Letter Rule: Although the Clean Air Act reserves to the states the right to determine how to achieve EPA air quality standards, that power is not diminished by allowing other states affected by a neighboring state's pollution to petition the EPA (D) for relief.

Alliance for Clean Coal v. Bayh

Instant Facts: An environmental group challenged an Indiana law conditioning approval of the state's plan to comply with national air quality standards on the continued use of Indiana-produced high-sulfur coal.

Black Letter Rule: State laws discouraging the use of coal produced in other states by conditioning approval of state implementation plans on the continued use of in-state coal and guaranteeing the recovery of costs for alternatives to out-of-state coal violate the Commerce Clause of the United States Constitution.

Engine Manufacturers Association v. South Coast Air Quality Management District

Instant Facts: The District (D) developed local rules for reducing vehicle emissions, and the Engine Manufacturers Association (P) contested them as violative of the Clean Air Act.

Black Letter Rule: No state or political subdivision thereof may set standards relating to the control of emissions from new motor vehicles or motor vehicle engines, or require certification, inspection, or other approval relating to the control of emissions as a condition precedent to the initial retail sale, titling, or registration of a motor vehicle, motor vehicle engine, or equipment.

Lead Industries Association v. EPA

(Industry Association) v. *(Regulatory Agency)*
647 F.2d 1130 (D.C. Cir. 1980)

UNDER THE CLEAN AIR ACT, EPA MAY NOT CONSIDER COSTS WHEN SETTING PRIMARY AIR QUALITY STANDARDS, AND MAY SET STANDARDS TO PROTECT AGAINST EFFECTS OF POLLUTION NOT *CLEARLY HARMFUL*

■ **INSTANT FACTS** Lead manufacturers and users sued EPA for setting the NAAQS for lead at too low a level.

■ **BLACK LETTER RULE** (1) Section 109 of the Clean Air Act precludes EPA from considering costs when formulating NAAQSs. (2) Statutory command that EPA set primary standards at a level protecting public from "adverse health effects" is not limited to effects known to be clearly harmful.

■ **PROCEDURAL BASIS**

Challenge, direct to Circuit Court, of an agency rulemaking.

■ **FACTS**

Clean Air Act [CAA] § 109 requires the EPA to establish primary National Ambient Air Quality Standards [NAAQSs] at a level "allowing an adequate margin of safety" to "protect the public health." NAAQSs [no one knows if the plural of this acronym is pronounced "Nacks" or "Nacksusses" by the way] are to be based on air quality criteria that reflect the latest scientific data "useful in indicating the kind and extent of all identifiable effects on public health or welfare which may be expected from the presence of [the] pollutant in the ambient air." CAA § 108(a)(2). Because of a successful citizen suit in 1976 (*NRDC v. Train*), EPA created a NAAQS for lead, setting the primary and secondary standard at 1.5 micrograms/square meter. Primary standards are to "allow an adequate margin of safety" to protect the public health. Secondary standards are supposed to protect the public from the pollutant's "known or anticipated adverse effects." The Lead Industries Association [LIA] and St. Joe Minerals Corporation [St. Joe] challenged the standard. St. Joe argued that the "adequate margin of safety" language should be read to require EPA to consider costs and feasibility of achieving its air quality standard for lead. St. Joe claimed that the new lead NAAQS would have a devastating effect on industry. LIA argued that Congress intended CAA to protect the public from only those effects of pollution which are "clearly harmful." EPA argued that LIA's interpretation was too limiting and would frustrate Congress' intent to create a precautionary statute.

■ **ISSUE**

(1) Does Clean Air Act § 109 require the EPA to consider costs and feasibility of proposed standards when EPA formulates NAAQSs? (2) Does the Clean Air Act require EPA to limit its air quality standards to protect the public from only those effects known to be "clearly harmful"?

■ **DECISION AND RATIONALE**

(J. Skelly Wright, Chief Judge) (1) No. Clean Air Act § 109 precludes EPA from considering costs and feasibility when formulating NAAQSs. The industry's argument that EPA must consider economic impacts of its air quality standards is "totally without merit." Industry cannot show any support for interpreting the Clean Air Act to require EPA to consider costs. In fact, the statute and its legislative history show that Congress intended EPA not to consider economic impacts when formulating NAAQSs. When Congress intended EPA to consider economic impacts and technological feasibility, as in § 111, it explicitly said so. Furthermore, the legislative history shows that Congress, fed up with a lack of progress on air quality, designed § 109 and others to be "technology-forcing" rules. (2) No. EPA does not need to limit its primary standards to a level preventing only "clearly harmful" effects of a pollutant. The statutory language requiring EPA standards to leave an "adequate margin of safety" refutes the idea that EPA is limited to standards which address only clearly harmful effects. Additionally, the legislative history of the Clean Air Act shows that Congress did not intend to limit EPA to setting standards only when the effects of pollution are clearly harmful. The statute is precautionary in nature. The Senate Report to EPA instructed the agency to set standards that guarantee "an absence of adverse effects." EPA need not wait for medical consensus on harms, because waiting allows only reaction not prevention. The rule is upheld.

Analysis:

The court in *Lead Industries* very strongly reinforces the "health-based" nature of air quality standards in the Clean Air Act. Health-based standards, the strictest type that Congress uses to direct agencies, are supposed to set standards that adequately protect the population regardless of cost or feasibility. Naturally, health-based standards are often opposed vigorously by industry. The *Lead Industries* court notes that Congress intended standards under CAA § 109 to be so strict that they would force industry to invent and implement new technologies in order to comply. A critic of the NAAQS, Professor Krier, has two strong criticisms of these regulations. First, setting unachievable standards results in delay and expense, often without producing the hoped for levels. Second, setting national standards for ambient air may be misguided when various environments and topographies can create such different impacts, on both the cost and benefit sides, in different locales. Thus, Krier argued for flexibility in standards. The court in *Lead Industries* was not swayed by any of industry's arguments, however, and interpreted the "adequate margin of safety" language to require very high standards on air quality.

■ CASE VOCABULARY

AMBIENT AIR: This is the free floating air in a region or over a city, for which EPA must set standards regardless of the sources of pollution contributing to that air; in the Clean Air Act, standards for ambient air are contrasted to those for stationary sources of pollution.

Whitman v. American Trucking Associations, Inc.

(*EPA Administrator*) v. (*Trucking Associations*)

531 U.S. 457, 121 S. Ct. 903, 149 L. Ed. 2d 1 (2001)

THE EPA IS NOT REQUIRED TO CONSIDER ECONOMIC COSTS IN SETTING AIR QUALITY STANDARDS

■ **INSTANT FACTS** As required by statute, the EPA Administrator (D) reviewed certain national ambient air quality standards (NAAQS) that had it had promulgated and revised the NAAQS for particular matter and ozone.

■ **BLACK LETTER RULE** The Administrator of the EPA cannot consider implementation costs in setting national ambient air quality standards under § 109(b) of the Clean Air Act (CAA).

■ **PROCEDURAL BASIS**

Certiorari to review, among other things, whether the Administrator (D) could consider the costs of implementation in setting NAAQS under § 109 (b)(1) of the CAA.

■ **FACTS**

The Administrator of the EPA (P) was required to review NAAQS it promulgated at five-year intervals and to make appropriate revisions. After reviewing the NAAQS for particular matter (PM) and ozone, the Administrator (D) determined that they needed to be revised. American Trucking Associations, Inc. (P), as well as other private companies and certain states, challenged the new standards. On certiorari, the Supreme Court considered, among other things, (1) whether the Administrator (D) could consider the costs of implementation in setting NAAQS under § 109(b)(1), and (2) whether the court of appeals had jurisdiction to review the EPA's interpretation of § 109(b)(1) in setting NAAQs, and if so, whether the EPA's interpretation was permissible.

■ **ISSUE**

May the EPA Administrator (D) consider the costs of implementation in setting air quality standards under the Clean Air Act?

■ **DECISION AND RATIONALE**

(Scalia, J.) No. The Administrator (D) may not consider the costs of implementation in setting NAAQS under § 109 (b)(1) of the CAA because the statute does not expressly condition the setting of NAAQS on this consideration. Several other provisions of the CAA expressly provide for the consideration of economic costs, but such consideration applies with regard to implementing the air quality standards, not establishing them. A showing of a textual commitment of authority to the EPA to consider costs in setting NAAQS would be sufficient to establish that the EPA was required to consider economic costs in setting NAAQS. However, to show a textual commitment, there must be clear showing that one is present. None of the phrases or terms in § 109(b)(1) is sufficient to show a textual commitment to considering economic costs in setting NAAQS. Finally, although a number of provisions in the CAA require attainment cost data to be generated, the purpose of these provisions is only to enable the Administrator (D) to assist states in carrying out their statutory role as implementers of the NAAQS.

Decision of the court of appeals affirmed with respect to its finding that the Administrator (D) was not required to consider the costs of implementation in setting NAAQS.

Analysis:

The Supreme Court in *Whitman* further determined that § 109(b)(1) did not lack any determinate criteria for establishing standards and, therefore, it provided an "intelligible principle" to guide the EPA's (P) exercise of authority in setting NAAQS. According to the Court, the requisite "intelligible principle" is only found lacking in statutes that either provide no guidance for the exercise of discretion or confer authority on the basis of no more precise standard than stimulating the economy by assuring fair competition. Section 109(b)(1) is neither of these types of statutes because its guiding language, "requisite to protect the public health," is appropriately within the scope of discretion of the EPA (P). The Court, therefore, reversed the court of appeals' decision and remanded for reinterpretation.

■ CASE VOCABULARY

BEST EVIDENCE: Evidence of the highest quality available, as measured by the nature of the case rather than the thing being offered as evidence. The term is usually applied to writings and recordings.

CERTIORARI: An extraordinary writ ISSUEd by an appellate court, at its discretion, directing a lower court to deliver the record in the case for review. The U.S. Supreme Court uses certiorari to review most of the cases that it decides to hear.

ENVIRONMENTAL PROTECTION AGENCY: A federal agency created in 1970 to coordinate governmental action to protect the environment.

PROMULGATE: To put (a law or decree) into force or effect.

Union Electric Company v. EPA

(Power Company) v. *(Regulatory Agency)*
427 U.S. 246 (1976)

EPA MAY NOT CONSIDER ECONOMIC IMPACTS OR TECHNOLOGICAL FEASIBILITY WHEN EVALUATING STATE IMPLEMENTATION PLANS (SIPs) UNDER CLEAN AIR ACT § 110

■ **INSTANT FACTS** Utility company challenged EPA approval of Missouri's state implementation plan because utility claimed the plan was economically and technologically impossible.

■ **BLACK LETTER RULE** Under Clear Air Act § 110, EPA may not consider economic impacts or technological feasibility when evaluating a state implementation plan.

■ **PROCEDURAL BASIS**

■ **FACTS**

Section 110 of the Clean Air Act [CAA] makes states responsible for creating state implementation plans [SIPs] detailing how the state will comply with EPA's national ambient air quality standards [NAAQSs]. The state must determine the levels of pollution for each statutorily defined air quality control region [AQCR] in the state. The state must then show EPA how the measures it proposes in its SIPs will meet the NAAQSs for each pollutant in each AQCR. When a NAAQS is promulgated, states must submit SIPs within three years. EPA must approve or reject the SIP within twelve months. According to CAA § 110(a)(2), if a SIP meets eight statutory criteria and the procedure creating the SIP involved reasonable notice and hearing, then EPA "shall approve" the SIP. Missouri found that SO_2 levels exceeded the NAAQS in the St. Louis region, and created a SIP that reduced SO_2. Union Electric Company [Union] challenged EPA's approval of the SIP because Union considered compliance economically impossible and technologically infeasible. EPA argued that the statute did not permit the agency to disapprove a SIP on grounds of technological or economic impossibility. CAA § 110(a)(2)(B) states that a SIP must contain provision for control devices "as may be necessary" to achieve the NAAQS. In an amicus brief, Appalachian Power Co.—another utility provider—argued that this provision directed EPA to reject SIPs more restrictive than the federal law demands.

■ **ISSUE**

Must EPA reject a state implementation plan [SIP] because that plan requires economically impossible or technologically infeasible measures?

■ **DECISION AND RATIONALE**

(Marshall, J.) No. The Clean Air Act does not require EPA to take economic or technological factors into consideration when evaluating SIPs. The statutory language and legislative history indicate that Congress intended the requirements to be very strict, "technology-forcing" measures. Congress intended to allow states flexibility in how they met these standards. CAA § 110(a)(2) explicitly outlines eight criteria that states must meet when creating their SIPs. If a SIP meets all the criteria, then EPA approval is mandatory. This, in turn, precludes EPA from evaluating other criteria. The "as may be necessary" language of CAA § 110(a)(2)(B) does not demand that EPA reject SIPs more stringent than the federal law demands. Rather, the "as may be necessary" clause simply directs states to include in their SIPs control measures adequate to meet the minimum demands of NAAQSs. If a state determines

that it wants stricter rules, EPA is not empowered to interfere by rejecting the SIP. The procedures through which the states create their SIPs are the proper places to consider the issues of economic and technological feasibility. The statute allows states to use whatever constellation of measures they see fit to meet the national standards. In addition, industries that face considerable difficulty in complying with SIPs may seek a variance to be passed on to EPA for approval. If an industry is denied an exemption or variance, the industry may seek redress in state court. Congress was aware that it was making strong rules when it passed CAA, and intentionally left to the states the power to determine how to comply with those rules. The EPA's approval of the Missouri SIP is upheld.

Analysis:

In this case, the Supreme Court recognized that the SIP provisions of the Clean Air Act are an interesting experiment in federalism. While the statute establishes strict national standards that every state must meet, it allows states to figure out how they will come into compliance. This means that a state can target a certain industry or pollution source, or the state may use many little measures combined to reach compliance levels. For example, some regions may benefit most from tighter pollution controls on automobiles, while others may need to get scrubbers on factory smokestacks. Conversely, a state might choose to relax standards on a given industry to make it attractive for that industry to stay put, and so find a way to comply with NAAQSs through other means.

■ CASE VOCABULARY

TECHNOLOGY-FORCING LEGISLATION: Legislative standards so strict that current technology cannot comply are called "technology-forcing" because industries must research and develop new methods or tools to be able to continue operating under the new standards.

Virginia v. EPA

(State) v. *(Federal Regulatory Agency)*

108 F.3d 1397 (D.C. Cir. 1997)

CLEAN AIR ACT DOES NOT AUTHORIZE EPA TO IMPOSE EPA'S CHOICE OF POLLUTION CONTROL MEASURES ON STATE IMPLEMENTATION PLANS

■ **INSTANT FACTS** Virginia challenged EPA's SIP call, which effectively ordered Virginia to adopt California's ozone emissions standards.

■ **BLACK LETTER RULE** Clean Air Act § 110 does not permit EPA to condition approval of a state implementation plan on the state's adoption of EPA's preferred control measure.

■ **PROCEDURAL BASIS**

Federal agency rulemaking challenged directly to United States Circuit Court.

■ **FACTS**

Due to changing conditions in emissions sources, Clean Air Act [CAA] § 110(k)(5) permits EPA to call on states to revise their SIPs from time to time. The "SIP call" is authorized when EPA finds that a SIP has become "substantially inadequate to attain or maintain" the national ambient air quality standards [NAAQS], to decrease interstate pollution, or if the SIP fails to comply with CAA in any other way. The 1990 Amendments to CAA created a Northeast Ozone Transport Commission [NOTC] to address the problem of automobile pollution in twelve northeastern states and D.C. (CAA § 184). The NOTC recommended the adoption of California's Low Emission Vehicle program, which contains strict ozone emission standards. Under both § 184 and the SIP call provision in § 110(k)(5), EPA issued an order for states in the region to the effect that their SIPs were "substantially inadequate" unless they adopted the California ozone rules or other, virtually infeasible provisions. Affected jurisdictions challenged the rule, in part on the grounds that EPA could not force any state to adopt EPA's choice of control measures.

■ **ISSUE**

Does CAA's SIP call provision give EPA authority to condition approve of a SIP on the adoption of EPA's choice of pollution control measures?

■ **DECISION AND RATIONALE**

(Randolph, Circuit Judge) No. The basic premise of CAA § 110 is that states are free to determine how they will come into compliance with the NAAQS established by EPA. Because the alternatives to adopting the California ozone standards are virtually impossible to implement, the states are being given no meaningful choice in the present case. No case has authorized EPA to hinge its approval of a SIP on the adoption of a particular control measure. If a state fails to produce an adequate SIP, it may be penalized; for example, restrictions may be placed on the state's use of federal highway funding. If the state deficiencies persist for 24 months, EPA must impose a federal implementation plan [FIP] for all areas of the state out of compliance. A 1975 Supreme Court decision, *Train v. Natural Resources Defense Council,* construed § 110 as saying that EPA must examine the ultimate effect of the state's choices of pollution limitations. If the ultimate effect is compliance, the Court continued, the State is free to pursue its course as it sees fit. In short, EPA determines the ends, while the states determine the means. This same division of responsibilities between the states and EPA continues under SIP calls. The creation of the NOTC by the 1990 Amendments did nothing to change the relationship of states and EPA. Section 184 grants a general authority to order adoption of specific NOTC recommendation, but this is trumped by other provisions of CAA that state that EPA may not force states to adopt automobile pollution standards other than national standards. The rule issuing SIP calls to the states and D.C. is vacated in its entirety.

Analysis:

This case is an excellent example of the challenges courts face when required to interpret specific provisions within large, comprehensive statutes. The problems for the court in *Virginia v. EPA* were compounded by the fact that some of the provisions in question come from amendments passed nearly twenty years after most of the overall Clean Air Act. The court had to determine whether the newer provisions were intended to fit within the original framework of the bill or were intended to supersede that framework. The court decided the former, that the amendment creating the NOTC was not intended to alter the general relationship of the federal agency (EPA) with the states.

■ CASE VOCABULARY

SIP CALL: This is the procedure, authorized by CAA § 110(k)(5), by which EPA can force a state to strengthen its state implementation plan (SIP) when EPA determines that the SIP is substantially inadequate to meet national standards.

Alaska Department of Environmental Conservation v. Environmental Protection Agency

(State Permitting Authority) v. *(Federal Regulatory Authority)*

540 U.S. 461 (2004)

THE EPA HAS AUTHORITY OVER STATE REGULATORY AGENCIES

The "Red Dog Mine" had two masters, Alaska and the EPA.
One master was okay with Red Dog's noxious gases,
but the other wasn't. I know just how that feels.

■ **INSTANT FACTS** The Alaska Department of Environmental Conservation (P) approved the construction of a new generator at the Red Dog Mine, but the EPA (D) blocked the construction based on the failure to comply with the Clean Air Act.

■ **BLACK LETTER RULE** The EPA's (D) authority under the Clean Air Act includes not only the power to mandate the inclusion of emissions-control designations in pre-construction permits, but also the power to determine whether the designations are in accord with the provisions of the Act.

■ **PROCEDURAL BASIS**

Supreme Court review of a judgment in favor of the EPA.

■ **FACTS**

The Red Dog Mine, located 100 miles north of the Arctic Circle, decided to expand its production of zinc concentrate, which required that the facility increase its onsite electrical generating capacity. The onsite construction of a new generator, in turn triggered the application of certain provisions of the Clean Air Act. The "PSD" (Prevention of Significant Deterioration) provisions of the Act required that the mine's new generating capacity be equipped with the "Best Available Control Technology" (BACT). The BACT requirements for a particular facility are determined on a case-by-case basis and limit emissions to the lowest level possible, based on what is feasible for the company. The Alaska Department of Environmental Conservation (ADEC) (P) was charged with determining the BACT requirements applicable to the Red Dog Mine. The ADEC (P) approved Red Dog's proposed plans for the new generator, but the EPA (D) objected to them, even after the ADEC (P) made amendments in response to the EPA's (D) initial objections. Acting under the authority of § 113(a)(5) of the Clean Air Act, the EPA (D) issued an order prohibiting construction of Red Dog's planned expansion.

■ **ISSUE**

Does the EPA's (D) authority under the Clean Air Act extend to determining whether a state permitting authority's BACT determination is reasonable?

■ **DECISION AND RATIONALE**

(Ginsburg, J.) Yes. The EPA's (D) authority under the Clean Air Act includes not only the power to mandate the inclusion of emissions-control designations in pre-construction permits, but also the power to determine whether the designations are in accord with the provisions of the Act.

The parties here agree that the EPA (D) may enforce the requirement that a PSD permit contain a BACT limitation, and it is undisputed that the EPA (D) may issue an order to stop a facility's construction if a permit contains no such BACT designation. But the ADEC (P) argues that the Clean Air Act assigns authority to the state permitting authority to determine the control technology qualifying as the "best available." In other words, the ADEC (P) argues, the EPA's (D) enforcement role is restricted to the requirement that a permit contain *any* BACT. It is true that Congress entrusted state agencies with the authority to make permitting decisions on a case-by-case basis. But Congress also entrusted the EPA (D) with the sweeping authority to enforce all Clean Air Act requirements, including those relating to BACT. There is no reason why Congress, having expressly endorsed such an expansive surveillance role for the EPA (D), would preclude the Agency from verifying substantive compliance with the BACT provisions and limit the EPA's (D) role as the ADEC (P) argues. We confirm the EPA's (D) authority to rule on the reasonableness of BACT decisions by state permitting authorities.

The question that remains is whether the ADEC's (P) decision here was reasonable. In this case, the ADEC (P) at one point found that certain technology was economically feasible for Red Dog, but then, just four months later, it found the same technology economically *un*feasible. There is no support in the record for such a switch in position. The ADEC's (P) BACT designation simply did not qualify as reasonable in light of the statutory guidelines. And it does not matter that changes would have also been implemented with regard to the existing generators, brining overall emissions levels to an acceptable standard. What matters is that the generator to be constructed did not meet the requirements of the Clean Air Act, and the EPA (D) therefore properly exercised its authority in stopping the construction. Affirmed.

Analysis:

The Clean Air Act requires that all facilities obtain a permit from ADEC (P) before beginning any new construction that will increase the facility's emission of pollutants. To receive a permit, the facility must show that it would use the Best Available Control Technology (BACT) to limit its emissions. Selective Catalytic Reduction (SCR) would have been most effective means of reducing the emissions from the mine's new generator in this case, but the ADEC (P) found that the cost of installing SCR would have had adverse economic impacts on the facility owner. Accordingly, the ADEC (P) issued a permit allowing the implementation of less-expensive technology in all of the mine's existing generators, as well as the proposed new generator, which would have resulted in an overall reduction in pollution comparable to leaving the old generators as they were and using SCR in just the new one. The EPA (D) reviewed the ADEC's (P) permit, however, and ordered ADEC (P) to withhold permission for the new construction, because SCR was the best available technology and the mine had not adequately demonstrated that SCR was economically unfeasible. The court of appeals affirmed the EPA's (D) orders, holding that the EPA (D) has the authority to review the ADEC's (P) findings and to make a final determination on whether BACT requirements are met.

■ CASE VOCABULARY

BEST AVAILABLE CONTROL TECHNOLOGY (BACT): An emissions limitation based on the maximum degree of control that can be achieved at a major stationary source. It is a case-by-case decision that considers energy, environmental, and economic impact. BACT can be add-on control equipment or modification of the production processes or methods.

PREVENTION OF SIGNIFICANT DETERIORATION (PSD): A Clean Air Act permitting program for new and modified major sources of air pollution such as power plants, manufacturing facilities, and other facilities that emit air pollution. PSD requirements apply to all pollutants that do not exceed the National Ambient Air Quality Standards (NAAQS) in an area.

United States v. Duke Energy Corp.

(Prosecuting Authority) v. *(Electric Company)*

411 F.3d 539 (4th Cir. 2005), *cert. granted*, May 15, 2006

ONLY INCREASES IN *PER-HOUR* EMISSIONS ARE "MODIFICATIONS" SUBJECT TO THE PREAPPROVAL REQUIREMENT

■ **INSTANT FACTS** The EPA (P) sued Duke Energy Corp. (D) for making modifications to its energy plants without obtaining prior approval under the Clean Air Act, but the trial court granted summary judgment to Duke (D) and the EPA (P) appealed.

■ **BLACK LETTER RULE** When Congress mandates a specific definition of a statutory term, an agency cannot interpret the meaning of the term differently under its regulations.

■ **PROCEDURAL BASIS**

On appeal from a grant of summary judgment in favor of Duke Energy (D).

■ **FACTS**

Duke Energy (D) operated eight electricity-generating plants in North and South Carolina. Between 1988 and 2000, Duke (D) engaged in a plant modernization program, implementing twenty-nine projects involving its coal-fired generating units. The projects were designed to allow the units to operate for more hours each day and to extend the life of the units. Duke did not obtain permits from the EPA (P) for these projects. The EPA (P) brought legal action, arguing that these projects constituted "major modifications" of Duke Energy's (D) furnaces, and thus required permits under the Clean Air Act's "PSD" provisions and the regulations promulgated thereunder. Duke (D) argued that no PSD requirements were triggered, because the modifications did not result in increased hourly emissions by the modified units. The EPA countered that, although per-hour emissions may not have increased, if the generating units were operating for a greater number of hours each day, the emissions increased overall, and thus a permit was required. The federal district court, applying the statutory definition of "modification," agreed with Duke Energy (D) and granted summary judgment in its favor. The EPA (P) appealed.

■ **ISSUE**

Did the EPA's (P) interpretation of "modification," which was contrary to the Clean Air Act's stated definition, apply in the PSD context, such that Duke Energy (D) was required to obtain prior approval for its plant modernization program?

■ **DECISION AND RATIONALE**

(Motz, J.) No. When Congress mandates a specific definition of a statutory term, an agency cannot interpret the meaning of the term differently under its regulations. When the interpretation of agency regulations is at issue, the court engages in a modified *Chevron* analysis. Under *Chevron U.S.A., Inc. v. Natural Resource Defense Council*, the court must determine whether Congress has directly spoken to the precise question at issue. The courts are the final authority on questions of statutory construction, and if the court determines that Congress has precisely addressed the issue at hand in the relevant statute, the statute resolves the issue. Only when there is silence with regard to a particular issue, or an ambiguity arises, is Congress deemed to have delegated authority to the appropriate agency to promulgate regulations on the issue.

Here, Congress has directly spoken to the precise question at issue. The question in this case is whether the statutory term "modification" can be interpreted differently with regard to PSD requirements than the EPA (P) interprets it in other contexts. But the Clean Air Act includes an explicit definition of "modification," and it explicitly requires that the definition be applied in the PSD context as well. Accordingly, there is only one conclusion here: the statute applies, and its definition of "modification" requires an increase in the *per-hour* level of emissions. It does not include the type of project performed by Duke Energy (D), in which the per-hour levels remained the same, although the total number of emission hours increased.

This result is consistent with the Supreme Court's decision in *Rowan Cos. v. United States*, 452 U.S. 247 (1981), in which the Court held that when Congress itself has provided substantially identical statutory definitions of a term in different statutes, the agency charged with enforcing the statutes cannot interpret the statutory definitions differently. Here, the EPA (P) argues that the New Source Performance Standards (NSPS) definitions should not be applied in the PSD context, because of the inherent differences between those contexts. We acknowledge that these differences exist, but when the same word or phrase is used in different parts of a statute, there is a presumption of uniform usage. This presumption relents under certain circumstances, but here the presumption is effectively irrebuttable because Congress, by creating identical definitions in both the NSPS and the PSD sections of the Clean Air Act, has affirmatively mandated that the terms be interpreted identically in the two programs. The different purposes of the NSPS and the PSD programs cannot override that mandate. The EPA (P) simply must interpret its regulations defining "modification" congruently. Under the applicable definitions, only a project that increases a plant's hourly rate of emissions constitutes a modification subject to preapproval, and thus the Duke (D) project was exempt. Affirmed.

Analysis:

After the Fourth Circuit decided this case, a nonprofit organization called Environmental Defense petitioned the United States Supreme Court for further review. Environmental Defense added a jurisdictional argument, claiming that the Fourth Circuit improperly heard the case. Under 42 U.S.C. § 7607(b), all appeals of air quality determinations that are national in scope must be filed in the United States Court of Appeals for the District of Columbia Circuit. The Supreme Court granted certiorari in 2006.

New York v. EPA

(State Government) v. *(Federal Regulatory Agency)*

413 F.3d 3 (D.C. Cir. 2005)

THE EPA'S INTERPRETATION OF "MODIFICATION" IS UPHELD BY THE COURT

■ **INSTANT FACTS** Various groups (P) challenged the definition of "modification" in a new EPA (D) regulation, which differed from earlier definitions of the term.

■ **BLACK LETTER RULE** When an issue of environmental concern requires a high degree of technical expertise, the court will defer to the informed discretion of the responsible federal agency, upholding the agency's decision unless it is unsupported by substantial evidence.

■ **PROCEDURAL BASIS**

Consideration of challenges to the EPA's new rule.

■ **FACTS**

Various governmental entities, energy firms, and industry associations challenged the EPA's (D) interpretations of "modification" for New Source Review (NSR) purposes, as used in a 2002 rule, arguing that it unlawfully differed from the definition applied for New Source Performance Standards (NSPS) purposes. The NSPS definition focused on the hourly rate of emissions, whereas the new NSR definition focused on net emissions measured in tons per year. The industry groups claimed that the term "modification," for purposes of mandating when pre-construction permits are required, must have the same meaning in both contexts. These petitioners argued, in essence, that the 2002 rule interpreted "modification" too broadly, whereas the government and environmental petitioners argued, by contrast, that the new rule's interpretation was too narrow.

■ **ISSUE**

Did the EPA's (D) 2002 interpretation of "modification" for NSR purposes impermissibly differ from the definition used in the NSPS context?

■ **DECISION AND RATIONALE**

(Per curiam.) No. When an issue of environmental concern requires a high degree of technical expertise, the court will defer to the informed discretion of the responsible federal agency, upholding the agency's decision unless it is unsupported by substantial evidence. Here, the industry group argues that because Congress used the same language in both the NSR and the NSPS statutory definitions of "modification," the same definitions must be applied in the regulatory context as well. They invoke the case of *Bragdon v. Abbott*, 524 U.S. 624 (1998), for the proposition that when Congress repeats a well-established term, it implies that Congress intended the term to be construed in accordance with preexisting regulatory interpretations. But that proposition does little good here, because the regulatory definitions differed even before the much earlier 1977 amendments. Given these long-standing definitional differences in the two contexts, it would take a pointed indication from Congress to support the idea that it expressly adopted one of them for NSR purposes. No such indication exists. Because the industry groups make no attack on the reasonableness of the EPA's (D) definition of "modification" for NSR purposes, no argument on that basis can be entertained. Accordingly, we defer to the EPA's

(D) reading of the term "modification" and deny the petitions of the government, environmental, and industry petitioners.

Analysis:

The holding in this case appears to contradict certain elements of the *Duke Energy* rationale. The *Duke Energy* court did acknowledge, however, that there may be cases involving ambiguities or rebuttable presumptions in which the courts will defer to agency interpretations. One thing different about this case than *Duke Energy* is the court in which it was brought. Under 42 U.S.C. § 7607(b), all appeals of air quality determinations that are national in scope must be filed in the United States Court of Appeals for the District of Columbia Circuit, as was the case here. The fact that *Duke Energy* was heard in the Fourth, rather than the D.C., Circuit was one ground for seeking review of that case in the Supreme Court.

Michigan v. EPA

(State Subject to EPA Regulations) v. *(Federal Regulatory Agency)*
213 F.3d 663 (D.C. Cir. 2000)

ONE STATE'S EMISSIONS CANNOT POLLUTE A DOWNWIND STATE'S AIR

I had a colossal storm brewing, but I stopped it because it was blowing pollutants across state lines and I fear the EPA.

stus.com

■ **INSTANT FACTS** Various states petitioned for review of an EPA (D) ruling that called for changes in SIPs deemed "cost-effective" by the EPA (D).

■ **BLACK LETTER RULE** The EPA (D) may consider both the health effects of pollution and the cost of abating it when determining whether a state's SIP fails to comply with the Clean Air Act.

■ **PROCEDURAL BASIS**

Review of an EPA (D) ruling applying to several jurisdictions.

■ **FACTS**

Prior to the 1990 amendments, § 110(a)(2)(D)(i)(I) of the Clean Air Act directed that the EPA insist on State Implementation Plans (SIP) that prevented sources within the state from emitting air pollution that would "prevent attainment or maintenance [of primary or secondary standards] by any other State." The amendment changed that language to require states to prohibit any source therein from "emitting any air pollutant in amounts which will ... contribute *significantly*" to nonattainment in a downwind state. The amendment did not spell out what constitutes "significant" as used therein. In 1998, the EPA (D) issued a final rule mandating that twenty-two states and the District of Columbia revise their SIPs to mitigate the interstate transport of ozone, based on the states' significant contribution to nonattainment in downwind states. The EPA's (D) rule required the reduction of nitrogen oxides (NOx, an ozone precursor) by the amount accomplishable through what the EPA (D) dubbed "highly cost-effective controls." Numerous petitions for review challenged various aspects of the EPA's (D) decision.

■ **ISSUE**

Did the EPA (D) properly consider both the health effects of the downwind pollution and the cost of abating it when determining that the twenty-three jurisdictions were "significant" contributors to other states' nonattainment?

■ **DECISION AND RATIONALE**

(Per curiam.) Yes. The EPA (D) may consider both the health effects of pollution and the cost of abating it when determining whether a state's SIP fails to comply with the Clean Air Act. The crux of the issue in these cases is the meaning of "significant" in the amended statute. The petitioners claim that § 110(a)(2)(D)(i)(I) of the Clean Air Act does not permit the EPA (D) to take into consideration the cost of reducing ozone. They argue that "significance" should be measured by the health effects of the emissions alone, no matter what the cost of reducing them. But the EPA (D) argues that health effects and cost factors must be considered together to determine what is a significant contribution to nonattainment by a downwind state. The EPA's (D) argument makes sense; there is no reason why the determination of "significance" must be based on one factor only, as the petitioners urge.

The petitioners also argue that the NOx budget program impermissibly intrudes on the states' right to create their own SIP in the first place. In reality, however, the EPA's (D) program reasonably establishes reduction levels and leaves the control-measure decision to the states. Unlike the rule invalidated in *Virginia v. EPA*, states implementing alternative control measures will not be penalized here. And since the challenged control measure does not mandate a specific, source-by-source emission limitation, the NOx budget plan does not run afoul of *Train v. NRDC*, which held that the states hold the power to determine which sources will be burdened by regulation and to what extent.

We do, however, vacate the EPA's (D) final rule with respect to those provisions that failed to provide adequate notice of a change in the definition of an electric generating unit and a change in the control level assumed for large stationary internal combustion engines. In all other respects, the petitions for review are denied.

Analysis:

In *Train v. NRDC*, 421 U.S. 60 (1975), relied on by the *Michigan* court, the United States Supreme Court considered a challenge to Georgia's procedures for revising source-specific emission limits adopted in an SIP. The *Train* Court held that the states have the authority under the CAA to initially propose specific emission limitations, and that that the EPA has only "a secondary role in the process of determining and enforcing the specific, source-by-source emission limitations." The *Train* decision and subsequent precedent make clear that § 110 left to the states the power to initially determine which sources would be burdened by regulation and to what extent. Thus, the court had to determine in this case whether the NOx budget program constituted an EPA-imposed control measure or emission limitation triggering the *Train* federalism bar—in other words, whether the program constituted an impermissible source-specific means rather than a permissible end goal. It concluded that it was a permissible end goal, and thus denied the petitions.

■ **CASE VOCABULARY**

FEDERALISM: The legal relationship and distribution of power between the national and regional governments within a federal system of government.

Appalachian Power Co. v. EPA

(Polluter) v. *(Federal Regulatory Agency)*

249 F.3d 1032 (D.C. Cir. 2001)

POLLUTERS MAY "TRADE" EMISSIONS ALLOWANCES WITH OTHER FACILITIES IN THE STATE

■ **INSTANT FACTS** States affected by other states' emissions sought relief from the EPA (D), which issued a ruling requiring the polluting states to reduce their emissions, and the polluters petitioned for review.

■ **BLACK LETTER RULE** Although the Clean Air Act reserves to the states the right to determine how to achieve EPA air quality standards, that power is not diminished by allowing other states affected by a neighboring state's pollution to petition the EPA (D) for relief.

■ **PROCEDURAL BASIS**

Review of an EPA (D) ruling applying to several jurisdictions.

■ **FACTS**

Several northeastern states alleged that nitrogen oxide emitted from neighboring states was harming their local air quality. In response, the EPA (D) promulgated a rule requiring many NOx-emitting facilities in the polluting states to conform to emission limits set by the EPA (D) and to participate in an emissions trading program. Numerous petitioners challenged the rule as arbitrary and capricious, technically deficient, and contrary to the states' autonomy to determine how to achieve mandated air quality standards.

■ **ISSUE**

Did the EPA's (D) rule requiring the subject states to reduce their emissions, either singly or as part of a trading program, violate the Clean Air Act?

■ **DECISION AND RATIONALE**

(Per curiam.) No. Although the Clean Air Act reserves to the states the right to determine how to achieve EPA air quality standards, that power is not impermissibly diminished by allowing other states affected by a neighboring state's pollution to petition the EPA (D) for relief. Section 126 of the Clean Air Act provides a mechanism by which downwind states may petition the EPA to directly regulate upwind sources of pollution if they contribute significantly to nonattainment of air quality standards by the affected states. The EPA (D) in this case found that such significant contribution existed, based on the NOx emissions and the relative cost of controlling them. The challenged rule promulgated by the EPA (D) allows facilities to "trade" emissions, meaning that if they may exceed their allotment, they may "buy" an additional allowance from other facilities; if they cannot buy any, they must reduce their emissions or shut down.

The EPA (D) maintains that its approach is consistent with the Clean Air Act and principles of federalism. The petitioners disagree, arguing that the EPA's (D) ruling shows inadequate deference to the states' right, in the first instance, to determine how to achieve the level of air quality mandated by the EPA. Although this right indisputably exists, states are not free to develop their plans free of *any* extrinsic legal constraints. Indeed, SIP development, like any other environmental planning process, commonly involves decision-making subject to various legal constraints. That § 126 of the Clean Air Act allows affected states to question the propriety of other states' SIPs does not affect a state's discretion under § 110. The petitions are, therefore, for the most part, denied.

Analysis:

In upholding the EPA's rule in this case, the court found that (1) the EPA (D) has authority under § 126 of the Clean Air Act to directly limit NOx emissions from upwind polluting power plants and other stationary sources, (2) this authority is in addition to the EPA's (D) authority under other provisions of the Clean Air Act to require states to limit such emissions, and (3) the EPA's finding that power plants and other stationary sources in the polluting states were significantly contributing to ozone attainment problems in certain downwind states was reasonable. The court did remand the rule to the EPA (D) to address a specific issue regarding the actual level of emissions permitted thereunder.

Alliance for Clean Coal v. Bayh

(*Environmental Group*) v. (*Indiana State Official*)

72 F.3d 556 (7th Cir. 1995)

INDIANA LAW DISCOURAGING THE USE OF LOW-SULFUR COAL PRODUCED OUT OF STATE VIOLATED THE COMMERCE CLAUSE OF THE UNITED STATES CONSTITUTION

■ **INSTANT FACTS** An environmental group challenged an Indiana law conditioning approval of the state's plan to comply with national air quality standards on the continued use of Indiana-produced high-sulfur coal.

■ **BLACK LETTER RULE** State laws discouraging the use of coal produced in other states by conditioning approval of state implementation plans on the continued use of in-state coal and guaranteeing the recovery of costs for alternatives to out-of-state coal violate the Commerce Clause of the United States Constitution.

■ **PROCEDURAL BASIS**

Appeal to United States Circuit Court from a District Court decision granting summary judgment that an Indiana law violated the United States Constitution.

■ **FACTS**

Coal-burning electric plants are a principal source of sulfur dioxide [SO2] pollution. The 1970 Clean Air Act [CAA] provided that newly built coal-burning electric plants could comply with emission requirements by either using low-sulfur coal or using scrubbers to reduce SO2. The 1990 CAA Amendments required plants to achieve even lower SO2 emission levels by the year 2000. The 1990 Amendments also provided for an "allowance" system by which plants could trade or sell pollution credits if they over-complied with emission standards. In response to the federal legislation, Indiana—a high-sulfur coal producing state—passed the Environmental Compliance Plans Act [ECPA] in 1991. ECPA benefited electric plants that submitted compliance plans that either continued or increased their use of Indiana coal. If the plan called for a lower use of Indiana coal, the plant had to justify the reduction through economic considerations including analysis of the impact the plan would have on coal-producing regions of Indiana. Alliance for Clean Coal (P) challenged the ECPA in United States District Court, seeking summary judgment that ECPA violated the Commerce Clause of the United States by discriminating against coal produced in other states. Indiana (D) argued that a competitive Midwest high-sulfur coal market was crucial for Indiana utilities to provide low-cost electrical service. The district court held the Indiana ECPA violated the United States Constitution by unfairly discriminating against interstate commerce.

■ **ISSUE**

Does an Indiana statute favoring the use of Indiana produced high-sulfur coal violate the Commerce Clause of the United States Constitution by discriminating against products solely based on their state of origin?

■ **DECISION AND RATIONALE**

(Cummings, Circuit Judge) Yes. The intent of the Indiana ECPA is to discriminate against coal produced in the western states. The fact that the law does not ban western coal, but rather encourages use of Indiana high-sulfur coal, does not save the law from its discriminatory intent. ECPA's effects on interstate commerce are not merely incidental. When a state law discriminates, the state has the burden of proving that the law is necessary to achieve a compelling state interest. Ensuring the competitiveness of the high-sulfur coal market does not rise to the level that justifies discriminating against interstate commerce. This case is controlled by *Alliance for Clean Coal v. Miller,* a 1995 case decided by the Seventh Circuit that invalidated the Illinois Coal Act. Like the Indiana ECPA, the Illinois law tried to discourage the use of western low-sulfur coal by assuring utilities that they will recoup the costs of installing scrubbers. The Illinois law was also similar to the Indiana ECPA in that it had provisions conditioning approval of the state's compliance plans on assessments of impact to the local coal and utility industries. The District Court decision holding the Indiana ECPA unconstitutional is affirmed.

Analysis:

This case provides another interesting example of how constitutional challenges occasionally enter into the Clean Air Act. The relevant portion of the case turns on questions outside the scope of what effect, if any, Indiana's law would have on SO2 emissions. Economic impact was a much more central issue in the case. It is noteworthy that the miners' union intervened on the side of the state seeking to uphold the state law. The state law was designed, at least in part, to keep the mining industry strong in Indiana. Utility company PSI Energy, Inc., on the other hand, intervened on the plaintiff side, supporting the Circuit Court's affirmance of the District Court's summary judgment that ECPA was unconstitutional. Perhaps the utility favored having the option to use coal from different sources without having to justify their choice as required by ECPA. Both of these intervenors highlight the sizable impact that environmental legislation can have on the economic prospects of companies and individuals up and down the energy production and consumption chains.

■ CASE VOCABULARY

EMISSIONS ALLOWANCE SYSTEM: This is a market-based approach to limiting pollution emissions that permits each source to emit a certain amount and then permits that source to sell its excess, unused allowance if it emits below its requirements. In theory, the system keeps a certain overall level of emissions in place while allowing those polluters for whom compliance is too expensive to purchase excess allowances from polluters who are able to over-comply.

Engine Manufacturers Association v. South Coast Air Quality Management District

(Trade Group) v. *(Emissions Standards Promulgator)*

541 U.S. 246 (2004)

"STANDARDS" INCLUDE MORE THAN REGULATIONS

This stinky truck is brought to you by the Clean Air Act.

stus.com

■ **INSTANT FACTS** The District (D) developed local rules for reducing vehicle emissions, and the Engine Manufacturers Association (P) contested them as violative of the Clean Air Act.

■ **BLACK LETTER RULE** No state or political subdivision thereof may set standards relating to the control of emissions from new motor vehicles or motor vehicle engines, or require certification, inspection, or other approval relating to the control of emissions as a condition precedent to the initial retail sale, titling, or registration of a motor vehicle, motor vehicle engine, or equipment.

■ **PROCEDURAL BASIS**

Supreme Court review of a judgment in favor of the defendant.

■ **FACTS**

South Coast Air Quality Management District (D) was responsible for developing and implementing an air quality management plan applicable to various motorized vehicles used in the area. The District (D) adopted six "fleet rules" designed to reduce the vehicles' emissions levels and achieve federal and state air quality standards. The Engine Manufacturers Association (P) sued the District (D), arguing that its fleet rules violated the Clean Air Act's proscription on the adoption of any state or local standard relating to the control of emissions from new motor vehicles or new motor vehicle engines. The district court upheld the rules, reasoning that when a state regulation does not compel manufacturers to meet a new emissions limit, but rather affects the *purchase* of vehicles, as the fleet rules did in this case, the regulation is not a state or local "standard" violative of the Act. The Ninth Circuit affirmed, and the District (D) sought further review in the Supreme Court.

■ **ISSUE**

Did the local fleet rules setting forth specifications as to what types of engines could be purchased violate the Clean Air Act?

■ **DECISION AND RATIONALE**

(Scalia, J.) Yes. Section 209(a) of the Clean Air Act provides that no state or political subdivision thereof may set standards relating to the control of emissions from new motor vehicles or motor vehicle engines, or require certification, inspection, or other approval relating to the control of emissions as a condition precedent to the initial retail sale, titling, or registration of a motor vehicle, motor vehicle engine, or equipment. The district court's determination that the fleet rules did not violate this statutory provision hinged on its interpretation of the word "standard" to include only regulations that compel manufacturers to meet specified emissions limits. Based on this interpretation, the court drew a line between purchase restrictions, which are allowed, and sale restrictions, which are preempted by the

Clean Air Act. But these conclusions find no support in the text or structure of the Act itself. Both the dictionary definition of "standard" and the use of that term throughout the Clean Air Act indicate that the term is more accurately interpreted to encompass "that which 'is established by authority, custom, or general consent, as a model or example; criterion; test.' " Thus, the fleet rules could be deemed standards.

In addition, treating sales restrictions and purchase restrictions differently makes no sense. The manufacturer's right to sell certain vehicles or engines is meaningless in the absence of the consumer's right to buy them. A command to consumers that they may buy only products that meet certain emissions standards is as much a "standard" as a command that only such products be manufactured. Accordingly, at least certain parts of the fleet rules are preempted by the Clean Air Act. This does not mean, however, that they are preempted in toto. Accordingly, the judgment is vacated and the case is remanded for further proceedings.

Analysis:

The South Coast Air Quality Management District is responsible for reducing air pollution in the Los Angeles area, which has one of the most significant air-quality problems in the United States. To accomplish its goals, the District's rules required owners of different types of fleet vehicles, such as street sweepers, garbage collection trucks, buses, and taxis, to purchase or lease only certain types of alternative-fuel vehicles that met stringent emissions specifications established by the California Air Resources Board, if such vehicles were commercially available. Despite the urgent need for local measures of this nature, the Court, in an eight-to-one opinion, held that these local standards were preempted by the federal Clean Air Act, although it did leave the door open for the adoption on remand of some of the District's proposals.

CHAPTER SIX

Water Pollution Control

United States v. Riverside Bayview Homes, Inc.

Instant Facts: The government sought to enjoin a housing developer from dumping landfill on property that the government believed was a wetland protected under the Clean Water Act.

Black Letter Rule: Wetlands adjacent to other protected bodies of water are "waters of the United States" under the Clean Water Act.

Solid Waste Agency of Northern Cook County v. U.S. Army

Instant Facts: The Solid Waste Agency selected an abandoned sand and gravel pit, with excavation trenches that had evolved into ponds, as a solid waste disposal site, but was denied a permit by the Army Corps of Engineers.

Black Letter Rule: The authority of the U.S. Army Corps of Engineers to issue permits, under § 404(a) of the Clean Water Act (CWA) does not extend to nonnavigable wetlands, unless they are adjacent to open waters.

Rapanos v. United States

Instant Facts: The plaintiffs discharged fill material into wetlands properties they owned in order to build a shopping mall and condominiums, and the government brought legal action against them because they did not obtain a permit before beginning development.

Black Letter Rule: The phrase "the waters of the United States," as used in the Clean Water Act, includes only those relatively permanent or continuously flowing bodies of water forming geographic features such as streams, oceans, rivers, and lakes, and does not include channels through which water intermittently flows or channels that provide periodic drainage for rainfall.

National Mining Association v. Army Corps of Engineers

Instant Facts: Various trade associations challenged the "Tulloch Rule" which expanded the definition of "discharge" to include any redeposit of dredged material within the waters of the United States, including any incidental fallback.

Black Letter Rule: Incidental fallback is not subject to the dredge and fill permit requirements of the Clean Water Act.

South Florida Water Management District v. Miccosukee Tribe of Indians

Instant Facts: The Indian Tribe (P) brought a citizen suit against the Water Management District (D) for failure to obtain a National Pollutant Discharge Elimination System (NPDES) permit for its pumping facility.

Black Letter Rule: The Clean Water Act requires a permit before a pollutant may be discharged into navigable waters.

NRDC v. Costle

Instant Facts: The NRDC (P) challenged as unlawful EPA (D) exemptions that excluded certain categories of point source polluters from the permit requirements of the Clean Water Act.

Black Letter Rule: The EPA (D) may not exclude any point source polluter from the Clean Water Act's permit requirements.

United States v. Plaza Health Laboratories, Inc.

Instant Facts: Villegas (D) disposed of numerous vials of human blood generated from his blood-testing laboratory business, Plaza Health (D), into the Hudson River. Upon discovery, Villegas (D) and Plaza Health (D) were indicted and convicted for violating the Clean Water Act.

Black Letter Rule: "Point source" as defined in the Clean Water Act does not include individuals.

Chemical Manufacturers Association v. NRDC

Instant Facts: An EPA (D) regulation allowed variances in effluent limitations to toxic dischargers for factors "fundamentally different" from those initially considered by the EPA (D) in promulgating the requirements.

Black Letter Rule: The Clean Water Act does not prohibit variances in effluent limitations for toxic dischargers.

Arkansas v. Oklahoma

Instant Facts: Oklahoma (P) challenged a permit granted by the EPA that authorized a plant in Arkansas (D) to discharge pollutants into a stream that emptied into the Illinois River in Oklahoma (P).

Black Letter Rule: The EPA may require an upstream discharger to comply with the water quality standards of downstream states.

PUD No. 1 of Jefferson County v. Washington Department of Ecology

Instant Facts: A proposed hydroelectric dam project planned to divert river water away from certain fisheries. In its water quality certification required by the Clean Water Act (CWA), the State imposed conditions on the project, including a minimum stream-flow requirement.

Black Letter Rule: States may condition certification issued pursuant to § 401 of the CWA upon any limitation necessary to ensure compliance with state water quality standards.

Pronsolino v. Nastri

Instant Facts: The Environmental Protection Agency (EPA) (D) required California to identify a certain river as a water body with insufficient pollution controls and to set "total maximum daily loads" (TMDLs) for pollution entering the river.

Black Letter Rule: The Clear Water Act (CWA) is best read to include waters impaired only by non-point sources of pollution in the § 303(d)(1) listing and TMDL requirements.

United States v. Riverside Bayview Homes, Inc.

(Army Corps of Engineers) v. *(Housing Developer)*

474 U.S. 121 (1985)

■ **INSTANT FACTS** The government sought to enjoin a housing developer from dumping landfill on property that the government believed was a wetland protected under the Clean Water Act.

■ **BLACK LETTER RULE** Wetlands adjacent to other protected bodies of water are "waters of the United States" under the Clean Water Act.

■ **PROCEDURAL BASIS**

Appeal to the United States Supreme Court from a denial of an injunction in action to prevent dumping of fill materials onto wetlands.

■ **FACTS**

Riverside Bayview Homes, Inc. (D), a housing developer, owned land adjacent to a lake. In preparation for construction of a housing development, Riverside (D) began to place fill materials on the property. Under §§ 301 and 502 of the Clean Water Act (CWA), any discharge of dredged or fill materials into "navigable waters" (defined as "waters of the United States") is prohibited unless authorized by permit by The Army Corps of Engineers (P) pursuant to § 404 of the CWA. In 1975, the Corps (P) promulgated regulations construing the CWA to cover all freshwater wetlands adjacent to other covered waters. The Corps (P), believing that Riverside's (D) land was an "adjacent wetland" under the 1975 regulations, sought to enjoin Riverside (D) from proceeding without a permit. The District Court held that the land was a wetland and granted the injunction. The Court of Appeals remanded the case for consideration in light of a subsequent 1977 regulation that removed the reference to periodic inundation and defined wetlands as those areas sufficient to support vegetation adapted to saturated soil conditions. On remand, the District Court again held the land was a wetland subject to the Corps (P) permit authority. Riverside (D) again appealed. The Court of Appeals reversed, holding that the 1977 regulations excluded land such as in the present case because it was not subject to frequent flooding from the adjacent navigable waters. The United States Supreme Court granted certiorari to the Corps (P) to determine the proper interpretation of the Corps' (P) regulations.

■ **ISSUE**

Are wetlands adjacent to other protected bodies of water "waters of the United States" under the Clean Water Act, even if the adjacent bodies of water do not regularly flood the wetlands?

■ **DECISION AND RATIONALE**

(White, J.) Yes. Wetlands adjacent to other protected bodies of water are "waters" under the Clean Water Act, even if the adjacent bodies of water do not regularly flood the wetlands. The Corps' (P) construction of the statute is entitled to deference if it is reasonable and not in conflict with the expressed intent of Congress. Congress intended to broadly define the waters covered by the CWA due to its concern for protection of water quality and aquatic ecosystems, and the Corps (P) has determined that adjacent wetlands play a key role in protecting and enhancing water quality. Thus, it is reasonable for the Corps (P) to interpret the term "waters" to include wetlands that are adjacent to waters as more conventionally defined. This conclusion holds true even for wetlands that are not inundated or flooded by the adjacent lakes, rivers or streams. Riverside (D) was, therefore, required to have a permit in this case. Reversed.

Analysis:

As the present case illustrates, "navigable waters" and "waters of the United States" are not defined by whether boats can actually navigate on them or whether the bodies of water are interstate in character. Not only are wetlands under the umbrella of the Clean Water Act, so are intermittent streams that only occasionally have water. These inclusions seem to contravene interpretations of the Commerce Clause of the U.S. Constitution whereby Congress' power is limited to activities that affect interstate commerce. However, Congress' jurisdiction over isolated bodies of water may be in jeopardy in light of 1995's *United States v. Lopez*, where the Supreme Court held that regulated activities must *substantially* affect interstate commerce, rather than just having a *potential* effect. Would *Riverside* have a different result today in light of *Lopez*?

■ CASE VOCABULARY

WRIT OF CERTIORARI: Petition for discretionary review of a case by the United States Supreme Court.

Solid Waste Agency of Northern Cook County v. U.S. Army Corps of Engineers

(Consortium of Suburban Chicago Municipalities) v. *(Engineering Service Provider to United States)*

531 U.S. 159, 121 S.Ct. 675, 148 L.Ed.2d 576 (2001)

THE ARMY CORPS OF ENGINEERS COULD NOT ISSUE A PERMIT FOR NONNAVIGABLE WETLANDS NOT ADJACENT TO OPEN WATERS

■ **INSTANT FACTS** The Solid Waste Agency selected an abandoned sand and gravel pit, with excavation trenches that had evolved into ponds, as a solid waste disposal site, but was denied a permit by the Army Corps of Engineers.

■ **BLACK LETTER RULE** The authority of the U.S. Army Corps of Engineers to ISSUE permits, under § 404(a) of the Clean Water Act (CWA) does not extend to nonnavigable wetlands, unless they are adjacent to open waters.

■ **PROCEDURAL BASIS**

Certiorari to review the U.S. Court of Appeals' finding that § 404(a) of the CWA extended the authority of the U.S. Army Corps of Engineers to ISSUE permits for the discharge of fill material to nonnavigable wetlands that were not adjacent to open waters.

■ **FACTS**

The Solid Waste Agency (P) selected an abandoned sand and gravel pit, with excavation trenches that had evolved into ponds, as a solid waste disposal site. It contacted the U.S. Army Corps of Engineers (R), and other federal agencies, to determine if a landfill permit was required. The Army Corps of Engineers (R) asserted jurisdiction over the site pursuant to § 404(a) of the Clean Water Act (CWA) because the site was used as a habitat for migratory birds, and it denied the permit. The Solid Waste Agency (P) challenged the Army Corps of Engineers' (R) jurisdiction over the site and its denial of the permit. The district court granted the Army Corps of Engineers summary judgment on the jurisdictional ISSUE. On appeal, the court of appeals held that Congress had authority to regulate intrastate waters and that the Migratory Bird Rule, which the Army Corps of Engineers (R) had stated extended § 404(a) of the CWA to intrastate waters that were habitats for migratory birds, was a reasonable interpretation of the CWA.

■ **ISSUE**

Does the authority of the U.S. Army Corps of Engineers to ISSUE permits under § 404(a) of the Clean Water Act extend to nonnavigable wetlands that are not adjacent to open waters?

■ **DECISION AND RATIONALE**

(Rehnquist, C.J.) No. The authority of the Army Corps of Engineers to ISSUE permits under § 404(a) of the Clean Water Act (CWA) does not extend to nonnavigable wetlands that are not adjacent to open waters because the text of the statute does not permit such authority. In *United States v. Riverside Bayview Homes, Inc.,* 474 U.S. 121 (1985), the Supreme Court determined that the Army Corps of Engineers had jurisdiction, pursuant to § 404(a), over wetlands. However, in *Riverside*, the wetlands actually abutted a nagivable waterway. In this case, they do not. Absent the nexus between wetlands

---

and navigable waters, the Army Corps of Engineers (R) has no jurisdiction under § 404(a). The fact that Congress had, in the past, failed to pass legislation that would have overturned the extension of jurisdiction in § 404(g) (which extended permit authority to adjacent wetlands, as well as navigable waters) was insufficient to indicate a legislative intent that wetlands not adjacent to navigable water were within the jurisdiction of the Army Corps of Engineers. The Migratory Bird Rule, in the absence of § 404(a) addressing authority over nonnavigable, nonadjacent wetlands, did not create jurisdiction over the site because nothing in the language of § 404(a) extended jurisdiction over an abandoned sand and gravel pit, even though it was a migratory bird habitat. Reversed.

■ DISSENT

(Stevens, J.) The Army Corps of Engineers (R) is entitled to § 404(a) jurisdiction because § 1362(7) of the CWA establishes its scope of jurisdiction to encompass all waters of the United States and does not limit that jurisdiction by requiring actual or potential navigability. Viewed in light of the history of federal water regulation, and the fact that the instructions of Congress in its conference report indicated that the definition of navigable waters under § 502(7) was to be give the broadest possible constitutional interpretation, the term "navigable waters" operates in § 404(a) as waters over which federal authority may be properly asserted. Even if the Congress did not extend jurisdiction in the CWA to reach beyond navigable waters and their navigable tributaries, Congress's rejection of efforts to cut back the extension of jurisdiction in § 404(g) was sufficient to indicate a legislative intent to grant that jurisdiction.

Analysis:

The fact that the decision here was reached only by a 5–4 majority creates some uncertainty as to whether the Court will assume the same position in future cases it reviews. Justice Stevens writes a compelling DISSENT, which just may indicate the direction the Court could take in the future, particularly in view of the fact that the Court could experience a significant turnover in the early twenty-first century.

■ CASE VOCABULARY

ENVIRONMENTAL PROTECTION AGENCY: A federal agency created in 1970 to coordinate governmental action to protect the environment.

NEXUS: A connection or link, often a causal one.

PROMULGATE: To put (a law or decree) into force or effect.

Rapanos v. United States

(Shopping Mall Developer/Wetlands Owner) v. *(Prosecuting Government)*

126 S. Ct. 2208 (2006)

"WETLANDS" ARE NOT "NAVIGABLE WATERS"

■ INSTANT FACTS The plaintiffs discharged fill material into wetlands properties they owned in order to build a shopping mall and condominiums, and the government brought legal action against them because they did not obtain a permit before beginning development.

■ BLACK LETTER RULE The phrase "the waters of the United States," as used in the Clean Water Act, includes only those relatively permanent or continuously flowing bodies of water forming geographic features such as streams, oceans, rivers, and lakes, and does not include channels through which water intermittently flows or channels that provide periodic drainage for rainfall.

■ PROCEDURAL BASIS

Supreme Court review of a federal circuit court decision affirming the district court's judgment in favor of the defendant.

■ FACTS

[The facts are not set out in the casebook. Briefly, the Clean Water Act makes it unlawful to discharge fill material into "navigable waters" without a permit, and it defines "navigable waters" to include "the waters of the United States." The Army Corps of Engineers, which issues permits for the discharge of fill material into navigable waters, interpreted "the waters of the United States" expansively to include not only traditional navigable waters, but also tributaries of such waters and wetlands "adjacent" to such waters and tributaries. The cases before the Court involved four Michigan wetlands lying near ditches or man-made drains that eventually emptied into traditional navigable waters. The United States brought civil enforcement proceedings against the petitioners, who had backfilled certain of these areas without a permit. The district court found federal jurisdiction over the wetlands because they were adjacent to "waters of the United States" or adjacent to "navigable waters." The Sixth Circuit affirmed.]

■ ISSUE

Did the courts below err in concluding that the wetlands in these cases constitute "navigable waters," such that the petitioners were required to obtain a permit under the Clean Water Act before discharging fill material into them?

■ DECISION AND RATIONALE

(Scalia, J.) Yes. The phrase "the waters of the United States," as used in the Clean Water Act, includes only those relatively permanent or continuously flowing bodies of water forming geographic features such as streams, oceans, rivers, and lakes, and does not include channels through which water intermittently flows or channels that provide periodic drainage for rainfall.

We first addressed the meaning of "the waters of the United States," as used in the Clean Water Act, in *U.S. v. Riverside Bayview Homes, Inc.*, 474 U.S. 121 (1985), in which we upheld the Corps' interpretation of this statutory phrase to include wetlands that abut traditional navigable waters. The petitioners contend here, however, that the waters must actually be navigable, or capable of navigation, to fall into the statutory category. While the meaning of "navigable waters" as used in the Act is broader than the traditional dictionary definition, the Clean Water Act authorizes federal jurisdiction only over "waters," which connotes relatively permanent bodies of water, as opposed to ordinarily dry channels through which water occasionally flows. The Act's use of the phrase "navigable waters" also suggests that it confers jurisdiction only over relatively permanent bodies of water. Moreover, the Clean Water Act itself categorizes the channels that carry intermittent flows of water separately from "navigable waters."

Riverside Bayview rested on an ambiguity in defining where "water" ends and its abutting ("adjacent") wetlands begin, which allowed the Corps to rely in that case on ecological considerations to resolve the ambiguity in favor of treating all abutting wetlands as waters. But isolated ponds are not "waters of the United States" and present no boundary-drawing problem justifying reliance on ecological factors. Thus, we conclude that only those wetlands with a continuous surface connection to bodies that are "waters of the United States" in their own right, such that there is no clear demarcation between the two, are "adjacent" to such waters and covered by the Act. Because the Sixth Circuit applied an incorrect standard to determine whether the wetlands at issue are covered "waters," and because of the paucity of the record, the cases are remanded for further proceedings.

■ CONCURRENCE

(Kennedy, J.) The Sixth Circuit recognized that waters and wetlands constitute "navigable waters" under the Act if they possess a "significant nexus" to waters that are navigable in fact or could reasonably be made navigable, but it did not consider all the factors necessary to determine whether the lands in question had the requisite nexus. The required nexus must be assessed in terms of the Act's goals and purposes. Congress enacted the Clean Air Act to "restore and maintain the chemical, physical, and biological integrity of the Nation's waters," and it pursued that objective by restricting dumping and filling in "waters of the United States." Wetlands can perform critical functions related to the integrity of other waters, such as by trapping pollutants, providing flood control, and storing runoff. Accordingly, wetlands have the requisite nexus, and are thus "navigable waters," if they, alone or in combination with similarly situated lands in the region, significantly affect the chemical, physical, and biological integrity of other covered navigable waters. If, however, their effects on water quality are speculative or insubstantial, they fall outside the term "navigable waters."

The Corps' theory of jurisdiction in these cases, based simply on adjacency to tributaries, goes beyond our holding in *Riverside Bayview*, so its assertion of jurisdiction cannot rest on that case. The overbreadth of the Corps' existing standard for tributaries thus precludes that standard's adoption as the measure of whether adjacent wetlands play an important role in the integrity of an aquatic system comprised of navigable waters as traditionally understood. Absent more specific guidance, the Corps must establish a significant nexus on a case-by-case basis when seeking to regulate wetlands based on adjacency to non-navigable tributaries. In the present cases, the record contains evidence pointing to a possible significant nexus, but neither the agency nor the reviewing courts considered the issue in these terms. Thus, I would remand the cases for further proceedings.

Analysis:

In one of the cases before the Court here, Rapanos had filled fifty-four acres of wetlands with sand in preparation for the construction of a shopping mall, without filing for a permit. In another case, Carabell had actually proactively sought a permit to build condominiums on nineteen acres of wetlands, but the request was denied. Neither of these parties prevailed in the lower courts. *Rapanos* was the first major environmental case heard by the newly appointed Chief Justice Roberts and Justice Alito. Five justices agreed to void the rulings against the plaintiffs, but the court was split over further details, with the four more conservative justices arguing in favor of a more restrictive reading of the term "navigable waters." Justice Kennedy did not fully endorse either position.

National Mining Association v. Army Corps of Engineers

(*Trade Groups*) v. (*Government Agency*)

145 F.3d 1399 (D.C. Cir. 1998)

INCIDENTAL FALLBACK IS NOT A DISCHARGE UNDER THE CLEAN WATER ACT

■ **INSTANT FACTS** Various trade associations challenged the "Tulloch Rule" which expanded the definition of "discharge" to include any redeposit of dredged material within the waters of the United States, including any incidental fallback.

■ **BLACK LETTER RULE** Incidental fallback is not subject to the dredge and fill permit requirements of the Clean Water Act.

■ **PROCEDURAL BASIS**

Appeal from judgment holding that incidental fallback is not subject to the dredge and fill permit requirements of the Clean Water Act.

■ **FACTS**

Section 404 of the Clean Water Act (CWA) authorizes the United States Army Corps of Engineers (D) to issue permits for the discharge of dredge and fill materials into navigable waters. In 1986, the Corps (D) issued a regulation defining the term "discharge of dredged material" to mean "any addition of dredged material into the waters of the United States" but expressly excluded "de minimis, incidental soil movement occurring during normal dredging operations." In 1993, following litigation of the same name, the Corps (D) instituted the "Tulloch Rule" which removed the de minimis exception and expanded the definition of discharge to cover "any addition of dredged material into, *including any redeposit of dredged material within*, the waters of the United States." Redeposit would include fallback, which is soils or sediments that fall from the bucket or other dredging mechanism back into the water. In effect, the new rule subjects virtually all excavation and dredging performed in wetlands subject to federal regulation. Various trade associations engaged in dredging and excavation, including the National Mining Association (P), mounted a facial challenge to the Tulloch Rule arguing that it exceeded the scope of the Corps' (D) regulatory authority under the CWA. The trial court held that incidental fallback is not subject to the dredge and fill permit requirements of the CWA, and the Corps (D) appealed.

■ **ISSUE**

Do the Clean Water Act's dredge and fill permit requirements apply to incidental fallback or de minimis redeposit of dredged materials back into the water?

■ **DECISION AND RATIONALE**

(Williams, Cir. J.) No. The Clean Water Act's dredge and fill permit requirements do not apply to incidental fallback or de minimis redeposit of dredged materials back into the water. Fallback is a practically inescapable byproduct of all mechanized land clearing, ditching or excavation. The Tulloch Rule would effectively require a permit for all of those activities. Section 404 only applies to "discharges," defined as the "addition of any pollutant to navigable waters." Fallback is not an addition of anything since it represents a net withdrawal or removal. Section 10 of the Rivers and Harbors Act of 1899, not the CWA, governs the removal of material. Some redeposits, such as those

---

pollutants moved from one body of water to another with different water quality, might be subject to regulation. However, the Tulloch Rule makes no effort to draw such a line since it covers *"any redeposit."* As a result, it outruns the Corps' (D) statutory authority under the CWA. Affirmed.

■ **CONCURRENCE**

(Silberman, Cir. J.) Fallback that was moved some distance away and then dropped, or that was held for some time and then dropped in the same spot might constitute an addition. However, the Tulloch Rule as it stands is unreasonable. To uphold the Rule would convert all dredging, which the Rivers and Harbors Act regulates, into discharge, which is regulated by the CWA.

Analysis:

The court does not specify what types of redeposits would be subject to regulation under § 404, only that regulating *"any* deposit" is too broad. The court further states that a reasoned attempt by the agencies to draw such a line would merit considerable deference. Suppose the regulation applied to "any *substantial* redeposit" or redeposits having "an *adverse environmental impact.*" Given the court's language, how much authority would the Corps (D) lose? Judge Silberman in his concurrence indicates that material that is "held for some time and then dropped back in the same spot" might constitute an "addition" and thus be subject to § 404. How could the passage of time make incidental fallback material more of an addition than it would be if it had fallen back immediately?

South Florida Water Management District v. Miccosukee Tribe of Indians

(Water Company) v. *(Concerned Citizen Group)*

541 U.S. 95 (2004)

MOVING POLLUTANTS BETWEEN BODIES OF WATER MAY NOT REQUIRE A PERMIT

She says I'm polluting my body. I say both my drink and my body are mostly water, so really I'm just moving pollutants between bodies of water.

stus.com

■ **INSTANT FACTS** The Indian Tribe (P) brought a citizen suit against the Water Management District (D) for failure to obtain a National Pollutant Discharge Elimination System (NPDES) permit for its pumping facility.

■ **BLACK LETTER RULE** The Clean Water Act requires a permit before a pollutant may be discharged into navigable waters.

■ **PROCEDURAL BASIS**

Supreme Court review of a circuit court ruling affirming a decision in favor of the plaintiff.

■ **FACTS**

South Florida Water Management District (D) operated a pumping station that transferred water from a canal into a reservoir. The Miccosukee Tribe (P) brought suit against the District, arguing that it was required to obtain a permit under the Clean Water Act. The trial court agreed with the Tribe (P) and the appellate court affirmed. The District (D) sought further review in the Supreme Court.

■ **ISSUE**

Did the court below properly grant summary judgment to the plaintiff on its claim that the District (D) violated the National Pollution Discharge Elimination System provisions of the Clean Water Act by failing to obtain a permit for its pumping activities?

■ **DECISION AND RATIONALE**

(O'Connor, J.) No. The Clean Water Act requires a permit before a pollutant may be discharged into navigable waters. Here, however, questions remain as to whether the transfer of a pollutant from one body of water to another triggers the permitting provisions of the Act.

The objective of the Clean Water Act is to restore and maintain the chemical, physical, and biological integrity of the nation's waters. To achieve that goal, the Act prohibits the discharge of any pollutants except as provided therein. The NPDES requires dischargers to obtain permits that specifically limit the amount of pollutants that they can release into the nation's waters. The Tribe (P) argues here that the District could not operate its pumping facility without obtaining such a permit, because the station moves phosphorous-laden water from one place to another. The District (D) argues, by contrast, that although phosphorous is a known pollutant and the waterways involved here qualify as "navigable waters," the real question is whether operation of the pump constitutes "discharge of a pollutant" within the meaning of the Act.

Importantly, the Clean Water Act requires permits only when there will be an addition of a pollutant to navigable waters. The Government therefore suggests a "unitary waters" approach here, under which the permitting provision is not triggered when a pollutant is merely transferred from one body of water to another. However, this argument was not raised below and thus cannot be considered here. Nor is there ample evidence in the record as to how the relationship between the pre-and post-pumping bodies of water should be assessed in this case, and as to whether they are truly distinct bodies of water. Because factual issues remain, the district court improperly granted summary judgment. The factual issues must be resolved, and the Government's unitary waters argument can be heard by the court on remand. Vacated and remanded for further proceedings consistent with this opinion.

Analysis:

Both the federal district court and the Eleventh Circuit rested their holdings in this case on the determination that the canal and reservoir were two distinct bodies of water. The Supreme Court, however, found that further development of the record was necessary to resolve the dispute over the distinction between the two. The Court acknowledged the possibility that, on remain, after reviewing the full record, the district court could conclude that the canal and the reservoir were not meaningfully distinct water bodies, in which case the pumping station would not need an NPDES permit.

NRDC v. Costle

(Environmental Group) v. *(EPA Administrator)*

568 F.2d 1369 (D.C. Cir. 1977)

NO POINT SOURCE POLLUTER IS EXEMPT FROM THE CLEAN WATER ACT'S PERMIT REQUIRE-MENTS

■ **INSTANT FACTS** The NRDC (P) challenged as unlawful EPA (D) exemptions that excluded certain categories of point source polluters from the permit requirements of the Clean Water Act.

■ **BLACK LETTER RULE** The EPA (D) may not exclude any point source polluter from the Clean Water Act's permit requirements.

■ **PROCEDURAL BASIS**

Appeal from an order granting NRDC's (P) motion for summary judgment in action seeking declaratory judgment that certain EPA (D) regulations were unlawful.

■ **FACTS**

In 1973, the EPA administrator issued regulations that exempted certain categories of point source polluters from the permit requirements of § 402 of the Clean Water Act. The exempted discharges included, among others, agricultural, silvicultural, and storm water runoff point sources. The EPA (D) reasoned that the exclusions allowed it to conserve its resources for more serious polluters. The National Resources Defense Council (NRDC)(P) sought a declaratory judgment that the regulations were unlawful under the CWA, arguing that Congress intended to prohibit the discharge of pollutants from *all* point sources unless a permit had been issued under § 402. The trial court granted NRDC's (P) motion for summary judgment. The EPA (D) appealed.

■ **ISSUE**

Does the EPA (D) have the authority to exclude certain categories of point source polluters from the permit requirements of the Clean Water Act?

■ **DECISION AND RATIONALE**

(Leventhal, Cir. J.) No. The EPA (D) does not have the authority to exclude certain categories of point source polluters from the permit requirements of the Clean Water Act. The wording of the CWA, its legislative history, and precedents are clear: the discharge of a pollutant without a permit is unlawful, and the EPA (D) administrator does not have the authority to make exceptions to this rule. The EPA's (D) argument that certain characteristics of runoff pollution make it difficult to promulgate precise effluent limitations is without merit. We conclude that the existence of uniform national effluent limitations is not a necessary precondition for incorporating the excluded point sources at issue into the permit program. If the EPA (D) fears that it will be overburdened by the number of permits that it will face without these exemptions, it has alternatives, such as granting area-wide or general permits. The EPA (D) does not, however, have the authority to exempt point sources from the permit program.

Analysis:

The court states that there is a "very practical difference" between a general permit and an exemption. Its rationale is that a general permit will undergo reconsideration at least every five years whereas an exemption slips through the cracks. If, as the EPA (D) argues, the point sources at issue in the present case create such administrative infeasibility, will the EPA's (D) reconsideration after five years be anything more than perfunctory? The CWA defines "point source" as any "discernible, confined and discrete conveyance" including, among others, pipes, ditches, and channels. The court never discusses which exempted sources were point sources, though some were arguably not.

■ **CASE VOCABULARY**

EFFLUENT: Waste discharged into a body of water.

SIVICULTURAL: Relating to the use of forest land for timber.

United States v. Plaza Health Laboratories, Inc.

(Prosecutor) v. *(Dumper)*

3 F.2d 643 (2d Cir. 1993)

A HUMAN BEING IS NOT A "POINT SOURCE" UNDER THE CLEAN WATER ACT

■ **INSTANT FACTS** Villegas (D) disposed of numerous vials of human blood generated from his blood-testing laboratory business, Plaza Health (D), into the Hudson River. Upon discovery, Villegas (D) and Plaza Health (D) were indicted and convicted for violating the Clean Water Act.

■ **BLACK LETTER RULE** "Point source" as defined in the Clean Water Act does not include individuals.

■ **PROCEDURAL BASIS**

Appeal from a conviction of knowingly discharging pollutants into a waterway without a permit in violation of the Clean Water Act.

■ **FACTS**

Villegas (D) was co-owner and vice president of Plaza Health Laboratories, Inc. (D), a blood-testing laboratory business. On at least two occasions, Villegas (D) loaded containers of numerous vials of human blood generated from his business into his personal car and deposited them at low tide within a crevice near his condominium and the Hudson River. The vials were subsequently found washed up on shore near Staten Island. Authorities later discovered additional plastic containers of vials near Villegas' (D) condo. All of the vials were eventually traced back to Plaza Health (D). Villegas (D) and Plaza Health (D) were convicted of knowingly discharging pollutants into a waterway from a point source without a permit in violation of the Clean Water Act. Villegas (D) appealed, arguing that the definition of "point source" does not include discharges that result from the individual acts of human beings.

■ **ISSUE**

May a human being constitute a "point source" as defined in the Clean Water Act?

■ **DECISION AND RATIONALE**

(Pratt, Cir. J.) No. A human being may not be a point source as defined in the Clean Water Act. The CWA does not expressly recognize a human being as a "point source." If Congress had intended to include human beings as point sources, it could have done so very simply. The CWA generally targets industrial and municipal sources of pollutants. The legislative history of the CWA further confirms the Act's focus on industrial polluters. Additionally, the CWA does not make structural sense when "human being" is included in the meaning of "point source." The term "point source" as applied to a human being is at best ambiguous, and in criminal prosecutions, the rule of lenity requires that ambiguities in the statute be resolved in the defendant's favor. The CWA did not clearly proscribe Villegas' (D) conduct and did not accord him a fair warning of the sanctions the law placed on that conduct. Under the rule of lenity, therefore, the prosecutions must be dismissed.

■ DISSENT

(Oakes, Cir. J.) The term "point source" has been broadly construed to apply to a wide range of polluting techniques, so long as the pollutants reach the navigable waters by human effort. Unlike nonpoint sources, a point source is not difficult to identify or to control. Villegas' (D) activities more closely resemble a point source discharge than a nonpoint source discharge because the source of the pollution was clear and would have been easy to control. Villegas' (D) stream of activity functioned as a "discrete conveyance" or point source. Under the majority's holding, a corporation could have its employees stand between the company trucks and the sea and dump pollutants without violating the CWA. I would read the CWA as ambiguous as applied to individual litterers, but not to disposers of industrial and municipal waste, the principal targets of the CWA.

Analysis:

The majority states that it finds no suggestion that Congress intended the CWA to impose criminal liability on an individual for the myriad, random acts of human waste disposal such as a passerby who flings a candy wrapper into the Hudson River, or a urinating swimmer. Does the majority intend to place such acts in the same category as those of the defendants in this case? Dumping vials of blood, some of which were infected with the Hepatitis-B virus, into a river is hardly a random act of human waste disposal. Would the majority agree, as the dissent points out, that a company could avoid the CWA by simply having its employees hurl the waste into the water themselves? Might the majority abandon its rule of lenity in that situation since the employees should have a "fair warning" of the criminal nature of their undertaking?

■ CASE VOCABULARY

RULE OF LENITY: Judicial doctrine by which courts decline to interpret ambiguous statutes in such a way as to increase the penalty.

Chemical Manufacturers Association v. NRDC

(Trade Group) v. *(Environmental Group)*

470 U.S. 116 (1985)

THE CLEAN WATER ACT DOES NOT PROHIBIT VARIANCES FOR DISCHARGES OF TOXIC POLLUTANTS

■ **INSTANT FACTS** An EPA (D) regulation allowed variances in effluent limitations to toxic dischargers for factors "fundamentally different" from those initially considered by the EPA (D) in promulgating the requirements.

■ **BLACK LETTER RULE** The Clean Water Act does not prohibit variances in effluent limitations for toxic dischargers.

■ **PROCEDURAL BASIS**

Appeal from holding that variances could not be granted for discharges of toxins into sewage treatment systems.

■ **FACTS**

Under the Clean Water Act (CWA) § 301(*l*), the EPA (D) may not "modify" any requirement of § 301 applicable to toxic pollutants. The EPA (D) granted variances in effluent limitations to toxic dischargers for factors "fundamentally different" (FDF) from those initially considered by the EPA (D) in setting the standards. The National Resource Defense Council (P)(NRDC) argues that § 301(*l*) should apply to all modifications in order to carry out the intent of Congress. The EPA (D) insists that § 301(*l*) prohibits only those modifications expressly permitted by other provisions of § 301 for nontoxic pollutants, namely those dealing with economic or water-quality grounds. The court of appeals held in favor of the NRDC (P), and the EPA (D) appealed.

■ **ISSUE**

Does the Clean Water Act's prohibition against modification of effluent standards for toxic pollutants prohibit variances for "fundamentally different factors" not considered by the EPA (D) in originally setting the standards?

■ **DECISION AND RATIONALE**

(White, J.) No. The Clean Water Act's prohibition against modification of effluent standards for toxic pollutants does not prohibit variances for "fundamentally different factors" not considered by the EPA (D) in setting the standards. The word "modify" in § 301(*l*) is not be construed in its broadest sense so as to forbid every change in the toxic waste standards. Congress intended § 301(*l*) to bar only waivers based on the economic capability of dischargers or on water quality considerations under §§ 301(c) and (g). These FDF variances will not contravene the goals of the CWA because they do not excuse compliance with a correct requirement, but acknowledge that not all relevant factors were sufficiently taken into consideration in the original requirement. Given the enormous burden of the EPA in setting effluent limitations, it is understandable that it may not be apprized of unique factors applicable to atypical plants during the rulemaking process. It is important that the EPA be given the flexibility that the FDF variance mechanism affords. Section 301 (*l*) does not prohibit FDF variances. Reversed.

■ DISSENT

(Marshall, J.) The plain meaning and the legislative history of the CWA show a clear Congressional intent to ban all modifications pertaining to toxic pollutants, not just those modifications authorized under § 301 for nontoxic pollutants. An FDF variance sets an individual requirement as opposed to categories of dischargers. This method does not force more effective pollution control technology as Congress intended.

Analysis:

The 1987 amendments to the CWA specifically addressed the FDF variance issue. The new section 301(n) sets forth permissible grounds for FDF variances for toxic pollutants. Note that the toxic pollutants at issue here are listed at 33 U.S.C. § 1317(a)(1). If the pollutant is not listed, it is not considered toxic for CWA purposes, even though the pollutant may be harmful.

Arkansas v. Oklahoma

(Upstream State) v. *(Downstream State)*

503 U.S. 91 (1992)

THE EPA MAY REQUIRE AN UPSTREAM DISCHARGER TO COMPLY WITH THE WATER POLLUTION REGULATIONS OF A DOWNSTREAM STATE

■ **INSTANT FACTS** Oklahoma (P) challenged a permit granted by the EPA that authorized a plant in Arkansas (D) to discharge pollutants into a stream that emptied into the Illinois River in Oklahoma (P).

■ **BLACK LETTER RULE** The EPA may require an upstream discharger to comply with the water quality standards of downstream states.

■ **PROCEDURAL BASIS**

Appeal from judgment overturning issuance of an NPDES permit.

■ **FACTS**

The EPA issued a National Pollution Discharge Elimination System (NPDES) permit to a plant in Arkansas (D) authorizing the plant to discharge pollutants into a stream. The stream eventually emptied into the Illinois River, which runs through Oklahoma (P). Oklahoma (P) challenged the permit in light of Oklahoma (P) water quality standards that prohibited any degradation of the Illinois River. After several administrative reviews upholding the permit, the Court of Appeals invalidated the permit. Arkansas (D) appealed.

■ **ISSUE**

Does the EPA have the authority to require an upstream discharger to comply with the water quality standards of a downstream state?

■ **DECISION AND RATIONALE**

(Stevens, J.) Yes. The EPA has the authority to require an upstream discharger to comply with the water quality standards of a downstream state. Although the CWA may not require such action, it clearly does not limit the EPA's authority to mandate such compliance. The EPA has broad discretion to establish conditions for NPDES permits to ensure compliance with the applicable water quality standards of all affected States. Consideration of state water quality standards is wholly consistent with the CWA's broad purpose of maintaining the integrity of the Nation's waters. We find nothing in the CWA's history to indicate that Congress intended to preclude the EPA from conditioning such permits on compliance with downstream water quality standards. The Court of Appeals should have deferred to the administrative findings that the discharges here would not lead to a detectable change in the water quality in Oklahoma (P). Accordingly, the Court of Appeals invalidation of the permit is reversed.

Analysis:

The Court here quoted with approval the EPA's Chief Officer statement that "unless there is some method of measuring compliance, there is no way to ensure compliance." Does this mean that new plants like the one in Arkansas (D) can come to the scene and be in compliance with the downstream state's water quality standards because there is no satisfactory method of measuring noncompliance? Should the Court consider other violators, such as those upstream from Arkansas (D), who make the added increment undetectable? In this case, the downstream water was already degraded. Could a downstream state with clean water effectively dictate the terms of NPDES permits in upstream states by adopting very stringent water quality standards?

■ CASE VOCABULARY

DE MINIMIS: of minimal importance, insignificant.

EUTROPHICATION: The process by which water receives increased amounts of dissolved nutrients such as nitrogen and phosphorous that promote excessive plant growth and oxygen depletion.

PUD No. 1 of Jefferson County v. Washington Department of Ecology

(*Dam Builder*) v. (*State Environmental Agency*)

511 U.S. 700 (1994)

A STATE MAY CONDITION ITS § 401 CERTIFICATION UPON ANY LIMITATION NECESSARY TO ENSURE COMPLIANCE WITH THE STATE'S WATER QUALITY STANDARDS

■ **INSTANT FACTS** A proposed hydroelectric dam project planned to divert river water away from certain fisheries. In its water quality certification required by the Clean Water Act (CWA), the State imposed conditions on the project, including a minimum stream-flow requirement.

■ **BLACK LETTER RULE** States may condition certification issued pursuant to § 401 of the CWA upon any limitation necessary to ensure compliance with state water quality standards.

■ **PROCEDURAL BASIS**

Appeal from judgment affirming the State's power to impose minimum stream flow conditions on § 401 certifications.

■ **FACTS**

A proposed hydroelectric dam project threatened to divert river water away from certain fisheries. To obtain the necessary federal license for the project, PUD (P) was required to obtain state certification of the project pursuant to § 401 of the CWA. The Washington Department of Ecology (D) conducted a study to determine the minimum stream flows necessary to protect the affected fisheries. As a result of the study, Washington (D) issued a § 401 water quality certification but imposed a variety of conditions on the project, including a minimum stream-flow requirement. Claiming that the certification condition exceeded Washington's (D) authority, PUD (P) sought administrative and judicial review. The Washington Supreme Court affirmed the State's power to impose the conditions, and PUD (P) appealed.

■ **ISSUE**

May a State condition its § 401 certification upon any limitation necessary to ensure compliance with the state's water quality standards or any other appropriate requirement of State law?

■ **DECISION AND RATIONALE**

(O'Connor, J.) Yes. A State may condition its § 401 certification upon any limitation necessary to ensure compliance with the state's water quality standards or any other appropriate requirement of State law. Even though the conditions imposed here may not relate to specific discharges as suggested by § 401(a)(1), Washington (D) has the authority under § 401(d) to impose conditions necessary to assure the compliance of the *applicant* and the *activities*. Washington's (D) authority is not unlimited, but water quality standards adopted pursuant to § 303 are among the permitted limitations that Washington (D) may use to ensure compliance in the § 401 certification process. Further, Washington (D) may require that a permit applicant comply with both the designated uses and the water quality criteria of the state standards. Washington's (D) minimum stream flow condition also complies with EPA antidegradation policy since it ensures that an existing instream water use will be maintained and protected. Affirmed.

■ CONCURRENCE

(Stevens, J.) This is an easy case because the CWA permits the States to impose stricter standards than federal law requires.

■ DISSENT

(Thomas, J.) Section § 401 should not be interpreted to allow states to impose conditions that have no relation to any possible discharge. A limitation on minimum stream relates to intake, not discharge. This broad interpretation permits § 401(d) to swallow § 401(a)(1). Under the Court's interpretation, state agencies may pursue their water goals in any way they choose so long as they tend to make the water more suitable for the uses the State has chosen.

Analysis:

In his dissent, Justice Thomas argues that the Court's reading of § 401 places no meaningful limitations on the State's authority to impose conditions on § 401 certifications. The majority, however, stated that the authority is not unbounded. The Court states that, pursuant to § 401(d), the State can only ensure that the project complies with "any applicable effluent limitations and *other limitations*, under [CWA § 301 and § 302]," and "with *any other appropriate requirement of State law.*" The Court reasons that the limitations at issue fall within these italicized portions. As long as the limitation had something to do with water quality, would there be any meaningful limitation on the State's ability to impose conditions?

Pronsolino v. Nastri

(Landowners) v. *(EPA Regional Administrator)*

291 F.3d 1123 (9th Cir. 2002)

THE EPA HAS AUTHORITY OVER WATERS WITH NON–POINT SOURCES OF POLLUTION

■ **INSTANT FACTS** The Environmental Protection Agency (EPA) (D) required California to identify a certain river as a water body with insufficient pollution controls and to set "total maximum daily loads" (TMDLs) for pollution entering the river.

■ **BLACK LETTER RULE** The Clear Water Act (CWA) is best read to include waters impaired only by non-point sources of pollution in the § 303(d)(1) listing and TMDL requirements.

■ **PROCEDURAL BASIS**

Appeal from a U.S. District Court finding that the EPA had authority to establish TMDLs for waters that fail to meet water quality standards solely as a result of non-point source pollution.

■ **FACTS**

The EPA (D) required California to identify a certain river as a water body with insufficient pollution controls and to set "total maximum daily loads" (TMDLs) for pollution entering the river. Section 303(d)(1)(A) of the CWA required listing and calculation of TMDLs for those waters within the states' boundaries "for which the effluent limitations required by § 301(b)(1)(A) and § 301(b)(1)(B) are not stringent enough to implement any water quality standard applicable to such waters." Effluent limitations pertain only to point sources of pollution (i.e., pipes, tunnels). Pronsolino (P) challenged the EPA's (D) authority to establish TMDLs for the river that was identified because that river failed to meet water quality standards solely as a result of non-point source pollution. The U.S. District Court rejected Pronsolino's (P) claim.

■ **ISSUE**

Must the "not stringent enough to implement any water quality standard" language of § 303(d)(1)(A) be interpreted to mean both that (1) application of the effluent (point sources of pollution) limitations will not achieve water quality standards, and (2) the waters at ISSUE are subject to the effluent limitations?

■ **DECISION AND RATIONALE**

(Berzon, J.) No. The language and the structure of the CWA, along with § 303(d), support the position that TMDLs are required for all waters that are not able to achieve water quality standards through technology-based controls on point sources of pollution. States must establish water quality standards for all waters, including waters that fail to meet water quality standards solely as a result of non-point source pollution. TMDLs are a primary information tool useful in helping to accomplish this goal. Although the CWA only authorizes federal regulations for point source pollution, it is necessary that states have access to TMDLs, as an information tool, for waters with non-point source pollution sources. Therefore, the "not stringent enough to implement any water quality standard" language of § 303(d)(1)(A) must be interpreted to apply to waters with non-point sources of pollution, as well as waters with point sources of pollution.

Analysis:

Even though the EPA has authority to establish TMDLs for waters impaired by non-point source pollution, the balance of federal-state control established in the CWA is not upset because the implementation and monitoring of the TMDLs is still left to the state. This is just one example of the separation of powers between state and federal governments where environmental ISSUEs are concerned. In most cases, the states and the federal government work together to achieve similar environmental objectives.

■ **CASE VOCABULARY**

ENVIRONMENTAL PROTECTION AGENCY: A federal agency created in 1970 to coordinate governmental action to protect the environment.

PROMULGATE: To put (a law or decree) into force or effect.

CHAPTER SEVEN

Land Use Regulation and Regulatory Takings

Village of Euclid v. Ambler Realty Co.

Instant Facts: A land owner challenged the constitutionality of a city's residential zoning ordinance.

Black Letter Rule: Under appropriate circumstances, a residential zoning ordinance is constitutional and does not exceed a city's police power.

Penn Central Transportation Co. v. City of New York

Instant Facts: The owner of Grand Central Terminal claimed that a New York City historic landmark preservation law barring it from building a 55–story office building above the Terminal constituted a "taking" of its property and required the City to pay it just compensation.

Black Letter Rule: Whether a law results in a taking turns on the character of the governmental action, its interference with reasonable investment-backed expectations, and its economic impact.

Lucas v. South Carolina Coastal Council

Instant Facts: A South Carolina law barred a landowner from building any permanent structures on his beachfront land. The landowner claimed this constituted a "taking" under the Fifth Amendment requiring South Carolina to pay him just compensation.

Black Letter Rule: A law that renders property valueless is a taking under the Fifth Amendment and requires just compensation to the landowner.

Palazzolo v. Rhode Island

Instant Facts: Palazzolo's (P) development proposals were rejected by state authorities (D) pursuant to a state coastal protection law that required the issuance of a permit prior to the development of coastal wetlands. The law was enacted after Palazzolo's (P) company had acquired certain waterfront property that he proposed to develop but before Palazzolo (P) acquired individual title to that property.

Black Letter Rule: A post-regulation acquisition of property does not serve as an automatic bar to regulatory takings claims.

Tahoe-Sierra Preservation Council, Inc. v. Tahoe Regional Planning Agency

Instant Facts: The Tahoe Regional Planning Agency (TRPA) (D) imposed two moratoria on virtually all residential development in an area subject to TRPA (D) jurisdiction until TRPA adopted a new land-use plan.

Black Letter Rule: A moratorium on development imposed during the process of devising a comprehensive land-use plan does not constitute a per se taking of property requiring compensation under the Takings Clause.

Dolan v. City of Tigard

Instant Facts: A city granted a store owner's application for a permit to redevelop her site subject to the owner dedicating land for a storm drainage system and for a pedestrian/bicycle pathway.

Black Letter Rule: To not constitute a taking, a land use condition must have "rough proportionality" to the proposed development.

Lingle v. Chevron, U.S.A., Inc.

Instant Facts: Chevron (P) argued that statutory limits on the rents that it could charge to gasoline retailers constituted an unconstitutional taking of its property.

Black Letter Rule: A plaintiff seeking to challenge a government regulation as an uncompensated taking of private property may proceed only by alleging a "physical" taking, a total regulatory taking, a *Penn Central* taking, or a land-use exaction.

Village of Euclid v. Ambler Realty Co.

(City) v. *(Land Owner)*

272 U.S. 365 (1926)

RESIDENTIAL ZONING ORDINANCE IS CONSTITUTIONAL UNDER CITY'S POLICE POWER

■ **INSTANT FACTS** A land owner challenged the constitutionality of a city's residential zoning ordinance.

■ **BLACK LETTER RULE** Under appropriate circumstances, a residential zoning ordinance is constitutional and does not exceed a city's police power.

■ **PROCEDURAL BASIS**

Certification to U.S. Supreme Court of challenge to zoning ordinance.

■ **FACTS**

In 1922, the Village of Euclid ("Euclid") (D) adopted a comprehensive zoning plan. Under the plan, certain areas were zoned for residential use only. The ordinance excluded apartment buildings, retail shops, hotels, and all other business uses. Ambler Realty Co. ("Ambler") (P) owned 68 acres of vacant land in that area that Ambler (P) had hoped to sell for industrial uses. Ambler (P) claimed the residential zoning would reduce the property's market value from $10,000 per acre to $2,500 per acre. The trial court invalidated the zoning ordinance because of its potential discriminatory effect on minorities and the poor.

■ **ISSUE**

Does a residential zoning ordinance exceed a city's police power?

■ **DECISION AND RATIONALE**

(Sutherland, J.) No, as long as the ordinance is not arbitrary or unreasonable, and is substantially related to the public health, safety, morals, and general welfare. Zoning is now necessary as a result of the tremendous increase and concentration of population. To determine whether a particular zoning ordinance exceeds a city's police power, we must look at the particular circumstances at issue. We also look at the analogies in nuisance law. Expert reports have shown that separate residential zones contribute to the public welfare. Residential zones improve fire safety, increase safety in home life, reduce street accidents, decrease noise and resulting nervous disorders, and preserve a favorable environment in which to raise children. Apartment houses are often parasites that interfere with the free circulation of air and sunlight. They also create more noise and traffic, and, in residential neighborhoods, come close to being nuisances. Here, Euclid's (D) ordinance is not arbitrary or unreasonable, and is substantially related to the public health, safety, morals, and general welfare. Therefore, it does not exceed Euclid's (D) police powers and is constitutional. Reversed.

Analysis:

Here the Court developed a fairly low standard for determining whether a zoning ordinance exceeds a city's police power. Under the Court's ruling, a challenger of a zoning ordinance has the burden of proving that the ordinance is arbitrary, unreasonable, and with no substantial relationship to the public health, safety, morals, or general welfare. This may be difficult for a challenger to do. The Court did not address the trial court's concern that the ordinance potentially discriminated against minorities and the poor. This potential discrimination would arise because poor people, who could afford to live only in apartments, would be excluded from the residentially-zoned areas. The Court does not look at Euclid's (D) motive in passing the ordinance. The Court also does not look at the adverse effect on Ambler's (P) property interests. The diminution of Ambler's (P) property value does not establish a "taking" as that term is used in the Fifth Amendment.

■ CASE VOCABULARY

SIC UTERE TUO UT ALIENUM NON LAEDAS: Use your own property in such as manner as not to injure that of another.

Penn Central Transportation Co. v. City of New York

(Owner of Landmark) v. *(City)*

438 U.S. 104 (1978)

LAW PREVENTING BUILDING ON CITY LANDMARK IS NOT A "TAKING"

■ **INSTANT FACTS** The owner of Grand Central Terminal claimed that a New York City historic landmark preservation law barring it from building a 55-story office building above the Terminal constituted a "taking" of its property and required the City to pay it just compensation.

■ **BLACK LETTER RULE** Whether a law results in a taking turns on the character of the governmental action, its interference with reasonable investment-backed expectations, and its economic impact.

■ **PROCEDURAL BASIS**

Certification to the U.S. Supreme Court of case seeking damages for taking property.

■ **FACTS**

Penn Central Transportation Co. ("Penn Central") (P) owns Grand Central Terminal in New York City (the "City") (D). The City passed a historic landmark preservation law prohibiting Penn Central (P) from building a 55-story office building above the Terminal. However, the law allowed Penn Central (P) to sell transferable development rights ("TDRs") to permit development on other property. Penn Central (P) claimed the law constituted a "taking" of its property rights and, pursuant to the Fifth Amendment, requested just compensation from the City (D).

■ **ISSUE**

Does a law barring construction on historic landmarks constitute a "taking" that requires just compensation?

■ **DECISION AND RATIONALE**

(Brennan, J.) No. We disagree with Penn Central's (P) argument that the City (D) has "taken" Penn Central's (P) right to the airspace above the Terminal, thus entitling it to compensation. The Fifth Amendment provides that private property shall not be taken for public use without just compensation. However, the Court has been unable to develop any set formula for determining when a "taking" occurs. In past decisions, we have looked at a law's economic impact on the claimant and whether the character of the government's action involves physically invading the property or just affecting the property's value. Here, with respect to the law's economic impact on Penn Central (P), denying Penn Central's (D) ability to exploit a property interest does not constitute a taking. Looking at the law's effect on Penn Central's (P) reasonable investment-backed expectations, we note that the law does not interfere in any way with the current primary use of the property as a railroad terminal. Indeed, the law allows Penn Central (P) to receive a reasonable return on its investment. Further, while the City (D) will not allow Penn Central (P) to build a 55-story office building on the Terminal, the City (D) has not prevented Penn Central (P) from building a smaller structure. In addition, Penn Central (P) may transfer its valuable air rights to other nearby land parcels.

Analysis:

Here the Court distinguishes between physical invasions of property, that are more easily considered "takings," and laws that merely diminish the value of property, which are not likely to be "takings." This distinction is easy to apply and takes into account that a government may be unable to function if it has to compensate landowners every time it does something that adversely impacts property values. While preserving historic landmarks may not promote public health and safety, it is a choice that society has made to enhance its historic and aesthetic interests. Moreover, as the Court emphasized, Penn Central (P) still maintained a substantial amount of value in the Terminal, including operating the Terminal, selling its TDRs, and possibly building a smaller office building on the Terminal.

Lucas v. South Carolina Coastal Council

(*Landowner*) v. (*State*)

505 U.S. 1003 (1992)

GOVERNMENT ACTION THAT RENDERS PROPERTY VALUELESS IS A TAKING UNDER THE FIFTH AMENDMENT

■ **INSTANT FACTS** A South Carolina law barred a landowner from building any permanent structures on his beachfront land. The landowner claimed this constituted a "taking" under the Fifth Amendment requiring South Carolina to pay him just compensation.

■ **BLACK LETTER RULE** A law that renders property valueless is a taking under the Fifth Amendment and requires just compensation to the landowner.

■ **PROCEDURAL BASIS**

Certification to U.S. Supreme Court of case seeking damages for taking property.

■ **FACTS**

In 1986, Lucas (P) bought two beachfront lots in South Carolina. In 1988, South Carolina (D) enacted the Beachfront Management Act (the "Act") to prevent beach erosion. The Act barred Lucas (P) from building any permanent habitable structures on his land. The trial court held that the Act rendered Lucas' (P) land valueless and constituted a taking that required South Carolina (D) to pay Lucas (P) just compensation. The South Carolina Supreme Court reversed, holding that the Act was an appropriate exercise of South Carolina's (D) police powers.

■ **ISSUE**

Does a law that renders property valueless constitute a "taking" under the Fifth Amendment?

■ **DECISION AND RATIONALE**

(Scalia, J.) Yes. While the Court has not set forth any exact formula for determining when a taking occurs, we have determined that a taking occurs in two circumstances. First, it is a taking when a law requires a physical intrusion on property, no matter how small. It is also a taking when a law leaves land without any economically viable use. Here, the South Carolina Supreme Court's reliance on South Carolina's (D) power to eliminate "harmful or noxious uses" of property was inappropriate. Since land use regulations can be seen as both preventing a harm or achieving a benefit, this analysis cannot be used to distinguish takings from non-takings. Instead, if a regulation renders property valueless, compensation is not necessary only if the banned uses of the property were not part of the title under the common law to begin with. For example, barring a landowner from creating a nuisance on his property would not require compensation, even if the property was rendered valueless. Here, on the other hand, Lucas (P) had a reasonable expectation, based on basic common law principles, that he could build houses on his property. The appropriate test for determining whether a taking has occurred is similar to a nuisance analysis. It requires weighing the degree of harm to public lands, resources or adjacent private property posed by the landowner's proposed activities; the social value of the landowner's activities; and the relative ease with which the proposed harm can be avoided.

Building houses on property is not a nuisance, so barring such building constitutes a taking. Reversed and remanded.

■ CONCURRENCE

(Kennedy, J.) I agree with the majority that a landowner's reasonable expectations are relevant in determining whether a regulation renders property valueless. However, I would not limit these expectations to the law of nuisance, but rather expand them to encompass our whole legal tradition. The government may respond to changing conditions and regulate land uses in ways that nuisance law may otherwise permit.

■ DISSENT

(Blackmun, J.) The government has the power to regulate property without compensation to prevent serious harm, no matter how adverse the financial effect on the owner may be. Until today, the Court has rejected the contention that the government's power to act without paying compensation turns on whether the prohibited activity is a common-law nuisance. Instead, the Court has relied on legislative judgments of what constitutes a harm. The Court ruling today does not objectively determine whether a taking occurs. Indeed, whether a law deprives land of all economically valuable use cannot be determined objectively, but depends on how the "property" is defined. Similarly, the law of nuisance is not objective, but is based on whether a land use is harmful.

■ DISSENT

(Souter, J.) I would dismiss the writ of certiorari on the ground that the trial court's determination that Lucas' (P) land was valueless was extremely questionable. This finding deprived the Court of its ability to clarify the meaning of "total taking."

Analysis:

This case addresses only "total takings," i.e., government action that renders property without any value at all. Whether property is without any value is difficult to determine. For example, a landowner may have reasonably expected to build a manufacturing plant on his land, but after a law is passed banning such building, the land may be appropriate only for an amusement park. Is the land without any value? From this opinion, it is unclear what a court should do when faced with property that is rendered nearly valueless, but not quite. In addition, the majority relies heavily on traditional common law nuisance law to determine whether a taking has occurred. In other words, the government must pay compensation unless it shows a justification under traditional nuisance principles. This is a pro-owner position in that it limits when a government action will not be considered a taking.

Palazzolo v. Rhode Island

(Waterfront Property Owner) v. *(State Government)*

533 U.S. 606, 121 S.Ct. 2448, 150 L.Ed.2d 592 (2001)

POST–REGULATION ACQUISITION OF WATERFRONT PROPERTY WAS NOT A BAR TO A PROPERTY OWNER'S TAKING CLAIM

■ **INSTANT FACTS** Palazzolo's (P) development proposals were rejected by state authorities (D) pursuant to a state coastal protection law that required the issuance of a permit prior to the development of coastal wetlands. The law was enacted after Palazzolo's (P) company had acquired certain waterfront property that he proposed to develop but before Palazzolo (P) acquired individual title to that property.

■ **BLACK LETTER RULE** A post-regulation acquisition of property does not serve as an automatic bar to regulatory takings claims.

■ **PROCEDURAL BASIS**

Certiorari to review a state supreme court decision that rejected Palazzolo's (P) regulatory takings claim on the basis that post-regulation acquisition of property serves as an automatic bar to regulatory takings claims.

■ **FACTS**

Sometime after Palazzolo's (P) company acquired certain waterfront property, a state coastal protection law was enacted that prohibited the development of coastal wetlands without the issuance of a permit. A few years later, Palazzolo's (P) company's corporate charter was revoked and he acquired individual title to the property. Palazzolo's (P) two development proposals for the property were rejected and he filed an inverse condemnation action in state court alleging a regulatory taking. At the time of the filing, an upland portion of the property retained some limited development value. The trial court rejected the takings claim and the state supreme court affirmed on the grounds that (1) the claims were not ripe, (2) the claims were barred by Palazzolo's (P) post-regulation acquisition of the property, and (3) the upland portion of the property retained some development value.

■ **ISSUE**

Does the post-regulation acquisition of property serve as an automatic bar to a regulatory takings claim?

■ **DECISION AND RATIONALE**

(Kennedy, J.) No. Permitting the post-regulation acquisition of property to serve as automatic bar to a regulator takings claim would, in effect, put an expiration on the Takings Clause because the state would be absolved of its obligation to defend any action restricting land use, no matter how reasonable, against any party who acquired the property after the regulation was enacted. The basic unfairness is evident when considering that an heir's regulatory takings claim, that was now ripe, would be barred because of post-regulation acquisition of the property while the previous owner, who acquired the property pre-regulation, had been unable to sustain takings claim action because of ripeness. The state supreme court is therefore reversed. The court is also reversed with regard to its finding that Palazzolo's

---

(P) takings claim was not ripe for review because, in denying Palazzolo's (P) development proposals, the state made it clear that he could not engage in any filling or developmental activity on his waterfront property. Palazzolo (P) was not, however, deprived of an economically beneficial use of the property because the upland portion of the property retained some development value, and the court below was not required to consider whether that property was distinct from the wetlands portion of the property.

■ **CONCURRENCE**

(O'Connor, J.) The regulation in place at the time title is acquired should be considered in evaluating a regulatory takings claim because it is relevant in determining the reasonableness of the property owner's investment-backed expectation.

■ **CONCURRENCE**

(Scalia, J.) The fact that a restriction existed a the time a purchaser took title to a property (other than restrictions forming part of the "background principles of the state's law of property and nuisance") should not have a bearing upon the determination of whether the restriction is so substantial as to constitute a taking.

CONCURRENCE IN PART, DISSENT IN PART (Stevens, J.) The case was ripe for review since the regulation, in and of itself, precluded Palazzolo (P) from filling and developing his wetland property. However, Palazzolo (P) had no standing to make a takings claim because he was not the owner of the property at the time the regulations were adopted and his only recourse would be to seek enjoinment of the regulations.

■ **DISSENT**

(Ginsburg, J.) Palazzolo's (P) claim was not ripe for review because the record was ambiguous concerning the extent of permissible development on Palazzolo's (P) land.

■ **DISSENT**

(Breyer, J.) The simple fact that a piece of property has changed hands does not always and *automatically* bar a takings claim.

Analysis:

The Court's decision that the post-regulation transfer of title does not automatically bar a takings claim opens up the possibility of significant new takings litigation. If this occurs, statutes might likely be drafted that bar post-regulation transfers under certain circumstances. Note, however, that the Court's decision was not without its detractors, given the number of separately written opinions.

■ **CASE VOCABULARY**

AMBIGUITY: An uncertainty of meaning or intention, as in a contractual term or statutory provision.

CONDEMNATION: The determination and declaration that certain property (especially land) is assigned to public use, subject to reasonable compensation; the exercise of eminent domain by a government entity.

EMINENT DOMAIN: The inherent power of a government entity to take privately owned property, especially land, and convert it to public use, subject to reasonable compensation for the taking.

RIPENESS: The circumstance existing when a case has reached, but has not passed, the point when the FACTS have developed sufficiently to permit an intelligent and useful decision to be made. The requirement that this circumstance must exist before a court will decide a controversy.

TAKING: The act of seizing an article, with or without removing it, but with an implicit transfer of possession or control. There is a taking of property when government action directly interferes with or substantially disturbs the owner's use and enjoyment of the property.

TAKINGS CLAUSE: The Fifth Amendment provision that prohibits the government from taking private property for public use without fairly compensating the owner.

Tahoe-Sierra Preservation Council, Inc. v. Tahoe Regional Planning Agency

(Council of Area Landowners) v. *(Government Planning Agency)*

535 U.S. 302, 122 S.Ct. 1465, 152 L.Ed.2d 517 (2002)

MORATORIA ON DEVELOPMENT DID NOT CONSTITUTE A COMPENSABLE TAKING

■ **INSTANT FACTS** The Tahoe Regional Planning Agency (TRPA) (D) imposed two moratoria on virtually all residential development in an area subject to TRPA (D) jurisdiction until TRPA adopted a new land-use plan.

■ **BLACK LETTER RULE** A moratorium on development imposed during the process of devising a comprehensive land-use plan does not constitute a per se taking of property requiring compensation under the Takings Clause.

■ **PROCEDURAL BASIS**

Certiorari to review a U.S. Court of Appeals decision that because the two moratoria had only a temporary effect on the landowner's (P) interest in the properties, the enactment of the moratoria did not constitute a taking.

■ **FACTS**

The TRPA (D) ISSUEd two moratoria on virtually all residential development in the area subject to the TRPA's (D) jurisdiction until the TRPA adopted a new land-use plan. The moratorium period on the residential development lasted for thirty-two months. A council of area landowners (P), along with some classes of area landowners (P), filed suit claiming that the two TRPA moratoria constituted takings without compensation, in violation of the Fifth Amendment. The District Court determined that, even though the property retained some value during the moratorium period, the temporary deprivation of economically viable use of their land constituted categorical takings for purposes of the Takings Clause. The U.S. Court of Appeals reversed, in part, and remanded on the ground that noncategorical takings occurred because the TRPA (D) moratoria had only a temporary effect on the landowners' (P) fee interest in their property.

■ **ISSUE**

Does a moratorium on development imposed during the process of devising a comprehensive land-use plan constitute a per se taking of property requiring compensation under the Takings Clause?

■ **DECISION AND RATIONALE**

(Stevens, J.) No. Prior decisions by the Court do not support the application of a per se rule that would require the payment of compensation if a temporary regulation, while in effect, denies a property owner all viable economic use of his or her property. Furthermore, the interest of facilitating informed decision-making by regulatory agencies also counsels against adopting a per se rule because the agency might hurry through the planning process, and consequently make a less than fully informed decision, in order to avoid paying compensation to owners who would be affected by a temporary regulation. In the absence of a per se rule, the default rule remains that, in the regulatory taking context, a more fact-specific inquiry is required to determine whether there is an obligation to compensate an owner who has been temporarily denied the economic use of his property. Affirmed.

■ **DISSENT**

(Rehnquist, C.J.) The ban on economic development of the landowners' properties lasted almost six years, not thirty-two months, because of a subsequent injunction prohibiting the approval of business properties. A moratorium of this length is not one of the longstanding, implied limitations of state property law. Because the moratorium on development did not resemble any "implied limitation" of state property law, it is taking that requires compensation.

Analysis:

The decision in *Tahoe-Sierra*, like the decision in *Palazzolo v. Rhode Island*, 533 U.S. 606 (2001), indicates that, even if moratorium on use is lengthy, landowners should take an ad hoc factual approach, rather than a per se approach, to support their position that there has been a taking that requires compensation. If the facts of a particular case support compensation, the landowner stands in a better position to be compensated.

■ **CASE VOCABULARY**

AD HOC: Formed for a particular purpose.

MORATORIUM: An authorized postponement, usually a lengthy one, in the deadline for paying a debt or performing an obligation. The period of this delay. The suspension of a particular activity.

PER SE: Of, in, or by itself; standing alone, without reference to additional FACTS. As a matter of law.

TAKING: The act of seizing an article, with or without removing it, but with an implicit transfer of possession or control. There is a taking of property when government action directly interferes with or substantially disturbs the owner's use and enjoyment of the property.

TAKINGS CLAUSE: The Fifth Amendment provision that prohibits the government from taking private property for public use without fairly compensating the owner.

Dolan v. City of Tigard

(Store Owner) v. *(City)*
512 U.S. 374 (1994)

TO PASS CONSTITUTIONAL MUSTER, A LAND USE CONDITION MUST HAVE ROUGH PROPORTION-
ALITY TO THE PROPOSED DEVELOPMENT

■ **INSTANT FACTS** A city granted a store owner's application for a permit to redevelop her site
subject to the owner dedicating land for a storm
drainage system and for a pedestrian/bicycle
pathway.

■ **BLACK LETTER RULE** To not constitute a
taking, a land use condition must have "rough
proportionality" to the proposed development.

■ **PROCEDURAL BASIS**

Certification to U.S. Supreme Court of case seeking damages for taking property.

■ **FACTS**

Dolan (P) owned a plumbing and electric supply store. She applied to the City of Tigard (the "City")
(D) for a permit to nearly double the size of her store and pave a parking lot. The City (D) granted the
application subject to certain conditions. The City (D) required Dolan (P) to dedicate part of her
property lying within a creek's 100-year floodplain for a public greenway and storm drainage system
and an additional strip of land adjacent to the floodplain as a pedestrian/bicycle pathway. The City (D)
determined that the bike path was necessary to lessen traffic congestion that Dolan's (P) new building
would cause. It also found that the floodplain dedication was necessary to reduce flooding in the
creek. Dolan (P) challenged the City's (D) order claiming that the dedication requirement constituted
an uncompensated taking of private property. The Oregon Supreme Court rejected Dolan's (P) claim.

■ **ISSUE**

Does a permit condition requiring a landowner to dedicate land to the city constitute a "taking" under
the Fifth Amendment?

■ **DECISION AND RATIONALE**

(Rehnquist, C.J.) Yes, unless the condition has "rough proportionality" with the proposed development. In general, land use regulations do not constitute a taking if they substantially advance legitimate
state interests. However, here, the regulation singles out an individual land parcel, rather than
classifying an entire area of the City (D), and it requires Dolan (P) to dedicate land to the City (D), rather
than limit how she can use the property. We must determine whether the permit conditions have an
"essential nexus" with "legitimate state interests." Preventing flooding along the creek and reducing
traffic congestion are legitimate state interests. A nexus exists between these interests and limiting
development within the creek's 100-year floodplain and creating a pedestrian/bicycle path. Next, we
look at whether the permit conditions bear the required relationship to the projected impact of Dolan's
(P) proposed development. This required relationship must be one of "rough proportionality," i.e., it
must be related both in nature and extent to the impact of the proposed development. Here, paving
Dolan's (P) property will increase the rate of storm water flow. However, the City (D) has not stated
why it needs a public greenway along the floodplain rather than a private one, whereby Dolan (P) could

exclude others from entering her property. With respect to the bicycle path, the City (D) has not quantified the increased traffic that the development would create or that the path may offset. The City (D) has only stated that the path could offset traffic. Therefore, the City (D) has not shown the required relationship between the permit requirement and Dolan's (P) new building. Reversed.

■ DISSENT

(Stevens, J.) The majority's "rough proportionality" test is inadequate. The inquiry should be whether a condition is so grossly disproportionate to the proposed development's adverse effects that it manifests motives other than land use regulation. Dolan (P) has never argued that the City (D) should have prohibited her from building on the floodplain rather than requiring her to dedicate the land to the City (D). In fact, by dedicating the land, Dolan (P) need not pay taxes or be responsible for torts on that parcel. Dolan's (P) failure to seek narrower relief should preclude that relief now. With respect to the bike path, the City (D) should not be required to quantify its effect. The assumption that traffic will be offset is perfectly reasonable. When there is doubt about the effect of development on the environment, the public interest must take precedence. The party challenging the government action should have the burden of proving that the conditions unreasonably impair the economic value of the proposed improvements.

■ DISSENT

(Souter, J.) In cases involving government police power, the government is assumed to have acted constitutionally. Therefore, the burden here should be on Dolan (P), not on the City (D). Furthermore, the record here shows the connection between the required condition and the impact of the development that the majority is looking for. The City (D) has adequately quantified the increased traffic flow that Dolan's (P) proposed development will cause to be 435 trips per day and has studied how the bike path will reduce such traffic.

Analysis:

The Court distinguishes *Nollan v. California Coastal Commission* [permit condition not reasonably related to project's environmental effects]. In *Nollan*, the state sought to condition a permit to build a house on the beach on the landowners granting the public an easement over their property. The state claimed the project interfered with visual access to the beach. The Court held that the condition did not have an "essential nexus" to the project's environmental effects and was, therefore, a taking. Here, on the other hand, the Court found there was an essential nexus. The Court went further here and held that there must also be rough proportionality between the condition and the proposed development. It is unclear what the Court requires the City (D) to prove in order to uphold the permit condition. On the one hand, the Court states that it does not require a precise mathematical calculation, yet, on the other hand, it held that the City (D) did not properly quantify the traffic that the bicycle path would offset.

■ CASE VOCABULARY

DEDICATION: Setting apart real property for public use.

Lingle v. Chevron U.S.A., Inc.

(*Governor of Hawaii*) v. (*Oil Company*)

544 U.S. 528 (2005)

REGULATIONS MAY EFFECT UNCONSTITUTIONAL "TAKINGS" OF PRIVATE PROPERTY

Wearing white trunks is the representative for the *Agins* test, and in this corner, representing the Supreme Court of the United States, is Justice O'Connor.

■ **INSTANT FACTS** Chevron (P) argued that statutory limits on the rents that it could charge to gasoline retailers constituted an unconstitutional taking of its property.

■ **BLACK LETTER RULE** A plaintiff seeking to challenge a government regulation as an uncompensated taking of private property may proceed only by alleging a "physical" taking, a total regulatory taking, a *Penn Central* taking, or a land-use exaction.

■ **PROCEDURAL BASIS**

Supreme Court review of an affirmance of judgment in favor of Chevron (P).

■ **FACTS**

[The facts are not discussed in the casebook. In essence, based on its concern over the effects of market concentration on retail gasoline prices, the Hawaii Legislature passed a law that limited the amount of rent that oil companies could charge to dealers leasing company-owned service stations. Chevron (P), one of the largest oil companies in Hawaii at the time, brought suit seeking a declaration that the rent cap effected an unconstitutional taking of its property. Based on the Supreme Court's decision in *Agins* v. *City of Tiburon*, the district court held that the rent cap effected an uncompensated taking in violation of the Fifth and Fourteenth Amendments because it did not substantially advance Hawaii's asserted interest in controlling retail gas prices. The Ninth Circuit affirmed, and the case went to the Supreme Court.]

■ **ISSUE**

Is the *Agins* "substantially advance[s]" formula an appropriate test for determining whether government regulation effects a Fifth Amendment taking?

■ **DECISION AND RATIONALE**

(O'Connor, J.) No. A plaintiff seeking to challenge a government regulation as an uncompensated taking of private property may proceed only by alleging a "physical" taking, a total regulatory taking, a *Penn Central* taking, or a land-use exaction. Because Chevron argued a "substantially advances" theory, it was not entitled to summary judgment on its takings claim.

This Court has recognized that government regulation of private property may be as onerous as a direct appropriation or ouster. But regulatory actions generally will be deemed takings for Fifth Amendment purposes only when the government requires an owner to suffer a permanent physical invasion of her property, or when regulations completely deprive an owner of all economically beneficial use of her property. Beyond these two categories, and the exceptional category of land-use exactions, regulatory takings challenges are governed by our decision in *Penn Central Transportation Co.* v. *New York City*. The inquiries in *Penn Central* and other relevant precedent aim to identify regulatory actions that are functionally equivalent to direct appropriations of or ousters from private property, each of them focusing on the severity of the burden that government imposes on property rights.

The "substantially advances" formula requires an inquiry in the nature of a due process test, which is out of place in the Court's takings jurisprudence. Although *Agins*' reliance on due process precedents is understandable when viewed in historical context, the language the Court selected was imprecise, suggesting a means-ends test that asks, in essence, whether a regulation of private property is effective in achieving some legitimate public purpose. Such an inquiry is simply not a valid method of determining whether property has been "taken" for Fifth Amendment purposes. The "substantially advances" inquiry reveals nothing about the magnitude or character of the burden the questioned regulation imposes on property rights, and it therefore fails to help identify those regulations whose effects are functionally comparable to government appropriations. The *Agins* test is therefore rejected here.

Although this Court applied a "substantially advances" inquiry in *Agins* itself, it has never found a compensable taking based on such an inquiry. Moreover, in most of the cases reciting the *Agins* formula, the Court has merely assumed its validity when referring to it in dicta. Accordingly, no precedent is disturbed by today's decision. Reversed and remanded.

Analysis:

The Court here unanimously decided that a property owner claiming a regulatory "taking" cannot simply allege that a regulation does not "substantially advance" a state interest. Justice O'Connor, writing for the Court, explained that the "substantially advances" test was an unfortunate example of how "a would-be doctrinal rule or test finds its way into our case law through simple repetition of a phrase—however fortuitously coined." The Court conceded that its takings jurisprudence "cannot be characterized as unified" and noted that the thrust of the case law was to identify regulatory actions that were functionally equivalent to appropriating private property or ousting the owner from his domain. The *Agins* "substantially advances" position was, the Court opined, "regrettable"—while means-ends tests may be appropriate in due process cases to determine whether a regulation is arbitrary or irrational, they are not valid in takings analysis, which involves a consideration of the regulation's burden on private property, regardless of its effectiveness in serving a public interest.

■ CASE VOCABULARY

JUST COMPENSATION: Under the Fifth Amendment, a payment by the government for property it has taken under eminent domain—usually the property's fair market value, so that the owner is theoretically no worse off after the taking.

TAKINGS CLAUSE: The Fifth Amendment provision that prohibits the government from taking private property for public use without fairly compensating the owner.

CHAPTER EIGHT

Environmental Impact Assessment

Calvert Cliffs' Coordinating Committee v. United States Atomic Energy Commission

Instant Facts: An environmental group sued the Atomic Energy Commission, charging that the Commission's rules governing the licensing procedures for nuclear power plants did not meet the requirements of NEPA.

Black Letter Rule: Atomic Energy Commission [AEC] rules requiring the creation of environmental reports did not comply with NEPA where those reports were required merely to accompany a nuclear power plant license application, but were not to be considered by AEC's licensing board.

Strycker's Bay Neighborhood Council Inc. v. Karlen

Instant Facts: U.S. Department of Housing and Urban Development challenged a Second Circuit ruling that it failed to comply with NEPA when it approved a housing project at an environmentally inferior site because alternatives sites would have entailed two-year delays.

Black Letter Rule: Agency determination that costs of delay outweighed environmental benefits did not violate NEPA.

Kleppe v. Sierra Club

Instant Facts: The Department of Interior challenged a Circuit Court ruling requiring a regional EIS for development of coal reserves in the northern Great Plains states.

Black Letter Rule: Multiple federal actions or proposals for action with respect to related activities within a geographical region do not require a regional EIS unless there is a proposal for comprehensive regional action or sufficient cumulative environmental impacts.

Thomas v. Peterson

Instant Facts: Conservationists sued to enjoin construction of a logging road and timber sales until the Forest Service prepared an environmental impact statement addressing the cumulative effects of the road and the sales.

Black Letter Rule: When separate federal actions may have connected or cumulative impacts, the responsible agency must prepare an environmental impact statement covering such impacts prior to undertaking any of the individual actions.

Sierra Club v. Peterson

Instant Facts: Conservationist challenged Forest Service approval of oil and gas leases that contained no provisions allowing the Forest Service to prevent drilling in certain areas.

Black Letter Rule: NEPA requires an EIS prior to any agency decision which would irreversibly or irretrievably commit resources to a federal action that could significantly affect the environment.

Hanly v. Kleindienst

Instant Facts: Local residents and businesses sued to enjoin construction of a federal jail and office complex in Manhattan when the responsible federal agency failed to prepare an environmental impact statement.

Black Letter Rule: (1) A proposed federal action may significantly impact the human environment if it either (a) deviates from the current character of the area where it will take place, or (b) combines with current impacts to create a cumulatively significant impact. (2) A federal agency must give the public notice and the opportunity to comment on proposed major federal actions prior to the agency's decision on whether the action requires preparation of an EIS.

Department of Transportation v. Public Citizen

Instant Facts: A public watchdog group brought legal action based on a federal agency's failure to consider the environmental impact of its regulations.

Black Letter Rule: When an agency has no ability to prevent a certain effect due to its limited statutory authority over the relevant actions, the agency cannot be considered a legally relevant "cause" of such effect; hence, under NEPA and the implementing regulations, the agency need not consider these effects in its EA.

Vermont Yankee Nuclear Power Corp. v. NRDC

Instant Facts: Power company appealed a Court of Appeals decision that the commission in charge of licensing nuclear power facilities consider energy conservation measures as an alternative to building a power plant.

Black Letter Rule: NEPA did not require the Atomic Energy Commission to consider energy conservation as an alternative to building a nuclear power plant in an EIS prepared for use in the plant licensing proceedings.

Sierra Club v. United States Army Corps of Engineers

Instant Facts: Conservationists challenged U.S. Army Corps of Engineers approval of a highway project based on an EIS that failed to consider evidence of marine life in an area to be filled.

Black Letter Rule: Court may not rule that an EIS was inadequate if the agency preparing the EIS adequately compiled and analyzed relevant data, ignored no pertinent data, and publicly disclosed its findings.

Marsh v. Oregon Natural Resources Council

Instant Facts: Conservationists sued to compel the U.S. Army Corps of Engineers to prepare a second supplement to the Corps' EIS concerning a dam project.

Black Letter Rule: Courts may not set aside an agency decision not to supplement EISs when that decision was based on factual findings and was not arbitrary or capricious.

Calvert Cliffs' Coordinating Committee v. United States Atomic Energy Commission

(Environmental Watchdogs) v. *(Federal Agency)*

449 F.2d 1109 (D.C. Cir. 1971)

NEPA REQUIRES AGENCIES TO CONSIDER ENVIRONMENTAL REPORTS AT EVERY IMPORTANT STAGE OF THE AGENCIES' DECISIONMAKING PROCESSES

■ **INSTANT FACTS** An environmental group sued the Atomic Energy Commission, charging that the Commission's rules governing the licensing procedures for nuclear power plants did not meet the requirements of NEPA.

■ **BLACK LETTER RULE** Atomic Energy Commission [AEC] rules requiring the creation of environmental reports did not comply with NEPA where those reports were required merely to accompany a nuclear power plant license application, but were not to be considered by AEC's licensing board.

■ **PROCEDURAL BASIS**

Challenge, direct to federal Circuit Court, of a federal agency rulemaking.

■ **FACTS**

The National Environmental Policy Act [NEPA] required all federal agencies to consider the environmental impacts of the agencies' actions. Section 101 of NEPA set forth the general requirement that the federal government protect the environment through "all practical means and measures." Section 101(b) specifically stated that federal officials had a duty to encourage "widest range of beneficial uses of the environment without . . . undesirable and unintended consequences" not inconsistent with "other essential considerations of national policy." NEPA required agencies to perform two specific procedures. First, Section 101(2)(C) required agency officials to prepare detailed environmental impact statements (EISs). The purpose of an EIS was to guide the agency's decisionmaking, advise other agencies, and inform the public. Section 102(2)(E) required agencies to "study, develop, and describe appropriate alternatives" to proposed actions. In direct response to NEPA, the Atomic Energy Commission [AEC] developed the following rules for the application process for acquiring a license to operate a nuclear energy facility. First, AEC required the license applicant to prepare a report on a proposed nuclear plant's environmental impact and on possible alternatives. Second, AEC would prepare an EIS, as required by NEPA § 102(2)(C), based on the applicant's report. Third, although the applicant's report and EIS would accompany the license application, the licensing board would not accept them into evidence and would not consider them in making its determination. Calvert Cliffs Coordinating Committee [CCCC], an environmental group, argued that the rules adopted by AEC failed to satisfy NEPA requirements. AEC argued that NEPA is vague and that AEC acted within its discretion under NEPA. AEC also argued that it did not need to consider air and water pollution caused by proposed plants because the Environmental Protection Agency would evaluate those areas.

■ **ISSUE**

Is a rule requiring the preparation of environmental reports sufficient for AEC to meet its requirements under NEPA when those reports must accompany a license application but are not to be considered in hearings?

■ DECISION AND RATIONALE

(J. Skelly Wright, Circuit Judge) No. AEC's contention that NEPA requires that an EIS merely accompany a license application made a mockery of NEPA § 102(2)(C). AEC seems to be advancing the absurd interpretation that § 102 just requires an EIS to travel around with other documents in a license application folder. NEPA § 102 states that agencies must comply with its provisions "to the fullest extent possible." This is a very high standard that reviewing courts must enforce. Thus, agency actions are not discretionary, and difficulty, delay and expense are not sufficient to overcome § 102 requirements. If an agency reaches a decision after the required consideration of environmental impact, a court will overturn the decision only if the decision was arbitrary. If, however, an agency makes any decision without full, good faith consideration of environmental costs and benefits, a reviewing court must reverse that decision. To comply to the fullest extent, an agency must consider the EIS "at every important stage in the decisionmaking process." NEPA requires that agencies balance environmental harms against economic and technical benefits on an individual, case-by-case basis. The agency given the responsibility of a given government action must perform the complete balancing analysis for that action. Thus, certification from EPA that the action does not violate EPA's air and water pollution standards does not relieve the responsible agency from its duty to balance all environmental costs against the benefits from the proposed license. As with the EIS, an agency must also "to the fullest extent possible" consider alternatives to proposed actions as required by § 102(2)(E).

Analysis:

This case was the first major NEPA decision issued by a federal court. Throughout the case, the court used this specific challenge to rules propounded by AEC to establish what the court saw as the contours of the whole NEPA act. Right at the beginning of the case, the court acknowledged that this was the first case in what the court predicted would be a flood of litigation over NEPA. Therefore, the court realized its important historical role as the first judicial body to review the act. Moreover, since this is the D.C. Circuit, the court knew that it would hear much of the litigation over NEPA and that other Circuits would look to it for guidance on the statute. This was, one imagines, a large factor in the court's careful consideration of the standards of review. The court clearly believes that Congress intended for NEPA to have teeth, to be tough and enforceable. This is the reason that the court denied AEC's contention that the act was intended to give agencies broad discretion. Rather than seeing the act's simplicity as providing agencies a largely blank canvas, the court saw the act's language as unambiguous: if an agency did not *fully* comply, the reviewing court was required to reverse the agency's decision.

■ CASE VOCABULARY

ENVIRONMENTAL IMPACT STATEMENT (EIS): This is the name given to the "detailed statement" on environmental impacts of proposed government actions that agencies must prepare under § 102(2)(C) of NEPA; the EIS must include analysis of alternatives and disclose any natural resources that would be lost as a result of the proposal.

Strycker's Bay Neighborhood Council, Inc. v. Karlen

(*Community Organization*) v. (*HUD Head*)

444 U.S. 223 (1980)

NEPA DOES NOT REQUIRE AGENCIES TO ELEVATE ENVIRONMENTAL FACTORS OVER OTHER COST AND BENEFIT CONSIDERATIONS

■ **INSTANT FACTS** U.S. Department of Housing and Urban Development challenged a Second Circuit ruling that it failed to comply with NEPA when it approved a housing project at an environmentally inferior site because alternatives sites would have entailed two-year delays.

■ **BLACK LETTER RULE** Agency determination that costs of delay outweighed environmental benefits did not violate NEPA.

■ **PROCEDURAL BASIS**

Appeal from a decision of the U.S. Court of Appeals Second Circuit that vacated a District Court decision in favor of HUD.

■ **FACTS**

Strycker's Bay Neighborhood Council Inc. [the "Council"] (P) sued to enjoin U.S. Department of Housing and Urban Development Administrator ["HUD"] (D) approval of a housing project planned for Manhattan's Upper West Side. The first time that the Second Circuit heard the case, it held that, to comply with the National Environmental Policy Act ["NEPA"], HUD (D) must consider alternatives to the housing project, but that NEPA did not require HUD (D) to prepare an EIS. The Second Circuit remanded the case to HUD (D), which prepared a report called Special Environmental Clearance. This report found that the projects social impacts were acceptable. The report incorporated a study of nine alternative sites. The study found that use of any of the alternative sites would create a delay of at least two years. HUD (D) concluded that the costs of the delays would outweigh any benefits from the alternative sites. The District Court approved the HUD report as "thorough," not arbitrary, and done "in full accordance with the law." On appeal, however, the Second Circuit vacated HUD's (D) decision for the second time. The Second Circuit found that NEPA provided "substantive standards necessary [for courts] to review the merits of agency decisions...." Specifically, the Second Circuit held that NEPA required that environmental factors, such as crowding, had determinative weight. Thus, the court rejected HUD's (D) argument that delay was sufficient reason to reject the alternative sites.

■ **ISSUE**

Did HUD fail to comply with NEPA standards by basing its approval of a housing project on a determination that delays caused by alternative sites outweighed environmental concerns?

■ **DECISION AND RATIONALE**

(Per Curiam) No. HUD (D) complied with NEPA's requirement by considering alternatives in this case. NEPA does not require agencies to elevate environmental factors over other costs and benefits. This conclusion is supported by *Vermont Yankee Nuclear Power Corp. v. NRDC* (1978). In *Vermont Yankee*, we found that NEPA creates national environmental *goals*, but imposes largely *procedural* requirements for federal agencies. NEPA's purpose is to guarantee that agency decisions are well-informed with respect to environmental concerns. The reviewing court's role is to make sure that an agency considered environmental factors in the decisionmaking process. The court may not substitute its substantive conclusions regarding the weight of environmental factors for the conclusions of the agency. The decision of the Second Circuit is reversed.

■ DISSENT

(Marshall, J.) The issue for the Circuit Court was whether NEPA permits an agency to approve an environmentally inferior site solely because alternatives would create delays. The answer to that issue is unclear in light of *Vermont Yankee*. We should examine HUD's (D) resolution of that issue to see if it was "arbitrary, capricious, or an abuse of discretion." Our decision in *Kleppe v. Sierra Club* (1976) held that NEPA required HUD (D) to take a "hard look" at the environmental concerns raised by the project. This Court should consider whether the agency failed to give proper consideration to environmental factors, and therefore acted arbitrarily or capriciously. *Vermont Yankee* cannot mean that a court must accept that an agency considered environmental factors even if the agency's "consideration" amounted to giving environmental factors no weight.

Analysis:

The Supreme Court decided this case without hearing oral arguments and approved the per curiam decision with little debate. Moreover, the tone of the opinion suggests that the Justices were impatient with the Second Circuit's ongoing remands. Because the Court felt that *Vermont Yankee* was controlling, the rationale in the per curiam opinion was very succinct. All of this makes the presence of Justice Marshall's dissent all the more thought provoking. The dissent makes its point rhetorically: is consideration really consideration (as contemplated by NEPA) when the result is the agency concluding that environmental factors don't count for a given decision. The dissent suggests that if the Court means to maintain the standard that the Court should at least look into whether HUD (D) clearly gave insufficient weight to the environmental factors in the present case. In the per curiam decision, the Court is not explicit about how it knows that HUD (D) gave sufficient consideration to environmental factors. The Court does mention that the District Court was satisfied that HUD (D) had conducted a thorough, good faith review. The point that the Supreme Court seems more intent on making, however, is that the reviewing courts should not impose their substantive evaluations about factors onto agencies. The Court seems to be reminding the lower courts that if the agency considered a two-year delay costly enough to trump the foreseeable environmental harm in this case, the agency may know its business better than the courts do. In the end, the Supreme Court's decision might be seen as more about how much deference reviewing courts should show to agencies than about the interpretation of NEPA.

■ CASE VOCABULARY

ARBITRARY OR CAPRICIOUS STANDARD: This is that standard that most courts use when reviewing agency rulings; the standard, sometimes referred to as the "abuse of discretion" standard, is very deferential to the agencies, and courts will not overturn agency actions unless the agency unreasonably exercised its discretion.

Kleppe v. Sierra Club

(Department of Interior head) v. *(Environmental Group)*
427 U.S. 390 (1976)

REGIONAL EIS IS REQUIRED ONLY WHEN AN AGENCY ACTS OR PROPOSES TO ACT ON A REGIONAL SCOPE OR WHEN VARIOUS LOCAL ACTS HAVE A CUMULATIVE ENVIRONMENTAL IMPACT

■ **INSTANT FACTS** The Department of Interior challenged a Circuit Court ruling requiring a regional EIS for development of coal reserves in the northern Great Plains states.

■ **BLACK LETTER RULE** Multiple federal actions or proposals for action with respect to related activities within a geographical region do not require a regional EIS unless there is a proposal for comprehensive regional action or sufficient cumulative environmental impacts.

■ **PROCEDURAL BASIS**

U.S. Supreme Court review of a D.C. Circuit decision remanding the case to the Department of Interior for development of a regional EIS.

■ **FACTS**

Section 102(2)(C) of the National Environmental Policy Act ["NEPA"] requires the creation of an Environmental Impact Statement ["EIS"] for "every recommendation or report on proposals for legislation and other major Federal actions significantly affecting the quality of the human environment." The Department of Interior ["Interior"] (D) authorized leases, mining plans, and right-of-ways concerning federal coal reserves in four states in the northern Great Plains. The Sierra Club (P) argued that, because Interior (D) was proposing a comprehensive federal plan for the region, NEPA required Interior (D) to create an EIS for the entire region. The Sierra Club also contended that, even if Interior's (D) plans did not constitute a comprehensive regional plan, NEPA required a regional EIS because the environmental impacts of various local actions were "intimately related." The D.C. Circuit did not rule on the Sierra Club's (P) second argument, but held in its favor on the first. The D.C. Circuit cited four factors for determining when NEPA requires a regional EIS: (1) the likelihood that the federal action will begin; (2) amount of information available about the action or proposal; (3) the extent to which the nation is irretrievably committing natural resources under the action: and (4) the level of potential environmental harm. The D.C. Circuit held that the second and fourth factors were established in this case and remanded the case to Interior (D) with orders to create a regional EIS. Interior (D) obtained U.S. Supreme Court review, arguing that there was no proposal for "major federal action" on the regional level. Interior (D) contended that, because there was no regional-level proposal for action, NEPA § 102(2)(C) was not triggered. The Sierra Club (P) reasserted their argument that a regional EIS was required because of the "intimately related" nature of the environmental impacts throughout the northern Great Plains area.

■ **ISSUE**

Does NEPA require the Department of Interior to create a regional EIS for various coal mining proposals within an area when the Department has a national coal policy and developed individual EISs for local actions?

■ DECISION AND RATIONALE

(Powell, J.) No. Interior (D) did not act or propose a major government action for the northern Great Plains region. The proposals that Interior considered were local in nature, e.g., issuing a lease, approving a mining plan, permitting a right-of-way. Interior understood that when one of these activities had the potential to "significantly [affect] the quality of the human environment," NEPA § 102(2)(C) required the creation of an EIS. Interior undertook several EISs on proposals for local action. Moreover, Interior (D) had prepared a national Coal Programmatic EIS covering the comprehensive policy of the Department for coal extraction throughout the country. In its findings, the District Court determined that there was no regional plan or proposal, and that the local projects were not coordinated or integrated into any comprehensive scheme. The D.C. Circuit did not change these finding. The D.C. Circuit, however, created its four-factor test for establishing when an EIS may be required under NEPA even though no formal proposal for federal action has been made. This test is not supported by NEPA. In *Aberdeen & Rockfish R. Co, v. SCRAP* (1975), we held that § 102(2)(C) requires that a final EIS must be available when the agency "makes a recommendation or report on a *proposal* for federal action." The D.C. Circuit's test would lead to too many unnecessary EISs being prepared. Finally, we agree with the Sierra Club (P) that there are times when NEPA may require preparation of a regional EIS where individual actions or proposals might lead to "cumulative or synergistic environmental impact[s]." In this case, however, Interior (D) determined that examining environmental impacts at the basin and drainage levels was more appropriate than at the comprehensive regional level. This determination is not arbitrary or capricious. The Court of Appeals for the D.C. Circuit decision is reversed, and the District Court decision is affirmed.

■ DISSENT

(Marshall, J.) The Court's decision is largely correct, but the Court should not strike down the D.C. Circuit's test for when an EIS may be required prior to a formal proposal for action. Such a test provides the courts a mechanism whereby they can remedy the situation of an inadequate or non-existent EIS in cases where government action is likely and environmental risk very high. Without such a mechanism, the courts have had to resort to costly and time-consuming injunctions. Such a test would help courts effectuate the goals of NEPA.

Analysis:

Taxpayers and Congress consistently snipe at revelations of redundant bureaucratic procedures between federal agencies or, even worse, within the same agency. The Court is clearly aware of how costly and time-consuming the preparation of environmental impact statements is in most cases. In this case, the court has to make several decisions about when NEPA requires an agency to prepare an EIS and the scope that an EIS must encompass. On the timing issue, the Court held that an agency did not have to have an EIS until the agency presented a formal proposal for legislation or major federal action. The Court's decision tries to make it possible for agencies to kick ideas around without worrying about the enormous EIS undertaking until the agency was really serious about acting.

Thomas v. Peterson

(Ranch Owner) v. *(Forest Service Chief)*
753 F.2d 754 (9th Cir. 1985)

NEPA REQUIRES A SINGLE EIS COVERING THE OVERALL IMPACT OF SEPARATE ACTIONS THAT ARE CUMULATIVE OR CONNECTED

■ **INSTANT FACTS** Conservationists sued to enjoin construction of a logging road and timber sales until the Forest Service prepared an environmental impact statement addressing the cumulative effects of the road and the sales.

■ **BLACK LETTER RULE** When separate federal actions may have connected or cumulative impacts, the responsible agency must prepare an environmental impact statement covering such impacts prior to undertaking any of the individual actions.

■ **PROCEDURAL BASIS**

Appeal to U.S. Court of Appeals from a District Court summary judgment in favor of Forest Service.

■ **FACTS**

The U.S. Forest Service (D) approved construction of an access road into an area of forest called "Jersey Jack." Because the Forest Service (D) determined that the road would not have a significant impact on the environment, it did not prepare an environmental impact statement ["EIS"] prior to approving the road. After approving the road, the Forest Service (D) also approved two timber sales in the area, again concluding that no EISs were necessary. Conservationists (P) sued to enjoin both the road and sales on several grounds, including the National Environmental Policy Act ["NEPA"]. Section 102(2)(C) of NEPA requires an EIS for "major Federal actions significantly affecting the quality of the human environment." After the Supreme Court's *Kleppe* decision, the Council for Environmental Quality ["CEQ"] issued two regulations that define when separate federal actions must be treated under one EIS. The first CEQ regulation requires a single EIS for all "connected actions." CEQ defines "connected actions" as actions that (a) automatically trigger other actions that may require EISs, (b) require other actions before or at the same time they occur, or (c) are interdependent parts of a larger action. The second CEQ regulation requires a single EIS for all "cumulative actions," defined as actions "which when viewed with other proposed actions have cumulative significant impacts." The Forest Service (D) argued that individual EISs or environmental assessments of the road and each of the two timber sales would be adequate to judge the cumulative impacts of the actions. The Forest Service (D) also argued that the timber sales were speculative and thus did not need to be assessed along with the road.

■ **ISSUE**

Are construction of an access road and timber sales in the area opened by the road so closely related as to require a single EIS covering the combined impacts of both the road and the sales?

■ **DECISION AND RATIONALE**

(Sneed, Circuit Judge) Yes. NEPA and the CEQ regulations require that the Forest Service (D) prepare a single EIS for the road and the timber sales. The timber sales and the road fall under CEQ's definition of connected actions. The road is being built to make timber sales possible, and the timber sales already approved cannot be carried out without the road. That meets the second and third definitions of connected actions. The Forest Service (D) has called the road a "logging road," and rejected the alternative of not building the road because without the road there would be no timber access. The Forest Service (D) cannot maintain that the road is not connected to the sales simply because the road may have other uses as well. There is also an inter-Service letter that links the road to the sales. The road and timber sales may also have cumulative effects. The Federal Fish & Wildlife Service, the EPA and state agencies have all maintained that separate impact statements will not sufficiently address cumulative impacts such as sediment deposits in the Salmon River and degradation of habitat for endangered species. The Forest Service's (D) claim that separate impact analyses for the road and each of the sales would be sufficient to assess the cumulative impacts is incorrect. It is too late to consider cumulative impacts after the road is already approved and built. Completion of the road makes approval of timber sales in the area more likely because the timber sales are designed to cover the cost of building the road. NEPA's purpose for requiring EISs is to assure that agencies have adequate information during the decision stage of proposed actions. The purpose of NEPA is frustrated by having the decision so chopped up that each little part does not require an EIS. If actions are related so closely that the CEQ regulations apply, then an agency cannot avoid preparing the more comprehensive EIS by characterizing some of the actions as speculative. On the NEPA issue, the case is reversed and remanded to the Forest Service for preparation of an EIS covering the combined impacts of the road and the timber sales.

Analysis:

In this case, the court wants to make sure that agencies prepare EISs of the proper scope, but to do so, the court must also address questions of timing. In other words, agencies must look forward to see how various actions might be interrelated in order to see whether an EIS will be required to cover their joint impacts. This might lead one to sympathize with the agencies. After all, we have all taken little steps in life that seemed insignificant on their own, only to look back and realize that we have done something quite monumental in hindsight. This is where the CEQ regulations come in. In the regulations, the court has a relatively objective and comprehensible standards which it can apply. This makes the medicine much easier for agencies to swallow. Now the court can say, "You don't have to guess at the mutual impacts of every possible action, but if the actions are close enough to count under the CEQ regulations, you had better consider them together."

■ CASE VOCABULARY

COUNCIL FOR ENVIRONMENTAL QUALITY [CEQ]: NEPA § 202 creates this three-member group in the Executive Office of the President to gather information, review federal programs, and give an annual report on the state of the environment; the Council's regulations may become binding on agencies by Executive Order.

Sierra Club v. Peterson

(*Conservation Group*) v. (*U.S. Forest Service Chief*)

717 F.2d 1409 (D.C. Cir. 1983)

AGENCIES MUST CONSIDER ENVIRONMENTAL IMPACT STATEMENTS PRIOR TO DECISIONS WHICH IRREVOCABLY COMMIT RESOURCES TO ACTIONS WHICH COULD CAUSE ENVIRONMENTAL IMPACT

■ **INSTANT FACTS** Conservationist challenged Forest Service approval of oil and gas leases that contained no provisions allowing the Forest Service to prevent drilling in certain areas.

■ **BLACK LETTER RULE** NEPA requires an EIS prior to any agency decision which would irreversibly or irretrievably commit resources to a federal action that could significantly affect the environment.

■ **PROCEDURAL BASIS**

Appeal from a U.S. District Court decision upholding the decision of the Forest Service and Department of the Interior.

■ **FACTS**

Oil and natural gas developers applied to the U.S. Forest Service [the "Service"] (D) and Department of the Interior (D) for oil and natural gas leases on Forest Service lands in Idaho and Wyoming known as the Palisades Further Planning Area. The Service (D) prepared an environmental assessment. On that basis, the Service (D) concluded that the leases would not cause significant environmental impacts, and that the Service (D) did not need to prepare an environmental impact statement ["EIS"] for the entire area. The Service (D) approved leases containing various stipulations allowing the Service (D) to require the lessees to get approval from the Service for various activities. For areas designated "highly environmentally sensitive," the leases contained No Surface Occupancy Stipulations ["NSO Stipulations"] that allowed the Service (D) to preclude certain activities. For the other areas, however, the leases contained no NSO Stipulations and thus, the Service (D) could not deny drilling permits requested by the lessees, although it could impose mitigating conditions on the drilling in those areas. Section 102(2)(C) of the National Environmental Policy Act ["NEPA"] requires agencies to prepare and consider an EIS for any proposed action that could significantly impact the environment. Sierra Club (P) sued to stop the leases contending that the Service (D) and the Department of the Interior (D) had violated NEPA by approving the leases prior to preparing and considering an environmental impact statement ["EIS"]. The District Court granted summary judgment for the agencies. Sierra Club (P) appealed regarding the leases with no NSO Stipulations.

■ **ISSUE**

Does an agency's approval of a lease which contained no clause allowing the agency to prevent oil and gas drilling on the leased lands violate NEPA when such lease is approved without first considering an EIS?

■ **DECISION AND RATIONALE**

(MacKinnon, Senior Circuit Judge) Yes. By approving leases that permitted oil and gas drilling without first considering an EIS, the Service (D) violated NEPA. The Service (D) claims that its environmental assessment was adequate to conclude that approval of the leases would cause no significant impact to the environment. Courts may overturn "no significant impact" findings only if the agency's determination was "arbitrary, capricious or an abuse of discretion." The D.C. Circuit uses a four-part test to review agencies' "no significant impact" findings: the agency must (1) take a "hard look" at the proposed action; (2) "identify the relevant areas of environmental concern;" (3) make a convincing case that the action will have insignificant impacts; and (4) in case of potential significant impact, show that changes in the proposed action have minimized the impacts. In this case, the Service fails on the third point. The Service (D) cannot support its conclusion that there would be no significant impact on the environment as the result of leases, when the Service (D) does not reserve the right to preclude drilling operations. The Service (D) contends that the lease stipulations will be sufficient to prevent environmental impacts until the lessee submits "site-specific exploration and development" plans. The Service (D) predicts that most of the leases will turn out not to be worth drilling or developing. With respect to the leases without NSO Stipulations, however, the Service (D) has permitted drilling, and its accompanying impacts, at the time it approved the leases. Therefore, NEPA requires the Service (D) to consider an EIS prior to approving the leases. The purpose of NEPA is to insure that agencies make fully informed decisions prior to the irrevocable commitment of resources to actions that will affect the environment. A two-step approach to the leases would be acceptable provided that the Service (D) retain the rights to prevent surface disturbances. But, if the Service (D) intends to issue leases without NSO Stipulations, it must prepare an EIS. The District Court's decision is reversed and the case remanded to the Service (D).

Analysis:

This is a case that surely must look much clearer in hindsight. Imagine for a moment all of the negotiations between the energy companies and the Forest Service. Imagine all the various branches of the Forest Service that would have to look at various aspects of these leases. Finally, imagine conservationists trying to monitor all of these developments and discover the impacts that the prospective exploration could have. All of that makes it clear why the courts have construed to NEPA to require EISs *before* major agency decisions are made. The lawyers for the oil companies are trying to get the best leases, i.e., with the fewest restrictions, for their clients, while different divisions within the Forest Service have their own reasons (e.g., political pressure, budget) for wanting to speed up or slow down the whole process. What the court is articulating in this opinion is a course of action that can really step in and protect the environment despite all these various conflicting forces.

Hanly v. Kleindienst

(Citizen) v. *(U.S. Attorney General)*

471 F.2d 823 (2d Cir. 1972)

SIGNIFICANCE OF ENVIRONMENTAL IMPACTS FROM FEDERAL ACTIONS IS JUDGED BY COMPARING THE IMPACT OF THE ACTION TO THE CURRENT SITUATION AND BY EVALUATING THE ABSOLUTE IMPACT OF THE ACTION. A FEDERAL AGENCY MUST PROVIDE PUBLIC NOTICE AND OPPORTUNITY TO COMMENT PRIOR TO DECIDING WHETHER PROPOSED ACTIONS REQUIRE THE AGENCY TO PREPARE AN EIS

■ **INSTANT FACTS** Local residents and businesses sued to enjoin construction of a federal jail and office complex in Manhattan when the responsible federal agency failed to prepare an environmental impact statement.

■ **BLACK LETTER RULE** (1) A proposed federal action may *significantly* impact the human environment if it either (a) deviates from the current character of the area where it will take place, or (b) combines with current impacts to create a cumulatively significant impact. (2) A federal agency must give the public notice and the opportunity to comment on proposed major federal actions prior to the agency's decision on whether the action requires preparation of an EIS.

■ **PROCEDURAL BASIS**

Appeal to federal Court of Appeals from a District Court decision denying injunctive relief to plaintiffs challenging the federal construction project.

■ **FACTS**

The General Services Administration ["GSA"] (D) planned to construct a jail and other buildings in association with the federal courthouse in Manhattan. Residents and businesses (P) near the courthouse site sought an injunction to halt the planned construction under the National Environmental Policy Act ["NEPA"]. Section 102(2)(C) of NEPA requires an Environmental Impact Statement ["EIS"] for any proposal for "major Federal actions significantly affecting the quality of the human environment." The Public Buildings Service of GSA (D), in charge of the courthouse project, operated under the guideline, issued by the Council on Environmental Quality ["CEQ"] that requires an EIS for any "proposed actions, the environmental impact of which [was] likely to be highly controversial." The District Court denied an injunction, agreeing with GSA (D) that the project would not significantly impact the environment and no EIS was required. On appeal, the Second Circuit upheld the District Court decision with respect to the office building part of the project, but reversed with respect to the jail facility. The Second Circuit ordered GSA (D) to study the jail project more thoroughly (specifically, noise, parking, traffic, and potential increases in crime in the neighborhood) to determine whether an EIS was needed. GSA (D) prepared a 25-page report about the jail [the "Assessment"] and decided that it need not prepare an EIS. The Assessment determined that the jail facility would not create significant increases in pollution or congestion, but did not examine the crime issue or address the proposed use of the jail as a drug treatment facility. Local residents and businesses (P) again challenged the project in federal court. The District Court again denied injunctive relief. The locals (P) appealed. The locals (P) also argued that GSA (D) also violated required procedures by not giving concerned citizens an opportunity to discuss the courthouse project before GSA (D) submitted its

Assessment. The locals (P) argued that three NEPA sections required public comment. Section 102(2)(A) requires that agencies consider "natural and social sciences and the environmental design arts" when assessing environmental impacts. Section 102(2)(B) requires agencies to take into account "unquantified environmental amenities and values" as well as economic and technical issues. Finally, § 102(2)(D) requires agencies to develop alternatives to its proposal for action. GSA (D) argued that these three provisions were triggered only if an EIS was required.

■ ISSUE

(1) Did GSA use the correct standard, under NEPA, to determine that a proposed federal jail did not pose a significant adverse effect on the human environment? (2) Does a federal agency have to provide opportunity for public comment before it may submit a report finding no need for an EIS?

■ DECISION AND RATIONALE

(Mansfield, Circuit Judge) (1) No. Because it did not evaluate projected increases in crime, use of the jail as a drug treatment facility and because factual findings in the Assessment were disputed, GSA acted arbitrarily in determining that it was not required to prepare and consider an EIS for the jail project. Any major federal action might be expected to have some environmental impact. However, by including the word "significantly" in NEPA § 102(2)(C), Congress intended to distinguish the level of environmental impact requiring preparation of an EIS from the level that might be expected from just any federal action. CEQ guidelines require EISs for actions expected to be "highly controversial." The term "controversial" here refers to situations where there is a dispute over the size, nature or impact of a proposed federal action, and not to the existence of community opposition to the project. Neither Congress nor CEQ has defined the term "significantly" as it is used in NEPA. Therefore, agencies must have some discretion in defining the term. The appropriate standard for reviewing GSA's actions is the "arbitrary or capricious standard." The proper test for determining whether an action will have a "significant" environmental impact is to examine (a) the extent to which the action will impact the environment beyond the current situation, and (b) the total quantitative impact on the environment including the extent to which the action combines with or contributes to existing impacts. For the most part, if a proposed use conforms to the character of the area, it will not create significant harms. Cumulative impacts must be studied, however, because in some cases, the proposed use will be the "straw that breaks the back of the environmental camel." In close cases, this two-factor test will encourage agencies to prepare EISs because the alternative could be lengthy litigation. Before determining that no EIS is required, GSA must complete further study on the effects on crime in the area of the proposed jail, the effects of the use of the jail as a drug treatment facility, and assess disputed findings of fact from its earlier assessment. (2) Yes. An agency must give the public notice of and opportunity to comment on any proposed major federal action before the agency may make a threshold decision that the proposal does not require an EIS. The sections of NEPA at issue (§§ 102(2)(A), (B), and (D)) are separate from § 102(2)(C), and are not required only when an EIS is required. If those sections were required only for "major Federal actions significantly affecting the human environment," then §§ 102(2)(C) and (D) would be redundant since both sections call for the study of alternatives to the proposed action. Section 102(2)(B) requires such procedures to assure that agencies will make fair and informed threshold findings. Public records also alert agencies to consider changes that might affect the environmental significance of their proposals. We think a formal public meeting such as those held on zoning disputes in many cities would be a good idea, but NEPA does not require such meetings. The agency may determine whether to use meetings or less formal methods of accepting public comment on a case-by-case basis. In the present case, GSA's (D) Assessment complied with § 102(2)(A) because GSA (D) used architects familiar with the aesthetic concerns and design requirements of the Manhattan area where the project was to be located. GSA (D) also complied with § 102(2)(D) because it did evaluate alternative sites for the project. The decision is remanded to GSA to undertake the proper evaluations and procedures.

■ DISSENT

(Friendly, Chief Judge) On one hand, the majority opinion raises the bar too high for what constitutes significant impacts, while, on the other, it makes an agency's task of determining that no EIS is required too burdensome. The problem with the majority's ruling is that it proposes an undertaking to show that no EIS is needed that is nearly as burdensome as preparing an EIS. Congress intended that agencies should prepare EISs whenever an action could fairly be argued to have a significant environmental impact, but likewise intended agencies to be free of the trouble and expense of EISs when an action carries no potential for significant harm. Thus, a low threshold is preferable because agencies would be better served to use their resources preparing an EIS in doubtful cases, than in preparing an equally elaborate report to show that an EIS is not needed. The CEQ guidelines support this interpretation when they state, "if there is potential that the environment may be significantly affected, the statement is to be prepared." When the CEQ guidelines direct agencies to create EISs in cases "likely to be highly controversial," CEQ means actions that will create public opposition, even if the environmental impacts are fairly predictable. The court should reverse and enjoin construction of the jail until GSA prepares and considers an EIS.

Analysis:

This is a very complex case that boils down to two different views of how best to implement NEPA's EIS provisions. The majority would have agencies—in this case GSA—create an EIS or justify its refusal to do so with an environmental assessment showing why an EIS is not required. The dissent's position is simpler: in close cases, prepare an EIS. Interestingly, both sides seem to be in favor of a strong interpretation of NEPA that restricts agency discretion. The debate between the majority and dissent positions leads to some empirical questions that outside observers could investigate to determine the effects that each of the positions would have. First, would the dissent's position lead to the creation of many additional EISs or just a few? Second, is the dissent's characterization of the assessment as nearly as burdensome as an EIS accurate? Finally, and most importantly, does the majority's two-factor test establish clear guidelines that agencies can understand and follow?

Department of Transportation v. Public Citizen

(Federal Regulatory Agency) v. *(Public Watchdog Group)*

541 U.S. 752 (2004)

THE INCREASE IN CROSS–BORDER TRUCKING RESULTED FROM THE PRESIDENT'S ACTION, NOT THE AGENCY'S, SO NO EIS WAS REQUIRED

I run a Federal agency, which may seem impressive, but usually Congress or the President tie my hands.

stus.com

■ **INSTANT FACTS** A public watchdog group brought legal action based on a federal agency's failure to consider the environmental impact of its regulations.

■ **BLACK LETTER RULE** When an agency has no ability to prevent a certain effect due to its limited statutory authority over the relevant actions, the agency cannot be considered a legally relevant "cause" of such effect; hence, under NEPA and the implementing regulations, the agency need not consider these effects in its EA.

■ **PROCEDURAL BASIS**

Supreme Court review of a judgment in favor of Public Citizen (P).

■ **FACTS**

The Federal Motor Carrier Safety Administration (FMCSA) is responsible for motor carrier safety and registration. The FMCSA has only limited discretion regarding registration, however; it must grant registration to all domestic or foreign motor carriers that are "willing and able to comply with" the applicable safety, fitness, and financial-responsibility requirements. The FMCSA has no statutory authority to impose or enforce emissions controls or to establish environmental requirements unrelated to motor carrier safety.

In 1982, Congress authorized the President to extend a two-year moratorium on new Mexican motor carriers operating in the United States. An international arbitration panel ruled in February 2001 that the moratorium violated the North American Free Trade Agreement (NAFTA), so President Bush declared his intention to lift it as soon as the FMCSA promulgated new regulations for such carriers, which it proposed in May 2001. In December 2001, Congress enacted Section 350 of the Department of Transportation and Related Agencies Appropriations Act, which barred the processing of applications by Mexican motor carriers to operate in the United States until the FMCSA adopted specific application and safety-monitoring regulations. In January 2002, the FMCSA issued an environmental assessment (EA) for the proposed Application and Safety Monitoring Rules. Because the FMCSA had concluded that the entry of the Mexican trucks was not an "effect" of its regulations, however, it did not consider any environmental impact that might be caused by the increased presence of Mexican trucks in the United States.

The environmental effects on which the EA focused were those likely to arise from the increased number of roadside inspections of Mexican trucks and buses due to the proposed regulations. The EA concluded that these effects were minor and could be addressed in the inspections process itself. The EA also noted that the increase in inspection-related emissions would be at least partially offset by the fact that the safety requirements would result in an overall reduction in the number of Mexican trucks operating in the United States. Based on these assessments, the EA concluded that the issuance of the proposed regulations would have no significant impact on the environment, and thus the FMCSA issued a finding of no significant impact (FONSI) and declined to prepare an environmental impact statement (EIS).

After the FMCSA issued its regulations in March 2002, the respondents sued, arguing that the regulations were promulgated in violation of the National Environment Policy Act (NEPA) and the Clean Air Act. The court agreed and set aside the rules. The court concluded that the EA was deficient because it failed to adequately consider the environmental impact of lifting the moratorium on the cross-border operation of Mexican motor carriers. According to the court, the FMCSA was required to consider these environmental effects because "the President's rescission of the moratorium was 'reasonably foreseeable' at the time the EA was prepared and the decision not to prepare an EIS was made." Due to this perceived deficiency, the court of appeals remanded the case for preparation of a full EIS.

■ ISSUE

Did the National Environmental Policy Act and the Clean Air Act require the FMSCA to evaluate the environmental effects of cross-border operations of Mexican-domiciled motor carriers, where the FMSCA's promulgation of new regulations would allow such operations to occur?

■ DECISION AND RATIONALE

(Thomas, J.) No. When an agency has no ability to prevent a certain effect due to its limited statutory authority over the relevant actions, the agency cannot be considered a legally relevant "cause" of such effect; hence, under NEPA and the implementing regulations, the agency need not consider these effects in its EA. Here, the FMSCA lacks discretion to prevent cross-border operations, so the National Environmental Policy Act and the Clean Air Act impose no environmental-impact assessment requirements on the FMSCA.

An agency's decision not to prepare an EIS may be set aside only if it is arbitrary and capricious. Respondents here argue that the issuance of a FONSI was arbitrary and capricious because the EA did not take into account the environmental effects of an increase in cross-border operations of Mexican motor carriers. The relevant question under NEPA is whether that increase, and the correlating release of emissions, is an "effect" of the FMCSA's rules; if not, the FMCSA's failure to address these effects in the EA did not violate NEPA, and the FONSI's issuance was not arbitrary and capricious.

Respondents argue that the EA must take the increased cross-border operations' environmental effects into account because the expenditure bar made it impossible for any Mexican truck to operate in the United States until the regulations were issued, and hence the trucks' entry was a "reasonably foreseeable" effect of the issuance of the regulations. But this argument overlooks the FMCSA's inability to countermand the President's lifting of the moratorium or otherwise categorically exclude Mexican trucks from operating in the United States. The FMCSA is subject to the mandate that it register any motor carrier willing and able to comply with various safety and financial responsibility rules. Only the moratorium prevented it from doing so with regard to Mexican trucks. NEPA requires a "reasonably close causal relationship" akin to proximate cause in tort law. Moreover, the policies underlying NEPA make clear that the causal connection between the proposed regulations and the entry of Mexican trucks is insufficient to make FMCSA responsible under NEPA to consider the environmental effects of entry.

Neither of the purposes of NEPA's EIS requirement—to ensure both that an agency has information to make its decision and that the public receives information so it might also play a role in the decision-making process—will be served by requiring FMCSA to consider the environmental impact at issue here. Since the FMCSA has no ability to prevent cross-border operations, it lacks the power to act on whatever information might be contained in an EIS. This analysis is not changed by the requirement that an agency evaluate the "cumulative impact" of its action, since that rule does not require the FMCSA to treat the lifting of the moratorium itself or the consequences from that lifting as an effect of its rules. Because the President, not the FMSCA, could authorize (or not authorize) cross-border operations of Mexican motor carriers, and because the FMSCA has no discretion to prevent the entry of Mexican trucks, its EA did not need to consider the environmental effects arising from the entry. Reversed and remanded.

Analysis:

NEPA requires that federal agencies provide "detailed information concerning significant environmental impacts." As this case demonstrates, however, not all federal actions require a full EIS. If the action is not likely to cause a significant impact, an agency may submit a simpler document called an Environmental Assessment (EA). EAs are permitted only when the agency determines that its action will give rise to "no significant impact." The Public Citizen case shows that "no significant impact" may also be read as "no significant impact *caused by the agency's action*."

■ CASE VOCABULARY

ENVIRONMENTAL IMPACT STATEMENT: A document that the National Environmental Policy Act (42 U.S.C.A. § 4332(2)(c)) requires a federal agency to produce for a major project or legislative proposal so that better decisions can be made about the positive and negative environmental effects of an undertaking.

Vermont Yankee Nuclear Power Corp. v. NRDC

(Nuclear Plant Owner) v. *(Conservation Group)*

435 U.S. 519 (1978)

NEPA DOES NOT REQUIRE AGENCIES TO CONSIDER EVERY ALTERNATIVE SUGGESTED IN ADMINISTRATIVE PROCEEDINGS

■ **INSTANT FACTS** Power company appealed a Court of Appeals decision that the commission in charge of licensing nuclear power facilities consider energy conservation measures as an alternative to building a power plant.

■ **BLACK LETTER RULE** NEPA did not require the Atomic Energy Commission to consider energy conservation as an alternative to building a nuclear power plant in an EIS prepared for use in the plant licensing proceedings.

■ **PROCEDURAL BASIS**

U.S. Supreme Court granted certiorari to review a decision of the D.C. Circuit court.

■ **FACTS**

Vermont Yankee Nuclear Power Corp. ["Vermont Yankee"] (D) applied to the Atomic Energy Commission ["AEC"] for a license to build and operate a nuclear power plant in Vernon. Vermont and Consumers Power (D) applied for a license to build and operate a nuclear plant in Midlands, Michigan. The AEC was responsible for preparing environmental impact statements ["EISs"] for use in licensing procedures. After AEC approved the Midlands license, conservation groups such as Saginaw intervened to have the license hearings reopened. The intervenors contended that AEC must consider energy conservation as an alternative to building the Midlands facility. AEC asked Saginaw to clarify its contentions, but Saginaw stated that it "had no conventional findings of fact to set forth" and that it had not chosen to respond to the proceeding. AEC denied Saginaw's request to re-open the hearings. The National Environmental Policy Act ["NEPA"] requires agencies preparing EISs to consider alternatives to the proposed federal action in § 102(2)(C)(iii). Elsewhere, NEPA directs agencies to "study, develop, and describe appropriate alternatives to recommended courses of action in any proposal which involves unresolved conflicts concerning alternative uses of available resources" (NEPA § 102(2)(E)). Conservationists (P) brought suit to force the AEC to consider energy conservation measures as an alternative to building the nuclear plant. The D.C. Circuit held that AEC was required to consider conservation. The D.C. Circuit ruled that NEPA required AEC to make independent investigations of alternatives brought to its attention by intervening parties, such as the conservationists in this case. The court found that the "threshold test" that AEC used to determine which alternatives warranted further consideration was too difficult for interested intervenors to meet. The court found, moreover, that NEPA created a duty for an agency to explain why alternatives did not warrant consideration in an EIS in those cases where the agency did not conduct further review. Consumers Power (D) sought review of the decision. The U.S. Supreme granted certiorari to hear the case and combined it with the Vermont Yankee appeal.

■ **ISSUE**

Does NEPA require AEC to consider energy conservation measures as an alternative to building a nuclear power facility in an EIS prepared for the purposes of evaluating the nuclear plant license application?

■ DECISION AND RATIONALE

(Rehnquist, J.) No. AEC did not violate NEPA when it declined to consider energy conservation in an EIS prepared for administrative proceedings on a license to build a nuclear power plant. The Atomic Energy Act of 1954 leaves decisions concerning the need for additional power in the hands of state public utility commissions and similar organizations. The AEC, on the other hand, is charged with overseeing nuclear safety, public health and issues of national security. NEPA requires examination of alternatives, but this term is not self-defining. As the Court of Appeals was also aware, time and money are too short to require investigation of every alternative in every instance. During the mid-1970s, the energy crisis made everyone acutely aware of the need for energy conservation. The Council for Environmental Quality and Federal Power Commission didn't promulgate regulations ordering agencies to consider energy conservation until 1973 and 1974. This was more than a year after the EIS at issue in this case was written and the hearings for which it was prepared were over. This goes to show that alternatives come and go. The AEC Licensing Board acted correctly given the information at its disposal. There was nothing before the Licensing Board to suggest that the project in question was not needed. The Court of Appeals erred in finding that AEC's threshold for considering alternatives was too high. While NEPA establishes a duty for agencies to consider alternatives, intervenors must present alternatives meaningfully and prove that the alternatives are significant enough to warrant consideration. Intervenor Saginaw's behavior in the administrative proceedings indicates a willingness to be obscure and difficult. AEC requires intervenors to show evidence "sufficient to require reasonable minds to inquire further," not to meet the heavy burden of presenting a prima facie case. Courts do not sit in judgment of the value or propriety of nuclear energy. Those policy decisions should be made by the legislature. NEPA exists to insure that agencies charged with implementing policy make informed decisions, but its guidelines are largely procedural. "Administrative decisions should be set aside... only for substantial procedural or substantive reasons as mandated by the statute, not simply because the court is unhappy with the result reached."

Analysis:

Like many of the U.S. Supreme Court decisions in the environmental law sphere, this case is very much about the scope of agencies' authority to set their own standards. The section of Justice Rehnquist's opinion relevant here is very deferential to the AEC, the responsible agency in this case. The conservationists' apparent foot-dragging and lack of cooperation as characterized in the opinion only strengthen this deference. The Court is clear that it considers the energy conservation challenge to be a peripheral, post-hoc attack on an otherwise properly conducted administrative proceeding. Even without a target as easy as Saginaw was here, however, the Court tends to give a lot of discretion to agencies. This is due, in part, to the role of agencies as fact-finders and experts in their areas of responsibility. Additionally, there are concerns over the separation of powers. In this case, the Court is concerned that the Court of Appeals has ruled against the AEC for policy reasons. Sending a message to the lower court, the Court's opinion states that it is for Congress to decide the energy policy and develop the laws that will implement that policy. Of course, the Court recognizes that NEPA requires the agencies charged with implementing policy to recognize environmental concerns, but the Court makes clear that it interprets NEPA as being "essentially procedural."

Sierra Club v. United States Army Corps of Engineers

(*Conservation Group*) v. (*Federal Agency*)

701 F.2d 1011 (2d Cir. 1983)

COURT MAY OVERTURN AGENCY DECISIONS BASED ON RELIANCE ON AN EIS CONTAINING FALSE INFORMATION OR PREPARED WITHOUT GOOD FAITH EFFORTS TO OBTAIN CORRECT INFORMATION

■ **INSTANT FACTS** Conservationists challenged U.S. Army Corps of Engineers approval of a highway project based on an EIS that failed to consider evidence of marine life in an area to be filled.

■ **BLACK LETTER RULE** Court may not rule that an EIS was inadequate if the agency preparing the EIS adequately compiled and analyzed relevant data, ignored no pertinent data, and publicly disclosed its findings.

■ PROCEDURAL BASIS

Appeal to the U.S. Court of Appeals from a District Court decision enjoining a construction of a federal highway project pending completion of a supplemental EIS.

■ FACTS

The U.S. Army Corps of Engineers [the "Corps"] (D) and the Federal Highway Administration ["FHWA"] (D) planned to construct a superhighway along the West Side of Manhattan. The project required a portion of the Hudson River to be filled in. The Corps (D) and FHWA (D) prepared an environmental impact statement ["EIS"] that concluded that the fill area was a "biological wasteland." Data indicated that striped bass lived in the fill area at greater levels than suggested in the EIS. The Environmental Protection Agency, the National Marine Fisheries Service, and the Fish and Wildlife Service also objected to the data in the EIS. Conservationists, such as the Sierra Club (P) sued in federal court to enjoin the project. Preparation of EISs is required by § 102(2)(C) of the National Environmental Policy Act ["NEPA"]. The District Court enjoined the project until the Corps (D) and FHWA (D) prepared a supplemental EIS. The District Court decision was appealed to the Court of Appeals.

■ ISSUE

May a court permissibly rule that an EIS is inadequate when the EIS contains false information or where the preparing agency made no effort to obtain accurate information?

■ DECISION AND RATIONALE

(Kearse, Circuit Judge) Yes. The District Court properly ordered preparation of a supplemental EIS concerning marine life because false statements concerning marine life in the EIS prepared by the Corps (D) and FHWA (D) indicate that the EIS was not prepared in good faith. Judicial precedent establishes that courts are permitted only very narrow review of EISs. In *Vermont Yankee*, the U.S. Supreme Court has ruled that NEPA is procedural in nature. Furthermore, in *Vermont Yankee* and *Strycker's Bay*, the Court stated that NEPA requires EISs in order to insure that agencies make well-informed decisions, but not necessarily those that reviewing judges would have made in the same circumstances. In *Kleppe v. Sierra Club*, the Court held that reviewing courts may only insure that agencies have taken a "hard look" at the environmental impact of its decisions. In *County of Suffolk v.*

Secretary of Interior, the Second Circuit held that an EIS must contain enough information for the public to make an informed decision and for the agency to be able to balance environmental risks against the benefits of any proposed actions. As the First Circuit said in *Silva v. Lynn*, EISs assure that agencies haven't "swept [environmental issues] under the rug." In short, the rule for a reviewing court is that the court cannot throw out an EIS "if the agency has made an adequate compilation of relevant information, has analyzed it reasonably, has not ignored pertinent data, and has made disclosures to the public. . ." In this case, however, the agencies have not met this test. For example, even after three other federal agencies questioned the accuracy of the EIS concerning marine life in the fill area, the Corps (D) and FHWA (D) did not conduct further studies or collect further information. Indeed, it appeared from that record that the agencies (D) preparing the EIS knew that the studies used for the EIS were flawed. The information for the EIS was so poor that the District Court correctly concluded that the EIS's conclusions "lacked substantial basis in fact" and that, by relying on the EIS, the agencies (D) could not possibly have given the environmental impact of the action full consideration. The District Court acted properly in enjoining the highway project until a supplemental EIS has been prepared. Proper enforcement of NEPA requires that the agencies prepare an adequate and reasonable EIS before proceeding with the project. Otherwise, the public could neither make an informed decision nor have any confidence that the agencies (D) considered the environmental impact of their actions. This decision does not hold that any inaccuracies in data are fatal to an EIS. If an agency's research is reasonable, an EIS is not necessarily inadequate simply because more information becomes available later. Furthermore, the conclusions reached by the Corps (D) or FHWA (D) in this case are not necessarily wrong, but the information contained in EIS is not sufficient to reasonably support those conclusions. The District Court decision enjoining the project and ordering preparation of a supplemental EIS is affirmed.

Analysis:

The court in *Sierra Club v. U.S. Army Corps of Engineers* cited many cases and went into detail to establish the standard by which it would determine that the EIS at issue here was inadequate. The court quite convincingly shows that the standard is quite deferential to agency discretion in preparation of EISs. In the decision, however, this exposition of the standard also has the effect of establishing that this court was not rushing in to overturn the EIS prepared by the Corps and FHWA. Indeed, by establishing how deferential the law requires it to be, the court highlighted just how flawed it considers this EIS to be. Without the outright use of inflammatory accusations, the Court of Appeals indicated that it believed that the agencies in this case did not act in "good faith." There are many areas of law, of course, where actions indicating intention on the part of a wrongdoer will be treated much more harshly than actions indicating mere negligence or poor judgment. It may be profitable to consider whether the court thought that the agencies had reached that level of action or not in this case. The strongest argument that the court is not accusing the agencies of intentional misconduct is found in the language that the court used to limit its holding in this case. The court stated specifically that it was not holding that the agencies conclusions were incorrect, but simply that the EIS did not contain adequate information on which to base reasonable conclusions. This limitation though also helps the court to avoid any appearance that it is overturning findings of fact on the part of the agencies.

Marsh v. Oregon Natural Resources Council

(Secretary of the Army) v. *(Conservationists)*

490 U.S. 360 (1989)

NEPA REQUIRES AGENCIES TO SUPPLEMENT ENVIRONMENTAL IMPACT STATEMENTS WHEN NEW INFORMATION INDICATES THAT REMAINING FEDERAL ACTION MAY CAUSE SIGNIFICANT ENVIRONMENTAL IMPACTS

■ **INSTANT FACTS** Conservationists sued to compel the U.S. Army Corps of Engineers to prepare a second supplement to the Corps' EIS concerning a dam project.

■ **BLACK LETTER RULE** Courts may not set aside an agency decision not to supplement EISs when that decision was based on factual findings and was not arbitrary or capricious.

■ **PROCEDURAL BASIS**

Appeal to the United States Supreme Court for review of a decision by the Ninth Circuit to requiring a federal agency to further supplement an EIS.

■ **FACTS**

The United States Army Corps of Engineers [the "Corps"] (D) planned and built three dams as components in a project in Oregon's Rogue River Basin during the 1970s and 1980s. The Corps (D) prepared a final environmental impact statement ["EIS"] in 1971. The Corps (D) prepared a supplement to the EIS in 1980. Later, the Corps (D) refused to prepare a second supplement. The National Environmental Policy Act ["NEPA"] requires an agency to prepare an EIS when the agency is considering actions that may cause significant environmental impact (§ 102 (2)(C)). In regulations instructing agencies on how to implement NEPA, the Council for Environmental Quality ["CEQ"] explains that supplemental EISs are required when agencies encounter "significant new circumstances or information relevant to environmental concerns and bearing on the proposed action or its impacts." The Corps (D) echoes this language in its own NEPA implementation guidelines, which require the Corps (D) to supplement an EIS when "new significant information, criteria or circumstances" arise concerning the environmental impacts of the Corps (D) actions. Conservationists such as the Oregon Natural Resources Council ["ONRC"] (P) sued in federal court to require the Corps (D) to produce a second supplement. ONRC (P) argued that memoranda by Oregon's Department of Fish and Wildlife and the U.S. Soil Conservation Service—both released after the first supplement—showed that the dam project would have greater environmental impacts than expected. The District Court held for the Corps (D), but the Ninth Circuit reversed. The decision was appealed to the U.S. Supreme Court, which accepted certiorari.

■ **ISSUE**

May a court set aside an agency decision not to supplement an EIS in light of new facts if the agency's decision was not arbitrary or capricious?

■ **DECISION AND RATIONALE**

(Stevens, J.) No. Because the Corps' (D) decision not to prepare a second supplement to the EIS was based on issues of fact, the court may not set that decision aside unless it was arbitrary or capricious. NEPA does not explicitly state when EISs must be supplemented. NEPA requires EISs for two reasons: (1) to insure that agencies make well-informed decisions with regard to the environment, and (2) so that the public has adequate information about the agencies' decisions. Thus, this Court held in *TVA v. Hill* that, for on going, long term projects, EISs must be prepared so long as "the remaining government action would be environmentally significant." We also owe deference to the CEQ regulations requiring supplemental EISs for significant new information. The appropriate test for when to supplement turns on the "value of the new information to the still pending decision-making process." On one hand, agencies cannot endlessly supplement EISs for every new piece of information that arises, or the EISs would never be completed. On the other hand, NEPA requires agencies to give environmental impacts a "hard look" during the decision-making process. The rule for when to supplement is much like the rule for when an EIS is required in the first place: If major federal action is still pending when new information indicating that the remaining action could significantly impact the human environment, the responsible agency must prepare a supplemental EIS. In this case, the Corps (D) argued that the applicable standard for courts when reviewing an agency's decision not to supplement is whether the decision was "arbitrary or capricious." The ONRC (P) argued that the reviewing court should make its own determinations as to the reasonableness of the agency's decision. The dispute in this case is over the Corps' (D) expert review of the information contained in the two post-1980 memoranda. This dispute is primarily factual and "requires a high level of technical expertise" on the part of the agency. It is not primarily a legal issue, such as the meaning of the word "significant" in the statute or the application of legal standards to undisputed facts. Therefore, the courts owe the agency decision a great deal of deference and should not set aside the decision unless it was "arbitrary or capricious." Although courts must not "automatically defer" to agencies, when the record shows that experts hold conflicting opinions, the court cannot substitute its choice of opinion for a reasonable choice on the part of the responsible agency. The Corps (D) is not required to supplement the EIS in this case. The Court of Appeals is reversed.

Analysis:

Marsh v. Oregon Natural Resources Council is another in a line of U.S. Supreme Court decisions interpreting NEPA in which the Court gives great deference to the factual decisions of federal agencies. In this case, the Court initially made a finding that, at times, NEPA does require agencies to prepare supplemental EISs. The Court refers to a "rule of reason" that it says leads to the conclusion that EISs must be supplemented basically under the same circumstances that would require EISs to be prepared initially. To get to the question of whether the Corps of Engineers would have to supplement the EIS in this case, however, the Court had to determine the appropriate standard for reviewing the Corps' decision not to supplement. Here, the Court made a further subdivision by way of applying the facts of the case. The Court concluded that the Corps' decision not to supplement was based primarily in findings of fact, i.e., the Corps' review of the new information. The Court rejected the ONRC argument that the Corps' decision was actually one of law, and should, therefore, be reviewed "de novo." How clear is it in this case (or in any NEPA case) that the agency was making factual findings and not legal ones?

■ CASE VOCABULARY

SUPPLEMENTAL ENVIRONMENTAL IMPACT STATEMENT (EIS): Sometimes abbreviated SEIS in court opinions, this is an EIS that is prepared after the so-called Final Environmental Impact Statement (FEIS) for a project has been issued because of new information that future stages of the project may significantly impact the environment; this is the case even if the project has been approved.

CHAPTER NINE

Preservation of Biodiversity

TVA v. Hill

Instant Facts: Citizens concerned that operation of a dam on the Little Tennessee River would jeopardize the existence of an endangered fish, filed a citizen suit to enjoin the dam's completion and operation.

Black Letter Rule: Upon finding that a federal agency action will jeopardize the existence or harm the critical habitat of an endangered species, the court should enjoin the action regardless of cost or degree of project completion.

National Association of Home Builders v. Babbitt

Instant Facts: County and contractors sued to overturn federal decision to regulate a hospital and road project in order to protect an endangered species of fly that was found only within California.

Black Letter Rule: Federal regulation of intrastate activities to protect endangered species is justified under the Commerce Clause when the regulation controls the channels of interstate commerce or substantially affects interstate commerce.

Gibbs v. Babbitt

Instant Facts: The Fish and Wildlife Service (FWS) (D) extended the takings prohibitions to the experimental red wolf populations but permitted the taking of red wolves on private land under certain conditions.

Black Letter Rule: Congress's power to regulate interstate commerce includes the power to regulate conduct that might harm red wolves on private land.

Thomas v. Peterson

Instant Facts: Local ranchers sued to enjoin construction of a logging road on the grounds that the Forest Service had not complied with ESA procedures prior to approving the road.

Black Letter Rule: An agency's failure to prepare a biological assessment once the agency is aware that endangered species are present in an area where the agency proposes to act is not a de minimis violation of ESA.

Roosevelt Campobello International Park Commission v. EPA

Instant Facts: Environmental advocates sought judicial review of EPA decisions not to have the EPA Administrator review an agency adjudication and not to reopen the record of the adjudication to receive new evidence on endangered species.

Black Letter Rule: An Administrative Law Judge who granted a Clean Water Act permit without ordering certain simulations to determine the permitted action's effects on endangered species violated his duty under ESA to consider the best available scientific data.

Carson-Truckee Water Conservancy District v. Clark

Instant Facts: A water district and power company sued to compel the Secretary of Interior to sell water from a federally operated dam.

Black Letter Rule: ESA § 7(a)(2) does not apply when federal agencies actively seek to conserve endangered species and does not limit agencies to only those actions necessary to avoid jeopardizing endangered species.

Babbitt v. Sweet Home Chapter of Communities for a Great Oregon

Instant Facts: Pro-logging plaintiffs sued the Secretary of Interior and Director of FWS claiming that those agencies' interpretation of the Endangered Species Act had harmed the plaintiffs' financial interest in logging.

Black Letter Rule: Secretary of Interior reasonably defined the term "harm" as used in § 9 of the Endangered Species Act as including modification or degradation of habitat essential to the survival of endangered or threatened species.

TVA v. Hill

(Federally-Owned Public Corporation) v. *(Environmentally-Concerned Citizen)*

437 U.S. 153 (1978)

ESA REQUIRES FEDERAL ACTIONS TO HALT ALL ACTIONS THAT JEOPARDIZE THE EXISTENCE OF AN ENDANGERED SPECIES OR DESTROY OR MODIFY HABITAT CRITICAL TO AN ENDANGERED SPECIES

■ **INSTANT FACTS** Citizens concerned that operation of a dam on the Little Tennessee River would jeopardize the existence of an endangered fish, filed a citizen suit to enjoin the dam's completion and operation.

■ **BLACK LETTER RULE** Upon finding that a federal agency action will jeopardize the existence or harm the critical habitat of an endangered species, the court should enjoin the action regardless of cost or degree of project completion.

■ **PROCEDURAL BASIS**

Appeal to the U.S. Supreme Court of a decision by the Court of Appeals to enjoin operation of a dam project that jeopardized the existence of an endangered species of fish.

■ **FACTS**

In 1967, the Tennessee Valley Authority ["TVA"] (D), a federally-owned public utility corporation, began work building the Tellico Dam on the Little Tennessee River. The dam, when completed, was to have transformed a clear, fast-flowing area of the Little Tennessee into a 30-mile long reservoir. Although construction on the dam was completed, the dam was enjoined from operating due to TVA's failure to create an environmental impact statement ["EIS"] adequate to satisfy § 102(C) of the National Environmental Policy Act ["NEPA"]. Only a few months before the NEPA injunction was to end, in 1973, a University of Tennessee ichthyologist [he must study the cause of itches—or is it fish] identified a previously unknown species of fish, the snail darter, in the area of the river to be affected by operation of the Tellico Dam. ["Snail darter" sounds a bit like "jumbo shrimp," doesn't it?] The discovery of the snail darter preceded congressional approval of the Endangered Species Act ["ESA"] by only four months. The Secretary of Interior [the "Secretary"] listed the snail darter, whose numbers were estimated to be between 10,000 and 15,000, as endangered in 1975. The Secretary determined that the snail darter lived only in the area to be inundated by the Tellico Dam, and that this "proposed impoundment of water...would result in total destruction of the snail darter's habitat." As a result, the Secretary designated the Tellico Dam area "critical habitat" for the snail darter. The Secretary issued a notice, directed at TVA (D), that all federal agencies must do everything necessary to insure that their actions do not harm or destroy critical habitat. In 1976, Hill (P) and others filed a citizen suit (authorized by § 11(g) of ESA) in federal court seeking an injunction for completion of the Tellico Dam. At trial, the District Court found that operation of Tellico Dam would adversely modify critical habitat and jeopardize the snail darter's existence. Nonetheless, the District Court disagreed with Hill (P) and the other plaintiffs that an injunction was mandatory under the circumstances. The Court of Appeals reversed and enjoined any activity at Tellico Dam that could harm the snail darter's critical habitat until Congress exempted Tellico Dam from the ESA or the snail darter was no longer endangered. TVA (D) appealed to the Supreme Court, arguing that it is unreasonable to apply ESA to federal projects "well under way" when Congress passed the Act.

■ ISSUE

Does ESA require courts to enjoin all federal actions, even those related to projects well under way when ESA was passed, that jeopardize the existence or harm the critical habitat of an endangered species?

■ DECISION AND RATIONALE

(Burger, Chief Justice) Yes. Because it would jeopardize the existence and harm the critical habitat of an endangered species, the court must enjoin the operation of the Tellico Dam. The statutory language of ESA § 7—that actions "funded," "authorized" or "carried out" by federal agencies must not jeopardize endangered species—is very clear, and admits of no exceptions due to cost or project completion. Applying the law to this case, TVA (D) is a federal agency. If TVA (D) were to close the gates on Tellico Dam, it would be carrying out an action that it authorized and funded, which—according to the Secretary of Interior—would jeopardize the snail darter, an endangered species. There is no doubt that this interpretation of the statute entails enormous cost and requires abandonment of anticipated projects. ESA's language, structure and legislative history, however, indicate that this strict interpretation was the intent of Congress. ESA was plainly intended "to halt and reverse the trend toward species extinction, whatever the cost." For example, Congress did not qualify its prohibitions against "taking" any endangered species. This was because, as the legislative history indicates, Congress was concerned about the loss of any species that might have an unknown use or unforeseen place in the ecosystem. Congress concluded, in the language of ESA, that the cost of losing endangered species is "incalculable." There is nothing in ESA that authorizes agencies to balance that loss against calculations of human benefit. Likewise, nothing in Article III of the U.S. Constitution empowers federal courts to balance those costs and benefits either. Operation of the Tellico Dam would clearly violate § 7 of ESA. The next question is what remedy is appropriate. Federal courts are empowered to grant equitable relief, but "a federal judge sitting as a chancellor is not mechanically obligated to grant an injunction for every violation of law." Traditionally, equitable remedies are discretionary and chancellors usually have balanced equities and hardships. That is what TVA (D) urges us to do in this case. This Court, however, has no expertise in endangered species, and Congress—exclusively empowered "to formulate legislative polices and mandate programs and projects"—has stated unequivocally that the scales are to be tipped in favor of protecting the snail darter. We will not pre-empt Congress by attempting to formulate public policy. The injunction issued by the Court of Appeals is affirmed.

Analysis:

TVA v. Hill is, by almost every account, the most important case in the history of the Endangered Species Act. The Court's decision firmly rejected the application of any balancing approach to ESA. As noted earlier, the Supreme Court often prefers not to take environmental law cases because they are extremely complex and fact sensitive. It is perhaps noteworthy, then, that the Court stated near the end of its opinion that it had no expertise in endangered species, but could decide this case because the intent of Congress was so clear. In its opinion, the Court mentioned several times how costly the project had been, and how great the benefits expected from it were. This was possibly the Court's way of assuring anyone reading the opinion that it knew how great the impact of this interpretation of ESA would be. In so doing, the Court gave clear instruction that future cases against § 7 could not be won by piling up huge sums on the cost side of the ledger.

■ CASE VOCABULARY

CHANCELLOR: The judge in a court of chancery (or equity) which followed somewhat different rules than a court of law; in modern times, the same courts hear cases for legal and equitable relief, so judges will follow the guidelines laid out for chancellors when hearing the latter.

National Association of Home Builders v. Babbitt

(Industry Lobby) v. *(Interior Secretary)*

130 F.3d 1041 (D.C. Cir. 1997)

USE OF ENDANGERED SPECIES ACT TO CONTROL INTRASTATE ACTIVITIES DOES NOT VIOLATE THE COMMERCE CLAUSE BECAUSE CONGRESS COULD REASONABLY CONCLUDE THAT PROTECTION OF ENDANGERED SPECIES WOULD SUBSTANTIALLY AFFECT INTERSTATE COMMERCE AND WOULD REQUIRE CONTROL OF THE CHANNELS OF COMMERCE

■ **INSTANT FACTS** County and contractors sued to overturn federal decision to regulate a hospital and road project in order to protect an endangered species of fly that was found only within California.

■ **BLACK LETTER RULE** Federal regulation of intrastate activities to protect endangered species is justified under the Commerce Clause when the regulation controls the channels of interstate commerce or substantially affects interstate commerce.

■ **PROCEDURAL BASIS**

Appeal from a federal District Court decision permitting application of federal Endangered Species Act to activities within the state of California.

■ **FACTS**

The federal Fish and Wildlife Service ["FWS"] (D) designated the Delhi Sands Flower-Loving Fly [the "Fly"] as an endangered species. The Fly's natural range was an eight-mile radius entirely within California. In order to protect the Fly's habitat, San Bernardino County [the "County"] (P) agreed to set aside land and alter construction plans to obtain FWS approval of County (P) hospital and power plant construction projects. After the FWS issued a permit for the construction, the County (P) announced that it would redesign an intersection near the proposed hospital. FWS (D) declared the proposed County (P) action a "taking" of the Fly under § 9(a) of the Endangered Species Act ["ESA"]. [Truly a fly in the ointment.] Section 9(a) bans any taking of an endangered or threatened species within the United States. In *Babbitt v. Sweet Home Chapter of Communities for a Greater Oregon*, the U.S. Supreme Court held that "takings" under § 9(a) included "significant habitat degradation." The County (P) sued in federal court, claiming that ESA § 9(a) was inapplicable. The County (P) argued that the Fly was found only in California and the Commerce Clause [U.S. Const. Art. I, § 8, cl. 3] does not give the federal government authority to regulate wildlife or nonfederal lands. The County (P) contended that the case was governed by *United States v. Lopez*, in which the U.S. Supreme Court ruled that the federal gun-free school zone law exceeded Commerce Clause authority [you will remember it as a very confusing case from Con Law I]. *Lopez* held that the Commerce Clause gives Congress authority to regulate in three areas: (1) the *channels* of interstate commerce, (2) the *instrumentalities* of interstate commerce, including persons and things in commerce, and (3) activities *substantially affecting* interstate commerce.

■ **ISSUE**

Does the Commerce Clause of the U.S. Constitution justify federal actions to protect an endangered species found only within a limited area of one state?

■ **DECISION AND RATIONALE**

(Wald, Circuit Judge) Yes. The action of the FWS (D) under ESA § 9(a)(1) to protect the Fly was justified because the protection of endangered species keeps the channels of interstate commerce free from an injurious use and substantially affects interstate commerce. Thus, § 9(a)(1) meets the first and third categories of activities that Congress is authorized to regulate in *Lopez*. The first *Lopez* category gives Congress authority to control the channels of interstate commerce. Protection of the Fly is an appropriate exercise of that power for two reasons. First, by prohibiting the "taking" of the Fly, the government may effectively ban transportation of the species. Second, by prohibiting the taking of the Fly, the government is "keep[ing] the channels of interstate commerce free from immoral or injurious uses" as the U.S. Supreme Court upheld in *Heart of Atlanta Motel, Inc. v. United States*. Moreover, it does not matter that the Fly is found only within California because *Heart of Atlanta Motel* (which was quoted in *Lopez*) states that Congress may regulate "purely local" activities to keep the channels of interstate commerce free from immoral or injurious uses. The third *Lopez* category permits Congress to regulate activities that substantially affect interstate commerce. According to *Lopez*, the activity to be regulated may be local and need not be defined as commerce. Unlike that of the gun-free school zone law at question in *Lopez*, the legislative history of ESA shows that Congress considered the effects of ESA on interstate commerce. When Congress passed § 9, permitting federal regulation to protect species located entirely within one state, it "could rationally conclude" that interstate commerce would be substantially affected for two reasons: (1) § 9 protects biodiversity, and (2) it "controls adverse effects of interstate commerce." Biodiversity is crucial to interstate commerce because plant and animal species constitute natural resources. Genetic material from plants and animals is used to enhance foods, create pharmaceuticals, and many other uses. Every time a species becomes extinct, we lose as yet undiscovered, potential products. While it is impossible to predict which species may yield useful materials, it is certain that "[i]n the aggregate...the extinction of species and the attendant decline in biodiversity will have a real and predictable effect on interstate commerce." Protection of the Fly under ESA § 9(a)(1) also affects interstate commerce by controlling destructive interstate competition. In *Hodel v. Virginia Surface Mining & Reclamation Ass'n* [also quoted in *Lopez*], the U.S. Supreme Court upheld the Surface Mining Act for the same reason. The Surface Mining Act sought to protect the landscape by regulating mining activities that occurred entirely within individual states. Both the ESA and the Surface Mining Act provisions are justified, however, because states would otherwise seek to attract destructive, albeit profitable, commercial activities by lowering environmental standards. The application of ESA § 9 to protect the Fly is affirmed.

■ **CONCURRENCE**

(Karen Lecraft Henderson, Circuit Judge) Although the court is correct in concluding that the "taking" provision of ESA § 9(a)(1) is a valid exercise of the Commerce Clause, some of the reasons the majority gives for its conclusion are incorrect. In each of the cases cited by the court as examples of valid regulations of the channels of commerce, the objects of the regulation (e.g., machine guns, lumber, public accommodations) were "connected to movement of person or things interstate." The Fly does not move interstate on its own or as a result of human activity, and regulations to protect the Fly are therefore, not "regulation[s] of the use of the channels of interstate commerce." The court argues that the protection of endangered species is justified because the potential loss of economically useful species substantially affects interstate commerce. It is impossible to conclude whether speculative, future losses substantially affect commerce or not. Section 9(a)(1) is, however, justified because the protection of the Fly affects "plainly interstate" commercial development. Although the court's argument is flawed, preserving biodiversity was one of Congress' goals for ESA. This is because Congress recognized the "interconnectedness" of all species within various ecosystems. Loss of a species affects all other species and, therefore, impacts "land and objects that are involved in interstate commerce." In addition to protecting endangered species, Congress intended ESA to protect the habitat in which such species exist. The legislative history of ESA shows that Congress intended to protect habitats by regulating commercial growth and development. Therefore, by requiring the County and its builders to redesign the intersection and the hospital for the protection of the Fly, the FWS is regulating commercial activity that substantially affects interstate commerce.

■ **DISSENT**

(Sentelle, Circuit Judge) It is unsettling that construction of a state of the art hospital and its supporting infrastructure is being held up for protection of this protected species of fly. The court's channels-of-commerce argument, which the concurrence does not support, is flawed. In *Lopez*, the Supreme Court found that a law regulating local ownership of guns was "not a regulation of the use of the channels of interstate commerce." Unlike the Fly, the guns being regulated in the Gun-Free School Zones Act did at least move through the channels of interstate commerce. The court then inverts the *Heart of Atlanta Motel* decision. The present case involves objects that move through interstate commerce and affect the Fly. Thus, the court decision would permit Congress to regulate not only that which substantially affects interstate commerce, but also "anything that is *affected* by commerce" as well. The court's arguments under the third *Lopez* category also fail. As the concurrence states, the speculative, potential economic value of endangered species cannot be said to substantially affect interstate commerce. Moreover, this logic creates a slippery slope, whereby Congress could be justified in regulating any activity that threatens to destroy anything, since—some day—we might discover how valuable that thing was. The concurring opinion's "ecosystem" argument also fails because ecosystems are not commerce. When the concurrence extends the argument to saying that in enacting ESA, Congress intended to protect "habitat," it is making the same mistake. The power to regulate "habitats" was not enumerated in the Constitution. The majority's argument that the *Hodel* case and the Surface Mining Act are analogous to the present case is wrong. Building a hospital is not at all like the destructive commercial activity of mining.

Analysis:

Every law student and lawyer remembers encountering the Commerce Clause in his or her first year Constitutional Law course. Many are struck at the breadth of subjects about which Congress has legislated under the umbrella of interstate commerce. Equally striking, however, is the number of laws that the U.S. Supreme Court has upheld by finding that they affected interstate commerce. The *Lopez* case that is so important to all three opinions here surprised many Court watchers because the Court refused to uphold a federal law on the basis of the Commerce Clause. After *Lopez*, many scholars speculated about the future of the Commerce Clause. Would it continue to be interpreted expansively or would the Court narrow its application further? This question is still being answered; in part, the three judges *in National Association of Home Builders v. Babbitt* are trying to answer exactly those questions. All three are keenly aware of the three categories of legislation that the Court said were justified by the Commerce Clause, yet none of the three can agree on how the facts in the case apply to them. Fortunately for the darling Delhi Sands Flower-Loving Fly, two of the judges at least agreed that § 9(a), the crucial portion of the ESA, substantially affected interstate commerce and controlled the channels of commerce.

■ CASE VOCABULARY

BIODIVERSITY: The number of different species of plants and animals that exist at any given time.

Gibbs v. Babbitt

(Private Landowners) v. *(Secretary of the Interior)*

214 F.3d 483 (4th Cir. 2000)

REGULATING CONDUCT THAT MIGHT HARM RED WOLVES ON PRIVATE LAND IS WITHIN CONGRESS'S COMMERCE CLAUSE AUTHORITY

■ **INSTANT FACTS** The Fish and Wildlife Service (FWS) (D) extended the takings prohibitions to the experimental red wolf populations but permitted the taking of red wolves on private land under certain conditions.

■ **BLACK LETTER RULE** Congress's power to regulate interstate commerce includes the power to regulate conduct that might harm red wolves on private land.

■ **PROCEDURAL BASIS**

Appeal from a federal district court judgment that upheld the Fish and Wildlife Service's (FWS) anti-taking regulations, as applied to red wolves occupying private land, as a valid exercise of power under the Commerce Clause.

■ **FACTS**

Regulation 17.84(c) provided significant restrictions on killing red wolves found on private lands. The anti-taking prohibitions were extended to experimental red wolf populations that were reintroduced into a two-state area. Gibbs (P) and other landowners challenged the federal government's authority to protect red wolves on private land and sought a declaration that Regulation 17.84(c) exceeded federal authority under the Commerce Clause. The district court held that Congress's power to regulate interstate commerce includes the power to regulate conduct that might harm red wolves on private land.

■ **ISSUE**

Does Congress's power to regulate interstate commerce include the power to regulate conduct that might harm red wolves on private land?

■ **DECISION AND RATIONALE**

(Wilkinson, J.) Yes. In *United States v. Lopez*, 514 U.S. 549 (1995), the Supreme Court recognized three broad categories of activities that Congress may regulate under its commerce power. One of these categories includes activities that "arise out of or are connected with a commercial transaction, which viewed in the aggregate, substantially affects interstate commerce." The taking of red wolves substantially affects interstate commerce because (1) the presence of red wolves in the state generates tourism; (2) red wolves are the subject of scientific research and scientific research generates jobs; and (3) as the red wolf population increases, there is the possibility of a renewed trade in their fur pelts. Since Regulation 17.84(c) is aimed to reverse the threatened extinction of the red wolf and conserve it for both current and future use in interstate commerce, Congress is within its commerce power authority to regulate conduct that might harm red wolves on private land. Affirmed.

■ **DISSENT**

(Luttig, J.) Because of the extremely small population of red wolves that live on private property, the killing of even all of these wolves would not have any substantial effect on interstate commerce. As such, the power to regulate conduct that might harm red wolves on private land is not within Congress's power to regulate interstate commerce.

Analysis:

The majority opinion went to great lengths to justify Congress's power to provide protections for red wolves on private lands. Given the extremely small population of red wolves, both on public and private lands, finding authority under the commerce clause based on their economic impact is a reach at a best. This decision appears to reflect more of a concern with its precedential impact (if Congress is found not to have authority, then the entire federal regulatory scheme for wildlife and natural resource conservation could be placed in peril), and the court therefore seems to struggle to find a way to support a decision it feels it must make.

■ CASE VOCABULARY

COMMERCE CLAUSE: U.S. Const. art. I. § 8, cl. 3, which gives Congress the exclusive power to regulate commerce among states, with foreign nations, and with Indian tribes.

INTERSTATE COMMERCE: Trade and other business activities between those located in different states; especially traffic in goods and travel of people between states.

Thomas v. Peterson
(Ranch Owner) v. *(Forest Service Chief)*
753 F.2d 754 (9th Cir. 1985)

PROCEDURAL REQUIREMENTS OF ESA MUST BE STRICTLY ENFORCED TO ENSURE AGENCY COMPLIANCE WITH ESA'S SUBSTANTIVE PROVISIONS

■ **INSTANT FACTS** Local ranchers sued to enjoin construction of a logging road on the grounds that the Forest Service had not complied with ESA procedures prior to approving the road.

■ **BLACK LETTER RULE** An agency's failure to prepare a biological assessment once the agency is aware that endangered species are present in an area where the agency proposes to act is not a de minimis violation of ESA.

■ **PROCEDURAL BASIS**

Appeal from a District Court decision granting summary judgment in favor of Forest Service Chief.

■ **FACTS**

Thomas (P), a rancher, and others, sued in federal District Court to enjoin the construction of an access road and timber sales in a formerly roadless area of National Forest known as "Jersey Jack." Thomas (P) made claims under the National Environmental Policy Act [that portion of the case is covered earlier in this chapter] and the Endangered Species Act ["ESA"]. The ESA requires federal agencies to avoid actions that might jeopardize the existence or habitat of endangered or threatened species. Under ESA § 7, agencies must follow a three-step procedure to ensure that they comply with ESA's substantive requirements. (1) An agency must inquire with the Fish & Wildlife Service ["FWS"] about the presence of endangered species in the area where the agency proposes to act. (2) If FWS indicates that such species are present, the agency must prepare a biological assessment to determine if the proposed action is likely to affect the species. (3) If the second step indicates that the species is likely to be affected, the agency must formally "consult" with FWS. In formal consultations, FWS issues a "biological opinion." Depending on the opinion's conclusion, FWS may require the agency to halt the action or to employ mitigating measures to protect the species. In District Court, the plaintiffs claimed that the Forest Service (D) failed to comply with the first step of the above procedure. The District Court found that the Forest Service (D) did not need to inquire because it was already aware that endangered Rocky Mountain Gray Wolves were present in the Jersey Jack area. Finding that the Forest Service (D) had performed enough study to satisfy the purposes of ESA, the District Court declined to enjoin the access road. *Citing Palila v. Hawaii Dept. of Land and Natural Resources,* the District Court also held that the plaintiffs had not met their burden of showing that the proposed action would have a prohibited effect on the endangered wolves. On appeal, Thomas (P) asserts that *TVA v. Hill* made injunctions mandatory whenever ESA is violated. The Forest Service (D) asserts that *TVA* does not apply to de minimis procedural violations. The Forest Service also argues that, because ESA contains substantive provisions, its procedural requirements need not be enforced as strictly as those of the National Environmental Policy Act ["NEPA"].

■ **ISSUE**

Is an agency's failure to prepare a biological assessment when the agency is aware of the presence of endangered species in the area of the agency's proposed action a de minimis violation of the Endangered Species Act?

■ DECISION AND RATIONALE

(Sneed, Circuit Judge) No.   Once the Forest Service (D) was aware of the presence of endangered species in the Jersey Jack area, it had a duty to prepare a biological assessment prior to approving the timber access road.   Without a biological assessment, it was impossible to know if the Forest Service (D) was required to "consult" with FWS.   Without consultation, it is impossible to determine that construction of the road will not violate ESA's substantive provisions.   Affidavits submitted at trial by the Forest Service (D) could not be substituted for the required biological assessment.   As to the procedural requirements of ESA and NEPA, "[a] failure to prepare a biological assessment is comparable to a failure to prepare an environmental impact statement."   In fact, since they ensure compliance with its substantive sections, the ESA's procedural rules should be enforced more stringently than those of NEPA should.   The District Court misapplied the *Palila* decision.   That case concerned "taking" an endangered species, not procedural violation of ESA.   The plaintiffs met the burden for establishing a procedural violation, which is to show that circumstances existed that triggered the agency's duty to perform the procedure and that the procedure did not occur.   Congress specifically directed agencies to work with FWS to evaluate impacts of agency actions on endangered species.   Courts should not make determinations of those impacts.   The District Court's decision not to enjoin the access road is reversed and the road is enjoined until ESA compliance is achieved.

Analysis:

As mentioned in the "Facts" section above, this is the same case that is covered earlier in the chapter in which the court found that the Forest Service had to prepare its NEPA environmental impact statement prior to approving the Jersey Jack road.   By strictly enforcing the procedural rules of ESA in this portion of the case, this court interprets the two laws as being very consistent.   This court finds in both NEPA and ESA that agencies fully consider the impacts *before* beginning proposed actions.   This is revealed by the court's insistence that ESA's procedural rules should be more stringently enforced because they provide assurances that the substantive portions of the Act will not be violated.   One concern raised by the § 7 inquiry and consultation provisions is that FWS could be quite Draconian and completely shut down the actions of other agencies.   In a study of approximately 100,000 consultations, however, the World Wildlife Fund found that less than 1/3 of one percent of FWS's opinions concluded that the proposed actions jeopardized an endangered or threatened species.

■ CASE VOCABULARY

PROCEDURAL PROVISIONS: These are the aspects of a law that tell agencies the steps that they must take in carrying out the law; these provisions are often in place so that outside parties can be comfortable that the agency is not acting on its own initiative.

SUBSTANTIVE PROVISIONS: These are the aspects of a law that tell agencies the actions they are required to do or not do; these provisions are in place to assure that the goal of the law is actually achieved.

Roosevelt Campobello International Park Commission v. EPA

(Environmental advocates) v. *(Federal Environmental Protection Agency)*

684 F.2d 1041 (1st Cir. 1982)

ESA REQUIRES AGENCIES TO CONSIDER THE BEST AVAILABLE SCIENTIFIC DATA AND INFORMA-
TION WHEN DETERMINING THAT A PROPOSED ACTION WILL NOT JEOPARDIZE ANY ENDANGERED
SPECIES

■ **INSTANT FACTS** Environmental advocates sought judicial review of EPA decisions not to have the EPA Administrator review an agency adjudication and not to reopen the record of the adjudication to receive new evidence on endangered species.

■ **BLACK LETTER RULE** An Administrative Law Judge who granted a Clean Water Act permit without ordering certain simulations to determine the permitted action's effects on endangered species violated his duty under ESA to consider the best available scientific data.

■ **PROCEDURAL BASIS**

Appeal to federal Court of Appeals from a decision of the EPA Administrator denying a reopening of the administrative record to receive new evidence on endangered species.

■ **FACTS**

A company named Pittston proposed building an oil refinery and oil shipping terminal in Eastport, Maine, an area largely unspoiled ecologically. The supertankers delivering the oil would have to pass through Canadian waters near the Roosevelt Campobello International Park. Barges and small tankers would carry refined products out of the refinery. After five years of hearings and review at the state and federal levels, the Environmental Protection Agency ["EPA"] recommended approval of Pittston's request for Clean Water Act discharge permits conditioned on state approval of the refinery. Later, EPA consulted with the Fish and Wildlife Service ["FWS"] and the National Marine Fisheries Service ["NMFS"] under § 7 of the Endangered Species Act ["ESA"]. At issue in the consultation was the impact of the refinery project on three endangered species: the right whale, the humpback whale, and the northern bald eagle. As a result of the consultation, EPA's regional office denied Pittston the Clean Water Act discharge permits. Pittston asked for and received an adjudicatory hearing on the matter. After a large-scale, five-week adjudication, the Administrative Law Judge ["ALJ"] overturned the EPA regional office. The ALJ ruled that the EIS was adequate and that the risk of an oil spill was too small to jeopardize the endangered species. The ALJ based his conclusion about the oil spill risk on three items of evidence. First, the Coast Guard testified that the channel leading to the proposed refinery would be safe for supertankers if certain conditions were met. The Council for Environmental Quality requested that the Coast Guard assist in "real time" simulations in the channel, but the Coast Guard—citing limited resources—declined to do so until final clearance had been given for the refinery's construction. Second, the ALJ cited computer simulations that confirmed the Coast Guard testimony and a study that recommended installation of certain navigational aids. Third, the ALJ conducted a detailed study of natural conditions—wind, fog, currents, etc.—that could influence the severity of oil spills in the area. Section 7(a)(2) requires agencies to use "the best scientific and commercial data available" when considering whether its actions could jeopardize any endangered species. Roosevelt

---

Campobello International Park Commission [the "Commission"] sought to have the EPA Administrator review the adjudication and to reopen the record to receive new information on the endangered whales. EPA denied the requests, and the Commission sought judicial review of the agency's decisions.

■ ISSUE

Did the Administrative Law Judge use the best available evidence in evaluating the risk of an oil spill despite declining to have the Coast Guard perform "real time" tanker simulations?

■ DECISION AND RATIONALE

(Coffin, Chief Judge) No. The ALJ "violated his duty to 'use the best scientific... data available' by not requiring the real time simulations to be conducted prior to approving the discharge permit. The standard of review for agency decisions is whether the decision was based on relevant factors and whether there has been a clear error in judgment." The court will also review the actions of the ALJ to determine whether the ALJ followed the required procedures. In *TVA v. Hill,* the U.S. Supreme Court stated that ESA seeks to prevent the loss of any endangered species, "regardless of the cost." Since state and federal agencies view the real time simulations as essential to the evaluation of oil spill risk, EPA cannot issue the Clean Water Act permits until the Coast Guard is able to conduct the simulations. Despite the obligation to consult with FWS and NMFS, an agency retains discretion to determine whether it has taken the steps required to insure that a proposed action will not jeopardize an endangered species: The consultation process, however, is more than a hoop through which the agency must jump. Courts reviewing agency decisions, for example, use biological opinions to assess an agency's degree of compliance with ESA. The 1979 Amendments that added the "best scientific evidence" requirement support this. The legislative history of the 1979 Amendments shows that § 7(a)(2) was put in place to insure that federal agencies would not proceed with proposed actions "in the face of inadequate knowledge or information...." The decision of the ALJ is set aside and the case is remanded.

Analysis:

For many people reading this case for the first time, the court's holding may have come as a surprise. In its opinion, the court seemed to show that the ALJ considered a great deal of credible evidence before rendering his decision. The court concluded though, that the ALJ should have ordered the real time simulations before granting the permits. So how does an ALJ, or more importantly, an Environmental Law student, recognize the best available scientific data? There are certainly a variety of factors to consider; how recent the study is, who conducted it, how solid is its methodology, etc. Each of these questions can be very difficult to answer and may be debated among experts. While the court did not address these issues in much detail in the *Roosevelt Campobello* decision, we can be certain that it considered the standard to be quite high. The court cited the *TVA v. Hill* decision for the proposition that cost should be no objective when enforcing ESA. The formulation of § 7(a)(2) that the court used in *Roosevelt Campobello* was disarmingly simple: there was a study that the ALJ could have ordered that would have made his conclusion somewhat more certain; the ALJ didn't do it; therefore, the ALJ violated § 7(a)(2).

■ CASE VOCABULARY

AGENCY ADJUDICATION: This is one procedure through which federal agencies reach decisions and issue orders; "formal" adjudications are "on the record" proceedings, somewhat like trials but usually lacking the strict rules of evidence and procedure.

Carson-Truckee Water Conservancy District v. Clark

(*Water District*) v. (*Interior Secretary*)

741 F.2d 257 (9th Cir. 1984)

ESA JUSTIFIES AGENCY ACTIONS TO ACTIVELY CONSERVE ENDANGERED SPECIES AND DOES NOT LIMIT AGENCIES TO ONLY THOSE ACTIONS NECESSARY TO AVOID JEOPARDIZING ENDANGERED SPECIES

■ **INSTANT FACTS** A water district and power company sued to compel the Secretary of Interior to sell water from a federally operated dam.

■ **BLACK LETTER RULE** ESA § 7(a)(2) does not apply when federal agencies actively seek to conserve endangered species and does not limit agencies to only those actions necessary to avoid jeopardizing endangered species.

■ PROCEDURAL BASIS

Appeal to federal Court of Appeals of a District Court decision ruling that the Secretary of Interior did not exceed his duties under ESA by refusing to sell water from a federally-operated dam for municipal and industrial use.

■ FACTS

Stampede Dam, on the Little Truckee River in California, is operated by the Secretary of the Interior ["Secretary"] (D) in a way that protects two endangered species of fish. The waters of Little Truckee River eventually drain into Pyramid Lake in Nevada, and the Washoe Project Act and other reclamation laws direct that water from Stampede Dam may be sold for municipal and industrial use in the Nevada cities of Sparks and Reno. Section 7(a)(2) of the Endangered Species Act ["ESA"], however, directs federal agencies to insure that their actions will not jeopardize the existence of any endangered species. Elsewhere ESA directs agencies to act in a manner that seeks "to conserve endangered and threatened species to the extent that they are no longer endangered or threatened." Section 7(a)(1) of ESA makes it mandatory for the Secretary (D) to use the programs he administers "to further the conservation purposes of ESA." The Secretary (D) refused to sell water for use in Sparks and Reno. Carson-Truckee Water Conservation District [the "Water District"] (P) and Sierra Pacific Power Company [the "Power Company"] (P) sued in federal District Court for declaratory judgment that the Secretary's (D) refusal to sell violated the Washoe Project Act. The District Court first held that the Secretary was, in fact, required to sell water to the Nevada cities. The District Court also found, however, that the Secretary's (D) duty to supply water to Indian Tribes and to comply with ESA trumped the duty to sell water to Sparks and Reno. The Secretary (D) determined that, after fulfilling these primary duties, no water was left to sell. The District Court upheld this determination, finding that it was not arbitrary or capricious. The Water District (P) and the Power Company (P) appealed the District Court ruling, arguing that, even though ESA trumps the Washoe Project Act, the Secretary (D) had exceeded his ESA duties. They argued that § 7(a)(2) constitutes the full extent of the Secretary's obligation under ESA.

■ ISSUE

Did the Secretary of the Interior exceed his statutory obligations under ESA by using water for conservation of endangered fish species and refusing to sell water for municipal and industrial use?

■ DECISION AND RATIONALE

(Pregerson, Circuit Judge) No. The Secretary's (D) duties under ESA are not limited to § 7(a)(2)'s requirement to avoid jeopardizing endangered species or their critical habitats. The suggestion of the Water District (P) and Power Company (P)—that the Secretary's duty begins and ends with § 7(a)(2)— produces a result inconsistent with the purposes of ESA because it ignores many other relevant sections of the Act. Section 7(a)(1) and other provisions of ESA direct the Secretary (D) to use programs under his control to advance conservation efforts. As the U.S. Supreme Court held in *TVA v. Hill,* ESA signals Congress' intent to make endangered species preservation a priority. As the Court stated in *TVA,* the purpose of ESA is "to halt *and reverse* the trend toward . . . extinction, whatever the cost." The Water District (P) and Power Company (P) are incorrect in asserting that § 7(a)(2) applies to this case, because the Secretary (D) is not proposing actions that jeopardize the endangered species of fish. On the contrary, the Secretary (D) is affirmatively protecting these species. Application of the proper sections of ESA justifies the Secretary's (D) decision to prefer protecting the fish until they are no longer listed as endangered or threatened species to selling water to recoup the costs of the project. The portion of the District Court's decision dealing with the Secretary's (D) decision not to sell water is affirmed.

Analysis:

Perhaps the most interesting aspect of the portion of the *Carson-Truckee* decision described here is the interplay between the various obligations of the Secretary of the Interior with regard to the Stampede Dam water. In the Western States, a first-in-time approach, called the Prior Appropriations Doctrine, determines most water rights. It is well established that the water rights of Indian Tribes are given precedence over almost all other uses. For this reason, the Pyramid Lake Paiute Tribe of Indians intervened in the case on the side of the Secretary. In the present case, however, we also add in the Washoe Project Act that covers water from the Stampede Dam. The role of this law is somewhat less clear. The Court of Appeals decision appeared to agree with the District Court that found that the Secretary is required to sell water (not reserved for the Indian Tribes or ESA purposes) to certain Nevada cities. Later, the court's opinion stated that "the Washoe Project Act anticipates but does not require the Secretary to sell water. . . ." Ultimately, this distinction was unimportant to the outcome of the *Carson-Truckee* case because the court held (indeed, the appellants conceded) that the ESA trumps the Washoe Project Act.

■ CASE VOCABULARY

TRUST OBLIGATION TO INDIAN TRIBES: Indian lands are held in trust by the federal government for the benefit of Indian tribes; the Secretary of the Interior acts as trustee in many cases, insuring that the lands are protected and used wisely.

Babbitt v. Sweet Home Chapter of Communities for a Great Oregon

(Interior Secretary) v. *(Pro-Logging Interest Group)*

515 U.S. 687 (1995)

THE PROHIBITION ON "HARMING" ENDANGERED SPECIES IN § 9(a)(1) OF ESA INCLUDES A PROHIBITION ON MODIFYING OR DEGRADING HABITAT ESSENTIAL TO THE SURVIVAL OF THE SPECIES

■ **INSTANT FACTS** Pro-logging plaintiffs sued the Secretary of Interior and Director of FWS claiming that those agencies' interpretation of the Endangered Species Act had harmed the plaintiffs' financial interest in logging.

■ **BLACK LETTER RULE** Secretary of Interior reasonably defined the term "harm" as used in § 9 of the Endangered Species Act as including modification or degradation of habitat essential to the survival of endangered or threatened species.

■ **PROCEDURAL BASIS**

Appeal from Court of Appeals decision setting aside the agency's interpretation of ESA.

■ **FACTS**

Section 9(a)(1) of the Endangered Species Act ["ESA"] makes it unlawful to "take" any animal listed as endangered by the Fish and Wildlife Service ["FWS"] (D). According to ESA, to "take" an endangered species means to kill, harass, harm, capture or collect. The Secretary of Interior [the "Secretary"] (D) issued a regulation interpreting "harm" (as used in § 9) to include modification or degradation of the species' habitat. When applied to the red-cockaded woodpecker [hereafter "Woody"] and the northern spotted owl—a threatened species—the regulation had the effect of preventing many logging operations in the Pacific Northwest. A group of lumber companies, families and landowners ["Sweet Home Chapter"] (P) challenged the Secretary's (D) definition of "harm." The Sweet Home Chapter (P) argued that the Secretary's (D) only option was to exercise his authority under ESA § 5 to purchase the lands on which the endangered and threatened birds were found. The Secretary (D) argued that, because the definition of harm included habitat degradation, anyone wishing to log the areas where the birds were found was required to obtain a permit for incidental taking as defined in ESA § 10. The Court of Appeals found in favor of the Sweet Home Chapter (P) holding that "harm" must refer to a direct application of force against the endangered species. The Secretary (D) appealed the decision to the U.S. Supreme Court.

■ **ISSUE**

Does the term "harm" as used in ESA § 9(a)(1) reasonably include modification and degradation of habitat?

■ **DECISION AND RATIONALE**

(Stevens, J.) Yes. The Secretary's (D) regulation, which defines "harm" to include degradation of habitat, is reasonable, comports with the statutory language of ESA, and is supported by later amendments to ESA. In *Chevron USA, Inc. v. NRDC*, this Court held that unless Congress "unambiguously manifest[ed] its intent" to adopt a particular definition of a term used in legislation, courts should defer to a reasonable definition of the term by the agency charged with carrying out the legislation. The Secretary's (D) definition of "harm" is reasonable for three reasons. First, it agrees with the ordinary use of the word. Webster's Third New International Dictionary, for example, defines harm as "to cause hurt or damage to; injure." This definition does not include any mention of the direct application of force. Furthermore, the canons of statutory construction direct courts to be reluctant to treat words in legislation as redundant. Unless Congress meant that "harm" included indirect injuries, the term would just overlap with "kill," "harass," "capture, " and "collect." Second, the purpose of ESA—stated in § 2—is "to provide a means whereby the ecosystems upon which endangered species and threatened species depend may be conserved. . . ." In *TVA v. Hill*, we recognized that this policy precluded completion of a dam because the operation of the dam would destroy the snail darter, an endangered species of perch. Although the Sweet Home Chapter (P) argued that activities causing only minimal or unforeseeable harm would not violate the statute, its attack on the "harm" provision would change the law in every case, even where a person intentionally altered habitat knowing that it could destroy an endangered species. Third, the fact that Congress added § 10 (by a 1982 amendment to ESA)—authorizing the Secretary (D) to issue permits for incidentally "taking" endangered species while engaging in an otherwise lawful activity—indicates that understood § 9 as barring indirect harm. It would be absurd to think that Congress meant that the Secretary (D) could allow "incidental" takings from activities that caused "direct" harm. The Court of Appeals definition of "harm"—that it means only direct application of force—is incorrect for three reasons. First, "taking" in § 9 encompasses other terms, such as "pursue" or "harass," that do not require direct application of force. Second, § 9 has a "knowing" requirement for violations, not an "intent" or "purpose" standard. Finally, the definition used by the Court of Appeals makes "harm" redundant with other words used to explain "taking" an endangered species. The Secretary's definition of "harm" as used in ESA § 9(a)(1) is upheld.

■ CONCURRENCE

(O'Connor, J.) The majority opinion is correct assuming that it is meant to include the following two elements. First, the meaning of habitat degradation in the Secretary's (D) regulation must be limited to actual and significant damage, not merely hypothetical injury, to "identifiable protected animals." Second, the Secretary's (D) regulation must be understood as containing the "ordinary principles of proximate causation." The dissent claims that the regulation goes too far because, by barring habitat degradation, the regulation is actually seeking to protect hypothetical, future animals. This is incorrect because injury includes "impairment," in this case, of breeding done by living animals. The dissent also argues that the regulation in question is not limited to harm proximately caused by habitat degrading activities. Typically, the courts will presume that Congress intends its legislation to be limited by accepted notions of proximate causation unless it explicitly abrogates such principles. This is a strict liability statute, but strict liability means liability without fault, not liability without causation. Proximate cause should be determined by finders of fact because it is highly fact sensitive, but as long as the Secretary's (D) regulation is presumed to be limited to "foreseeable" consequences of habitat degradation, it should not be set aside because it might possibly be misapplied.

■ DISSENT

(Scalia, J.) The Court's holding in this case could bring financial ruin upon simple farmers whose lands will, in essence, be requisitioned for "national zoological use." The Secretary's (D) regulation fails to comport with the statute for three reasons. First, it prohibits habitat modification that is merely the cause-in-fact of harm to protected animals, without regard to whether the harm was foreseeable. Second, the regulation applies to acts and omissions; the statute should be interpreted to cover only acts causing harm. Third, the regulation is too expansive in that it covers "impair[ment of] essential behavior patterns, including *breeding*" (emphasis in original). Impairment of breeding does not harm individual animals; it harms *populations* of animals. "None of these three features of the regulation can be found in the statutory provisions that authorize it." Moreover, these features deviate from the accepted meaning of "take" as a legal term of art describing "a class of acts (not omissions) done directly and intentionally (not indirectly and by accident) to particular animals (not populations of animals) . . . ." The majority opinion is incorrect that a narrow definition of "harm" is redundant to the terms "kill" and "wound." One might, however, "feed an animal poison, spray it with mace, or chop down the very tree in which it is nesting" and thereby do "harm" to the animal without killing or wounding it. The majority claims that one can infer that Congress intended § 9 to cover habitat degradation from the amendment that became § 10 in 1982. This is incorrect because habitat degradation is only one possible "otherwise lawful activity" that could incidentally cause a "taking." One example that Congress has mentioned in another statute is the "incidental" taking of sea turtles by shrimp fishermen. Although the Court and the concurrence both claim that the regulation is limited by the principle of proximate cause, their interpretations rob the statute of this feature. "In fact 'proximate' causation simply *means* 'direct' causation." The Court, however, upholds a definition of "harm" that includes indirect injuries. The regulation clearly defines "harm" as "(1) an act which (2) actually kills or injures wildlife," and this is equivalent to "but for" causation.

Analysis:

This is one of many interesting cases in which the Supreme Court is called upon to decide the meaning of a word as that word is used in a statute or regulation. This task raises many thorny issues. The majority opinion, for example, approached the definition of "harm" offered in the Secretary of Interior's regulation from several different directions. First, to establish that the Secretary's definition was reasonable, the majority cited a dictionary as evidence of how the word "harm" is normally used. Next, the opinion compared the term to other terms that the statute uses to define a "taking" of an endangered species. The majority then employed a canon of construction that directs courts to treat different words in any statutory provision as having different meanings, rather than treat statutory terms as surplusage. After this, the opinion looked at the stated purpose of the statute, to establish that the Secretary's definition advanced that purpose. Finally, the majority inferred from a later amendment that Congress must have meant both "direct and indirect" harm when it first used the word "harm." After all of this, if you are anyone other than William Safire, you are tempted to ask, "What do we mean when we say a word 'means' something?"

■ CASE VOCABULARY

CANONS OF CONSTRUCTION: These are rules that guide courts in interpreting ambiguous statutory language; the example from the present case, known as *noscitur a sociis* (meaning that words gather meaning from the words around it) directs courts to interpret statutory language so as to avoid redundant meanings.

CHAPTER TEN

Environmental Enforcement

Sierra Club v. Cedar Point Oil Co.

Instant Facts: In a successful citizen suit brought pursuant to the CWA, the trial court assessed the penalty at $186,070, the economic benefit to the polluter for not properly disposing of the polluted water.

Black Letter Rule: The court may, in its discretion, limit civil penalties for violation of the Clean Water Act to the economic benefit to the polluter.

Harmon Industries v. Browner

Instant Facts: Upon discovery of its violations of the RCRA, Harmon (P) implemented a cleanup plan with the Missouri Department of Natural Resources. While Harmon (P) was cooperating with the MDNR, the EPA (D) initiated an administrative enforcement action of its own.

Black Letter Rule: The EPA may not initiate enforcement actions under the RCRA in those states where it has previously authorized the state to act.

United States v. Weitzenhoff

Instant Facts: Weitzenhoff (D) and Mariani (D) regularly instructed two of their sewer plant employees to dispose of sludge by pumping it directly into the ocean.

Black Letter Rule: A polluter is criminally liable under the CWA when he knowingly engages in prohibited conduct, regardless of whether he knows that his conduct is illegal.

Sierra Club v. Morton

Instant Facts: The Sierra Club (P), on behalf of its members, sought to enjoin agency approval of a proposed resort development.

Black Letter Rule: Mere interest in a controversy, absent any actual injury, is not enough to give a party standing to seek judicial review of agency action.

Lujan v. Defenders of Wildlife

Instant Facts: Defenders of Wildlife (P) challenged the Secretary of the Interior's (D) interpretation that § 7 of the Endangered Species Act applied only to actions within the United States. Two members of Defenders (P) submitted affidavits that they had studied endangered species abroad in the past and would deprived of doing so in the future.

Black Letter Rule: A person seeking review of agency action must show an actual or imminent injury from that action.

Norton v. Southern Utah Wilderness Alliance

Instant Facts: A wilderness preservation group claimed that the Bureau of Land Management failed to properly safeguard certain wilderness areas by allowing off-road vehicle use therein.

Black Letter Rule: The authority of a federal court under the Administrative Procedures Act to "compel agency action unlawfully withheld and unreasonably delayed" extends only to claims involving a specific "agency action"—a rule, order, license, sanction, or relief—that the agency was required by law to take.

Gwaltney of Smithfield Ltd. v. Chesapeake Bay Foundation

Instant Facts: For several years, Gwaltney (D), a meat packing plant, repeatedly violated the conditions of its NPDES permit. After Gwaltney (D) remedied the violations, the Chesapeake Bay Foundation (P) filed a citizen suit pursuant to § 505 of the Clean Water Act.

Black Letter Rule: The Clean Water Act authorizes citizen suits for present violations, but not for violations that occurred entirely in the past.

Friends of the Earth v. Laidlaw Environmental Services

Instant Facts: For years, Laidlaw Environmental Services (D) violated the discharge limits of its NPDES permit. Between the commencement of a lawsuit by Friends of the Earth (P) and the trial court's judgment, Laidlaw (D) achieved substantial compliance with its permit.

Black Letter Rule: A defendant's post-complaint compliance with its permit does not render suits for civil penalties under the CWA moot or defeat plaintiff's standing.

Atlantic States Legal Foundation, Inc. v. Eastman Kodak Co.

Instant Facts: Eastman Kodak Co. (D) discharged pollutants into local waters under a state permit system, which specified effluent limitations for approximately 25 pollutants. Atlantic States Legal Foundation (P) alleged Kodak (D) discharged pollutants not listed in its state permit.

Black Letter Rule: The Clean Water Act only limits the discharge of those pollutants listed in the polluter's permit.

Sierra Club v. Cedar Point Oil Co.

(Environmental Group) v. *(Polluter)*

73 F.3d 546 (5th Cir. 1996)

THE COURT MAY LIMIT CIVIL PENALTIES UNDER THE CLEAN WATER ACT TO REFLECT ONLY THE ECONOMIC BENEFIT TO THE POLLUTER

■ **INSTANT FACTS** In a successful citizen suit brought pursuant to the CWA, the trial court assessed the penalty at $186,070, the economic benefit to the polluter for not properly disposing of the polluted water.

■ **BLACK LETTER RULE** The court may, in its discretion, limit civil penalties for violation of the Clean Water Act to the economic benefit to the polluter.

■ **PROCEDURAL BASIS**

Appeal from a judgment assessing civil penalties for violation of the Clean Water Act.

■ **FACTS**

The Sierra Club (P) brought a successful citizen suit against Cedar Point Oil Co. (D) for discharging polluted water without a permit in violation of the Clean Water Act (CWA). Section 309(d) of the CWA subjects violators to a maximum civil penalty of $25,000 per day for each violation. In determining the amount of the penalty, the court may consider factors such as the seriousness of the violation, the economic benefit (if any) resulting from the violation, any history of such violations, any good faith efforts to comply with the applicable requirements, the economic impact of the penalty on the violator, and such other matters as justice may require. The trial court found that the maximum penalty under § 309(d) was $20,225,000 by multiplying $25,000 per day by 809 days of unpermitted discharge. The trial court found that the economic benefit to Cedar Point (D) from the violation was $186,070, the amount that Cedar Point (D) saved by not properly disposing of the polluted water. Weighing the statutory factors, the trial court found that the maximum penalty was inappropriate and assessed the penalty at $186,070. Sierra Club (P) appealed, arguing that the trial court abused its discretion in assessing a penalty that reflected only the economic benefit to Cedar Point (D).

■ **ISSUE**

Is it an abuse of discretion for the court to assess a civil penalty for violation of the Clean Water Act that reflects only the economic benefit to the polluter?

■ **DECISION AND RATIONALE**

(Judge Not Stated). No. It is not an abuse of discretion for the court to assess a civil penalty for violation of the Clean Water Act that reflects only the economic benefit to the polluter. After calculating the maximum penalty as a starting point, the court should determine if the penalty should be reduced from the maximum by reference to the statutory factors of § 309. The Supreme Court has described the process of weighing the statutory factors in calculating civil penalties as "highly discretionary" with the trial court. It is clear the trial court considered all of the statutory factors before settling on an amount based only on economic benefit. As such, we perceive no abuse of discretion. Affirmed.

Analysis:

With respect to the statutory factors, the trial court found that Cedar Point's (D) violation was moderately serious, that it received a substantial economic benefit from its noncompliance, that it had been violating the CWA since operations on the well in question began operating, and that it had not demonstrated good faith in attempting to comply with the CWA. Given that most of the statutory factors weighed against Cedar Point (D), would you consider the reduction from $20,225,000 to $186,070 to be an abuse of discretion even though the assessment of penalties is "highly discretionary"? Some argue that limiting the penalties to that of the polluter's economic benefit actually decreases the incentive to comply voluntarily because the polluter only pays (assuming he is caught) what he would have paid to comply in the first place. Of course, this argument fails to consider the harm to the polluter in terms of public opinion (especially a corporate polluter) and the administrative and criminal penalties imposed by the CWA.

Harmon Industries v. Browner

(Polluter) v. *(EPA Administrator)*

191 F.3d 894 (8th Cir. 1999)

THE EPA MAY NOT DUPLICATE ENFORCEMENT ACTIONS PURSUANT TO THE RCRA WHERE IT HAS PREVIOUSLY AUTHORIZED THE STATE TO ACT

■ **INSTANT FACTS** Upon discovery of its violations of the RCRA, Harmon (P) implemented a cleanup plan with the Missouri Department of Natural Resources. While Harmon (P) was cooperating with the MDNR, the EPA (D) initiated an administrative enforcement action of its own.

■ **BLACK LETTER RULE** The EPA may not initiate enforcement actions under the RCRA in those states where it has previously authorized the state to act.

■ **PROCEDURAL BASIS**

Appeal from judgment holding that the EPA's enforcement action for civil penalties violated the Resource Conservation and Recovery Act and principles of res judicata.

■ **FACTS**

After discovering that it had been discarding volatile solvent residue in violation of the Resource Conservation and Recovery Act (RCRA), Harmon (P) voluntarily implemented a cleanup plan with the Missouri Department of Natural Resources (MDNR). Meanwhile, the EPA (D) initiated an administrative enforcement action of its own seeking over $2.3 million in penalties. Harmon (P) and the MDNR subsequently entered into a consent decree whereby MDNR released Harmon (P) from any claim for monetary penalties. Harmon (P) unsuccessfully challenged the EPA's (D) claim before an ALJ and Environmental Appeals Board panel. Thereafter, Harmon (P) appealed to federal district court which held that the EPA's (D) enforcement action for civil penalties violated the RCRA and principles of res judicata. The EPA (D) appealed.

■ **ISSUE**

May the EPA institute its own enforcement actions against suspected environmental violators under the RCRA after the commencement of a state-initiated enforcement action?

■ **DECISION AND RATIONALE**

(Hansen, Cir. J.) No. The EPA may not institute its own enforcement actions against suspected environmental violators under the RCRA after the commencement of a state-initiated enforcement action. Under 42 U.S.C. § 6926(b), states may apply to the EPA (D) for authorization to administer and enforce a hazardous waste program. If authorization is granted, the state's program then operates "in lieu of" the federal government's hazardous waste program. The EPA (D) cannot rescind this authorization unless the EPA (D) finds, among other things, that the state is failing to adequately enforce the requirements of federal law. As provided by § 6926(d), any action taken by a state under this program has the "same force and effect" as action taken by the EPA (D). Despite having authorized a state to act, the EPA (D) frequently files its own enforcement actions against suspected violators even after the commencement of a state-initiated enforcement action, a practice known as overfiling. While the EPA's (D) assertion that the "in lieu of" language only applies to the program and not its enforcement, the administration and enforcement of the program are inexorably intertwined. RCRA reveals a congressional intent for an authorized state program to supplant the federal hazardous waste program in all respects, including enforcement. This intent is evinced within the language of § 6926(b) which allows the EPA (D) to repeal a state's authorization if the state is failing to provide adequate enforcement. If the state fails to initiate an enforcement action after receiving notice as required by § 6928(a)(2), the EPA (D) may institute its own action pursuant to § 6928(a)(1). Further, nothing in RCRA suggests that the "same force and effect" language of § 6926(d) applies to issuance of permits but not their enforcement. Congress intended to delegate primary enforcement of EPA-approved hazardous waste programs to the states. Therefore, we find that the EPA's (D) practice of overfiling, in those states where it has authorized the state to act, oversteps the federal agency's authority under the RCRA. Affirmed.

Analysis:

In light of the court's decision in *Harmon*, what are EPA's options if it believes that the state is not adequately enforcing the requirements of federal law? As the court mentions, the EPA may withdraw the state's authorization to administer the program after timely notice and a reasonable period of time for the state to take corrective action. How likely is it that EPA will revoke the state's program authorization? The EPA has never taken such action in the nearly thirty years of delegated programs.

■ CASE VOCABULARY

RES JUDICATA: A matter adjudged. Rule which provides that once a court of competent jurisdiction has rendered a final judgment, that judgment is conclusive upon the parties to the case as to the issues determined therein.

United States v. Weitzenhoff

(Prosecutor) v. *(Polluter)*

35 F.3d 1275 (9th Cir. 1993)

"KNOWINGLY" REFERS TO KNOWLEDGE OF THE CONDUCT, NOT KNOWLEDGE THAT THE CONDUCT IS ILLEGAL

■ **INSTANT FACTS** Weitzenhoff (D) and Mariani (D) regularly instructed two of their sewer plant employees to dispose of sludge by pumping it directly into the ocean.

■ **BLACK LETTER RULE** A polluter is criminally liable under the CWA when he knowingly engages in prohibited conduct, regardless of whether he knows that his conduct is illegal.

■ **PROCEDURAL BASIS**

Appeal from conviction on six counts of conspiracy and knowingly discharging waste in violation of the Clean Water Act.

■ **FACTS**

Weitzenhoff (D) and Mariani (D), managers of a sewage treatment plant, instructed two employees at the plant to dispose of waste activated sludge (WAS) on a regular basis by pumping it from the storage tanks directly into the ocean. The discharges, most of which occurred at night, violated the plant's permit effluent limitations. In response to complaints by lifeguards at a nearby beach and health inspector inquiries, Weitzenhoff (D) and Mariani (D) repeatedly denied that there was a problem at the plant. Further evidence showed that Weitzenhoff (D) instructed a plant employee to keep quiet about the discharges. Following an investigation by the FBI, Weitzenhoff (D) and Mariani (D) were charged in a thirty-one-count indictment with conspiracy and substantive violations of the Clean Water Act (CWA). The jury found them guilty on six of those counts. Weitzenhoff (D) and Mariani (D) appealed, contending that the trial court erred in its interpretation of the CWA's "knowingly" requirement.

■ **ISSUE**

Are criminal sanctions to be imposed on individuals who knowingly engage in conduct that results in a permit violation, whether or not they are cognizant of the requirements or the existence of the permit?

■ **DECISION AND RATIONALE**

(Fletcher, Cir. J.) Yes. Criminal sanctions are to be imposed on individuals who knowingly engage in conduct that results in a permit violation, whether or not they are cognizant of the requirements or the existence of the permit. Section 1319(c)(2) of the CWA makes it a felony offense to knowingly discharge pollutants into navigable waters without an NPDES permit. The legislative history of the CWA and decisions interpreting analogous public welfare statutes lead us to conclude that "knowingly" refers to the acts made criminal rather than a violation of the regulation. In the absence of clear contrary congressional intent, public welfare offenses are not to be construed to require proof that the defendant knew he was violating the law. In this case, as the permittees, the defendants are clearly in the best position to know their own permit status and that the dumping of sewage into our nation's waters may pose a danger to public health and welfare. The criminal provisions of the CWA are clearly designed to protect the public at large from the potentially dire consequences of water pollution, and as such they

---

fall within the category of public welfare legislation. Thus, the government did not need to prove that Weitzenhoff (D) and Mariani (D) knew that their acts violated the permit or the CWA. Affirmed.

■ DISSENT

(Kleinfeld, Cir. J.) If we read the statute in an ordinary way, the state of mind required is knowledge that one is violating a permit condition. The court incorrectly reads the statute as though it says "knowingly discharges pollutants." By not requiring a criminal state of mind, we reduce the moral authority of our system of criminal law. Our decision will send sewer plant workers to prison if, unbeknownst to them, their plant discharges exceed permit limits. Although the opinion suggests otherwise, it is possible that Weitzenhoff (D) and Mariani (D) honestly and reasonably believed that their NPDES permit authorized the discharges. The classification of the CWA as a public welfare statute is a modernized version of malum prohibitum which makes the rule of lenity especially important. Offenses that require no mens rea are generally disfavored. If Congress makes a crime a felony, the usual presumption that a defendant must know the facts that make his conduct illegal should apply.

Analysis:

The dissent here argues that the court's decision will subject innocent sewer plant workers to imprisonment who unknowingly violate the plants permit requirements. The defendants in this case were managers of a sewage plant who directed their employees to discharge 436,000 pounds of sludge into the ocean. This was done at night, the employees were instructed not to reveal the discharges, and the defendants repeatedly denied the discharges when confronted by health officials. Do you agree that the court here would equate the actions of innocent sewer workers with the highly culpable actions of these midnight dumpers? The dissent's hypothesis on the impact on ordinary sewer workers is also undermined by the discretion exercised by prosecutors in pursuing convictions. EPA guidance documents direct agency investigators to focus only on the most significant and egregious violators, considering such factors as deliberate misconduct and efforts to conceal violations.

■ CASE VOCABULARY

MALUM IN SE: Conduct that is inherently wrong based on principles of natural moral law.

MALUM PROHIBITUM: Conduct that is wrong because law prohibits it.

MENS REA: A guilty mind or criminal intent; the mental state that accompanies a crime.

Sierra Club v. Morton

(Environmental Group) v. *(Secretary of the Interior)*
405 U.S. 727 (1972)

AN ORGANIZATION MUST HAVE MORE THAN A MERE INTEREST IN A PROBLEM IN ORDER TO HAVE STANDING TO SUE

■ **INSTANT FACTS** The Sierra Club (P), on behalf of its members, sought to enjoin agency approval of a proposed resort development.

■ **BLACK LETTER RULE** Mere interest in a controversy, absent any actual injury, is not enough to give a party standing to seek judicial review of agency action.

■ **PROCEDURAL BASIS**

Appeal from reversal of injunction in action seeking to enjoin agency approval of a development plan.

■ **FACTS**

The United States Forest Service invited bids from developers for the construction and operation of a ski resort and summer recreation area in Mineral King Valley, a natural area in the Sierra Nevada Mountains. A proposal by Walt Disney Enterprises to build a $35 million resort was approved by the Forest Service. A highway and power line that would traverse Sequoia National Park was also proposed by the State of California and submitted for approval to Morton (D), Secretary of the Interior. The Sierra Club (P) sued as a membership corporation with "a special interest in the conservation and the sound maintenance of the national parks, game refuges and forests of the country" to enjoin approval of the project. The trial court granted the requested injunction, but the court of appeals reversed for the Sierra Club's (P) lack of standing. The Sierra Club (P) appealed.

■ **ISSUE**

Is an organization's mere interest in a controversy sufficient to establish standing to seek judicial review of an agency action relating to that controversy?

■ **DECISION AND RATIONALE**

(Stewart, J.) No. An organization's mere interest in a controversy is not sufficient to establish standing to seek judicial review of an agency action relating to that controversy. The question of standing depends upon whether the party has alleged such a personal stake in the outcome of the controversy. The Sierra Club (P) relies on § 10 of the Administrative Procedure Act (APA) which provides that "[a] person suffering legal wrong because of agency action, or adversely affected or aggrieved by agency action within the meaning of a relevant statute, is entitled to judicial review thereof." To have standing under § 10, the challengers must allege that the action caused them "injury in fact." Aesthetic, environmental, and economic harm may amount to injury in fact, but the test requires that the party seeking review be among the injured. It is clear that an organization whose members are injured may represent those members in a proceeding for judicial review. But the Sierra Club (P) failed to allege that it or its members would be affected in any of their activities or pastimes by the proposed development or that its members even use Mineral King Valley for any purpose. The Sierra Club's (P) mere interest in this action is not sufficient by itself to render it "adversely affected" or "aggrieved" within the meaning of the APA. The court of appeals was correct in holding that the Sierra Club (P) lacked standing to maintain this action. Affirmed.

■ **DISSENT**

(Douglas, J.) We should fashion a federal rule that gives the threatened inanimate object standing to sue in its own name.

Analysis:

According to the Court, all that the Sierra Club (P) had to allege was that one of its members used the area for recreation and would suffer harm from the development. Why was the Sierra Club (P) not more specific in its pleadings? Was the Sierra Club (P) testing the Supreme Court to see how tenuous the actual injury could be in cases such as this? The Sierra Club (P) did score a victory with the Court's recognition that injury to aesthetic and environmental values may be sufficient to confer standing even if the injury is shared by many. On remand, the Sierra Club (P) amended its complaint to allege that its members used the area. It also added another claim under the newly-enacted National Environmental Policy Act (NEPA). The environmental impact statement required by NEPA recommended that the project be significantly scaled down. Ironically, the ski resort was never built.

■ **CASE VOCABULARY**

IPSO FACTO: By the mere fact itself.

Lujan v. Defenders of Wildlife

(Secretary of the Interior) v. *(Environmental Group)*

504 U.S. 555 (1992)

A PERSON MUST HAVE AN ACTUAL OR IMMINENT INJURY TO HAVE STANDING TO SUE

■ **INSTANT FACTS** Defenders of Wildlife (P) challenged the Secretary of the Interior's (D) interpretation that § 7 of the Endangered Species Act applied only to actions within the United States. Two members of Defenders (P) submitted affidavits that they had studied endangered species abroad in the past and would deprived of doing so in the future.

■ **BLACK LETTER RULE** A person seeking review of agency action must show an actual or imminent injury from that action.

■ **PROCEDURAL BASIS**

Appeal from ruling that Defenders of Wildlife (P) had standing in action challenging agency's interpretation of provisions of the Endangered Species Act.

■ **FACTS**

Section 7 of the Endangered Species Act (ESA) requires all federal agencies to consult with the Secretary of the Interior (D) to insure that the projects that they fund do not jeopardize endangered species. Defenders of Wildlife (P) challenged a rule promulgated by the Secretary (D) interpreting § 7 as being applicable only to actions within the United States. In response to the Secretary's (D) motion for summary judgment for lack of standing, two of Defenders' (P) members submitted affidavits that they had observed endangered species abroad in past years and would now be deprived of that opportunity in the future. The court of appeals held that Defenders (P) had standing, and the Secretary (D) appealed.

■ **ISSUE**

Does a person have standing to challenge an administrative agency action if he cannot demonstrate an actual or imminent injury?

■ **DECISION AND RATIONALE**

(Scalia, J.) No. A person does not have standing to challenge an administrative agency action if he cannot demonstrate an actual or imminent injury. The affidavits submitted by Defenders' (P) members show only that they have observed endangered species abroad in past years and that they intend to return at some unspecified time in the future. Defenders' (P) affidavits contain no facts showing how damage to the species will produce "imminent" injury to the affiants. Past exposure does not in itself show a present case or controversy if unaccompanied by any continuing, present adverse effects. Further, these "some day" intentions to return, without any description of concrete plans or specification of when that will be, do not support a finding of the "actual or imminent" injury that our cases require. Defenders (P) proposes its "ecosystem nexus" theory of standing whereby any person who uses any part of a contiguous ecosystem adversely affected by the activity has standing even if the activity is located a great distance away. We have held, however, that a plaintiff claiming environmental damage must use the area affected by the challenged activity. Even though the ESA protects ecosystems, it does not create rights of actions in those who have not been injured in fact. Likewise, someone's interest in studying or working with the endangered animals anywhere in the world, described by Defenders (P) as the "animal nexus" and "vocational nexus," is not enough to establish appreciable harm. The court of appeals also found that the citizen suit provisions of the ESA create a procedural right to consultation in all persons and that this right satisfies the injury in fact requirement. We reject this view. A plaintiff raising only a generally available grievance about government, and seeking relief that no more directly and tangible benefits him than it does the public at large, does not state an Article III case or controversy. Reversed.

■ CONCURRENCE

(Kennedy, J.) Although insufficient in this case, similar nexus theories might support a claim to standing in other cases. Congress has the power to define injuries and articulate chains of causation that will give rise to a case and controversy where none existed before. Although the ESA purports to allow any person to sue for violations of the ESA, it does not establish that there is an injury in any person by virtue of the violation.

■ CONCURRENCE

(Stevens, J.) Since Congress did not intend for § 7 of the ESA to apply to foreign activities, I must concur. However, any person who has visited the critical habitat of an endangered species, has a professional interest in preserving the species and its habitat, and intends to revisit them in the future has standing to challenge agency action that threatens their destruction.

■ DISSENT

(Blackmun, J.) A reasonable finder of fact could conclude that Defenders' (P) affiants will soon return to the project sites, thereby satisfying the "actual or imminent" injury standard. By requiring a description of concrete plans or specification of when the return visit will be, the Court demands an empty formality since the affiants can simply purchase plane tickets to return to the project areas. The Court's use of a geographical proximity requirement to negate Defenders' (P) "ecosystem nexus" theory ignores the fact that many environmental injuries cause harm distant from the area immediately affected.

Analysis:

The Court has articulated four requirements for standing: that the challenged action will cause plaintiff some actual or threatened injury-in-fact; that the injury is fairly traceable to the challenged action; that the injury is redressable by judicial action; and that the injury is to an interest arguably within the zone of interests to be protected by the statute alleged to have been violated. The first three are constitutionally mandated by the Case or Controversy requirement of Art. III and, as such, cannot be altered by Congress. In his concurrence, Justice Kennedy wrote that Congress has the power to define injuries and articulate chains of causation that will give rise to a case and controversy where none existed before. Does this mean that Congress can determine what constitutes injury and who is harmed by certain actions? The Court criticized Defenders' (P) affiants for not having specific, concrete travel plans to return to the affected foreign areas. What purpose would be served by requiring the plaintiffs to buy plane tickets? Would that weed out those who are genuinely harmed from those who are not?

Norton v. Southern Utah Wilderness Alliance

(Secretary of the Interior) v. *(Wilderness Preservation Group)*

542 U.S. 55 (2004)

A COURT MAY COMPEL AGENCY ACTION ONLY UNDER CERTAIN CIRCUMSTANCES

■ **INSTANT FACTS** A wilderness preservation group claimed that the Bureau of Land Management failed to properly safeguard certain wilderness areas by allowing off-road vehicle use therein.

■ **BLACK LETTER RULE** The authority of a federal court under the Administrative Procedures Act to "compel agency action unlawfully withheld and unreasonably delayed" extends only to claims involving a specific "agency action"—a rule, order, license, sanction, or relief—that the agency was required by law to take.

■ **PROCEDURAL BASIS**

Supreme Court review of the Tenth Circuit's reversal of the district court's dismissal of the plaintiff's claims.

■ **FACTS**

This case involves three separate claims asserting that the Bureau of Land Management (BLM) failed to take required action with regard to off-road vehicle use in wilderness preservation areas. The Southern Utah Wilderness Alliance (P) argued that by permitting off-road vehicle use in certain wilderness areas, the Bureau of Land Management (BLM) violated the terms of a land use plan and its statutory mandate to preserve such areas. The BLM contested the claim, arguing that lawsuits based on agency action or inaction are reserved for actions to compel a discrete final action, like issuing a regulation, and that to permit challenges to day-to-day management decisions would require the courts to determine whether discretionary agency actions complied with general statutory standards, which is beyond the scope of their authority. The federal district court dismissed the plaintiff's claims, and the plaintiff appealed. The Tenth Circuit reversed, finding the BLM's reading of the statute to be too narrow. The appellate court held that when an agency has an obligation to carry out a mandatory, non-discretionary duty and either fails to meet an established deadline or unreasonably delays in carrying out the action, the failure to carry out that duty is itself a final agency action. The case went to the Supreme Court.

■ **ISSUE**

Does the authority of a federal court under the Administrative Procedures Act to "compel agency action unlawfully withheld and unreasonably delayed" extend to the review of the U. S. Bureau of Land Management's stewardship of public lands under certain statutory provisions and its own planning documents?

■ **DECISION AND RATIONALE**

(Scalia, J.) No. The authority of a federal court under the Administrative Procedures Act to "compel agency action unlawfully withheld and unreasonably delayed" extends only to claims involving a specific "agency action"—a rule, order, license, sanction, or relief—that the agency was required by law to take.

The APA authorizes suits by persons suffering legal wrongs due to agency action, or persons adversely affected by agency action. Failures to act are sometimes, but not always, remediable under the APA. The APA provides that a reviewing court must compel agency action if it was unlawfully withheld or unreasonably delayed. Some "agency action"—a rule, order, license, sanction, or relief—must lie at the heart of the complaint. The denial of any of these agency actions may also give rise to a claim, as may the "failure to act." The "failure to act" is not the same thing as a denial. The latter is the agency's way of saying "no" to a request, whereas the former is simply the omission of an action without a formal rejection. A "failure to act," to be actionable, must be read as a failure to take one of the five agency actions listed above.

In addition, to be actionable, a failure-to-act claim must be based on action that the agency was *required* to take. In other words, a court may not compel agency action that is not mandated by law. Matters within an agency's discretion cannot be dictated by a reviewing court. Here, one of the applicable statutes is mandatory as to the object to be achieved—the preservation of wilderness areas—but it leaves a lot of discretion to the agency with regard to how to achieve that objective. Courts are limited in their review of agency decisions in order to limit judicial interference; they may not usurp agency roles.

The other applicable statute requires that the BLM act in accordance with land use plans. Land use plans are a preliminary step in the overall process of managing public lands; they are not a final agency decision or action. A land use plan is more like a statement of priorities. It may guide and constrain actions, but it does not prescribe them. A land use plan thus cannot be made the basis of a lawsuit against an agency. Allowing legal enforcement of land use terms would constitute impermissible judicial interference with agency discretion. Reversed and remanded.

Analysis:

Justice Scalia, writing for a unanimous Court in this case, rejected the claim that the Department of Interior (DOI) failed to prevent the degradation of wilderness areas as required by law, because although the applicable statute does require the prevention of degradation, it gives the agency discretion in determining how to achieve that objective. The environmentalist group wanted the Court to compel the agency to comply with the statutory non-degradation mandate, but that type of order, according to Justice Scalia, would cause undue judicial interference with the agency's exercise of discretion. Justice Scalia similarly rejected the argument that the agency could be compelled to comply with a land use plan, which provided that the agency would monitor off-road vehicle use. The land use plan, however, did not prescribe certain actions that must be taken, and hence there was no specific agency action that could be compelled.

Gwaltney of Smithfield Ltd. v. Chesapeake Bay Foundation

(Meat Packing Plant) v. *(Environmental Group)*

484 U.S. 49 (1987)

THE CLEAN WATER ACT DOES NOT AUTHORIZE CITIZEN SUITS FOR PAST VIOLATIONS

■ **INSTANT FACTS** For several years, Gwaltney (D), a meat packing plant, repeatedly violated the conditions of its NPDES permit. After Gwaltney (D) remedied the violations, the Chesapeake Bay Foundation (P) filed a citizen suit pursuant to § 505 of the Clean Water Act.

■ **BLACK LETTER RULE** The Clean Water Act authorizes citizen suits for present violations, but not for violations that occurred entirely in the past.

■ PROCEDURAL BASIS

Appeal from decision affirming that § 505 of the Clean Water Act authorizes citizen suits for wholly past violations.

■ FACTS

Gwaltney of Smithfield (D), a meat packing plant, was issued a NPDES permit to discharge certain pollutants pursuant to the Clean Water Act (CWA). For several years, Gwaltney (D) repeatedly violated the conditions of the permit. By May 1984, it had remedied the violations. In June 1984, the Chesapeake Bay Foundation (P) filed a citizen's suit alleging that Gwaltney (D) has violated and would continue to violate its NPDES permit. Section 505 of the CWA authorizes citizen suits against any person "alleged to be in violation" of the Act. Gwaltney (D) moved for dismissal of the action for lack of subject matter jurisdiction, arguing that § 505 requires that the defendant be violating the Act at the time of suit and that its violations had ceased weeks before the suit was filed. The trial court rejected this argument, holding that § 505 authorizes citizen suits for wholly past violations. It's alternative holding was that Chesapeake (P) had established subject matter jurisdiction by alleging in good faith that Gwaltney (D) was continuing to violate its permit when the suit was filed. The court of appeals affirmed, but declined to rule on the trial court's alternative holding. Gwaltney (D) appealed.

■ ISSUE

Does § 505 of the Clean Water Act authorize citizen suits for wholly past violations?

■ DECISION AND RATIONALE

(Marshall, J.) No. Section 505 of the Clean Water Act does not authorize citizen suits for wholly past violations. The most natural reading of § 505's "to be in violation" is a requirement that the citizen-plaintiff allege a state of either continuous or intermittent violation, that is, a reasonable likelihood that a past polluter will continue to pollute in the future. The language and structure of the rest of the citizen suit provisions in § 505 support that the interest of the plaintiff is forward-looking. This includes the pervasive use of the present tense throughout § 505, as well as the notice requirement, which requires that citizens give 60 days notice of their intent to sue to the alleged violator. The purpose of the notice requirement is to give the alleged violator an opportunity to comply, which would be gratuitous if citizens could target wholly past violations. Further, permitting citizen suits for wholly past violations would supplant government action rather than supplement it. Because we agree that § 505 confers jurisdiction over citizen suits when the citizen-plaintiffs make a good-faith allegation of continuous or intermittent violation, we remand the case to the court of appeals for further consideration. Proof of these allegations is not required to establish jurisdiction under § 505 since the language reads "*alleged to be in violation.*" However, the good-faith requirements of Rule 11 of the Federal Rules of Civil Procedure and longstanding principles of mootness adequately protect defendants from frivolous allegations and maintenance of the suit after full compliance has been met. Remanded.

■ CONCURRENCE

(Scalia, J.) The Court creates a peculiar new form of subject-matter jurisdiction by allowing a plaintiff who makes a good-faith allegation that the violations will continue to commence a lawsuit without requiring the plaintiff to prove the allegation when contested. The court of appeals on remand should resolve not only whether the allegation of a continuing violation on the day of the suit was made in good faith, but also whether Gwaltney (D) was in fact in violation.

Analysis:

In his dissent, Justice Scalia states that, according to the Court's interpretation, the plaintiff can never be called on to prove his jurisdictional allegation. Is this entirely accurate? The Court said that Congress intended a good-faith allegation to suffice for jurisdictional purposes. It then said that its standing cases recognize that allegations of ongoing injury are sufficient to invoke the jurisdiction of the court. The factual accuracy of the allegations may be challenged, however, by the defendant in a motion for summary judgment on the standing issue. The plaintiff would then offer evidence to support the allegation. If the defendant fails to make a showing after the plaintiff's offer, the case proceeds to trial on the merits, where the plaintiff must prove the allegations in order to prevail. The Court sums this up by stating that the Constitution does not require that the plaintiff offer this proof as a threshold matter in order to invoke the trial court's jurisdiction. It seems that the majority's view just lets the plaintiff stay in the game a little longer. According to the majority, the plaintiff's good-faith allegations will get him past a motion to dismiss, but the plaintiff will ultimately have to offer supporting evidence at the summary judgment stage or prove it at trial.

Friends of the Earth v. Laidlaw Environmental Services

(Environmental Group) v. *(Polluter)*

120 S.Ct. 693 (2000)

POST-COMPLAINT CORRECTIVE ACTION DOES NOT DEFEAT STANDING OR RENDER A CLAIM MOOT

■ **INSTANT FACTS** For years, Laidlaw Environmental Services (D) violated the discharge limits of its NPDES permit. Between the commencement of a lawsuit by Friends of the Earth (P) and the trial court's judgment, Laidlaw (D) achieved substantial compliance with its permit.

■ **BLACK LETTER RULE** A defendant's post-complaint compliance with its permit does not render suits for civil penalties under the CWA moot or defeat plaintiff's standing.

■ **PROCEDURAL BASIS**

Appeal from reversal of judgment awarding civil penalties in action for violation of the Clean Water Act's NPDES permit program.

■ **FACTS**

Between 1987 and 1995, Laidlaw Environmental Services (D) violated its NPDES permit nearly 500 times by discharging greater than permitted quantities of mercury into a nearby river. After institution of litigation by Friends of the Earth (P), but some two years before judgment was rendered, Laidlaw (D) achieved substantial compliance with the terms of its discharge permit. In 1997, the trial court rendered civil penalties against Laidlaw (D) but declined to issue injunctive relief. Friends (P) appealed seeking increased penalties, and Laidlaw (D) appealed arguing that Friends (P) lacked standing to bring suit. The court of appeals reversed for mootness, and Friends (P) appealed.

■ **ISSUE**

Does a defendant's compliance with its permit after the commencement of litigation render claims for civil penalties under the Clean Water Act moot or defeat plaintiff's standing?

■ **DECISION AND RATIONALE**

(Ginsburg, J.) No. A defendant's compliance with its permit after the commencement of litigation does not render claims for civil penalties under the Clean Water Act moot, nor does it defeat plaintiff's standing. The relevant showing for purposes of Article III standing is not injury to the environment, as Laidlaw (D) avers, but injury to the plaintiff. The trial court properly found that Friends (P) had sufficient injury to establish standing. It is undisputed that Laidlaw's (D) unlawful conduct was occurring at the time the complaint was filed. The civil penalties that Friends (P) sought had a deterrent effect that made it likely that the penalties would redress their injuries by abating current violations and preventing future ones. Thus, we are satisfied that Friends (P) had standing under Article III. Turning to the issue of mootness, a defendant's voluntary cessation of a challenged practice does not deprive a federal court of its power to determine the legality of the practice. A defendant claiming that its voluntary compliance moots a case bears the formidable burden of showing that it is absolutely clear that the challenged conduct could not reasonably be expected to recur. Since the effects of Laidlaw's (D)

---

compliance on future recurrences are disputed facts, the case is remanded for further consideration. Reversed and remanded.

Analysis:

Standing is often confused with mootness. This confusion is understandable, given the Supreme Court's statements that mootness is "standing set in a time frame." The personal interest that must exist at the commencement of the litigation (standing) must continue throughout the suit's existence (mootness). Standing doctrine functions to ensure, among other things, that the scarce resources of the federal courts are devoted to those disputes in which the parties have a concrete stake. By the time mootness is an issue, the case is ongoing and has often been litigated for years. In its discussion of standing, the Court discusses the ability of civil penalties to redress Friends' (P) injuries. Redressability, one of the constitutional requirements for standing, is the ability of the relief sought to fix the problem. Affidavits supporting redressability should show how an order to the defendant would allow the affiant to avoid the injury or how likely it is that third parties will modify their conduct following a court order against the defendant.

Atlantic States Legal Foundation, Inc. v. Eastman Kodak Co.

(Environmental Group) v. *(Polluter)*

12 F.3d 353 (2d Cir. 1993)

THE CLEAN WATER ACT ONLY LIMITS POLLUTANTS LISTED IN THE DISCHARGE PERMIT

■ **INSTANT FACTS** Eastman Kodak Co. (D) discharged pollutants into local waters under a state permit system, which specified effluent limitations for approximately 25 pollutants. Atlantic States Legal Foundation (P) alleged Kodak (D) discharged pollutants not listed in its state permit.

■ **BLACK LETTER RULE** The Clean Water Act only limits the discharge of those pollutants listed in the polluter's permit.

■ **PROCEDURAL BASIS**

Appeal from dismissal of action for discharging pollutants in violation of the Clean Water Act.

■ **FACTS**

Eastman Kodak Co. (D) operated an industrial facility in New York. Kodak (D) discharged wastewater into a local river and creek under a State Pollutant Discharge Elimination System (SPDES) permit. The SPDES permit set specific effluent limitations for approximately 25 pollutants. Atlantic States Legal Foundation (P) brought suit alleging that Kodak (D) had violated §§ 301 and 402 of the Clean Water Act (CWA) by discharging large quantities of pollutants not listed in its SPDES permit. The trial court denied Atlantic States' (P) motion for partial summary judgment, but it granted Kodak's cross-motion for summary judgment. Atlantic States (P) appealed.

■ **ISSUE**

Does the Clean Water Act prohibit discharges of pollutants not listed in the national or state discharge permits of the polluters?

■ **DECISION AND RATIONALE**

(Winter, Cir. J.) No. The Clean Water Act does not prohibit discharges of pollutants not listed in the national or state discharge permits of the polluters. Section 301 of the CWA prohibits discharges of any pollutant except as in compliance with other provisions of the CWA, including § 402. Section 402(c) allows the suspension of the national permit system upon the submission of an approved state program. Section 402(k), the so-called "shield provision," defines compliance with an NPDES or SPDES permit as compliance with § 301 for purposes of the CWA's enforcement provisions. Atlantic States' (P) view that the permits permit the discharge of identified pollutants and prohibit the discharge of unidentified pollutants is incorrect. The regulatory scheme makes it clear that polluters may discharge pollutants not specifically listed in their permits so long as they comply with the reporting requirements and abide by any new limitations when imposed on such pollutants. As the EPA points out, it is impossible to identify and rationally limit every chemical or compound present in the discharge of pollutants. The EPA addresses such discharges by amending the permit to list and limit a pollutant when necessary to safeguard the environment. EPA policy statements consider the possibility of large discharges of unlisted pollutants but take the position that the EPA will not take enforcement action as

---

long as the permittee complies with the CWA's notification requirements. We shall defer to the EPA's reasonable interpretations of the CWA. Affirmed.

Analysis:

The EPA commented that there is still some possibility that a permittee may discharge a large amount of a pollutant not listed in its permit and that the EPA will not be able to take enforcement action as long as the permittee complies with the CWA's notification requirements. EPA noted that this possibility constituted a "regulatory gap" and that the final regulations control discharges only of the pollutants listed in the permit application, which consist primarily of the listed toxic pollutants and designated hazardous substances. Does the court's decision mean that a discharger with a permit can legally discharge any material not specifically restricted in its permit? Given the mandatory notification requirements of the CWA and the permitting authority's ability to amend the water quality-based limits to address deviations from the water quality criterion, does the discharger really have a carte blanche to discharge unlisted pollutants? The court also noted that it is impossible to identify and rationally limit every chemical or compound present in the discharge of pollutants. Would compliance with the CWA be impossible if the court had accepted Atlantic States' (P) view? What if the permit, in addition to its specific limitations, included permission to discharge "any pollutants not listed in the CWA as toxic or hazardous"?

CHAPTER ELEVEN

Protection of the Global Environment

Beanal v. Freeport–McMoran, Inc.

Instant Facts: An Indonesian citizen sued an American mining company in federal court for environmental abuses in Indonesia.

Black Letter Rule: A federal court does not have subject matter jurisdiction over a suit for a U.S. company's environmental abuses in another country.

Beanal v. Freeport-McMoran, Inc.

(Indonesian Citizen) v. *(U.S. Mining Company)*
197 F.3d 161 (5th Cir. 1999)

FEDERAL COURT HAS NO JURISDICTION OVER CLAIM FOR U.S. COMPANY'S ENVIRONMENTAL ABUSES IN ANOTHER COUNTRY

■ **INSTANT FACTS** An Indonesian citizen sued an American mining company in federal court for environmental abuses in Indonesia.

■ **BLACK LETTER RULE** A federal court does not have subject matter jurisdiction over a suit for a U.S. company's environmental abuses in another country.

■ PROCEDURAL BASIS

Appeal of district court decision granting motion brought under Rule 12(b)(6) of the Federal Rules of Civil Procedure.

■ FACTS

Freeport-McMoran, Inc. and Freeport-McMoran Copper & Gold, Inc. ("Freeport") (D) operate copper, gold, and silver mines in Indonesia. The mines allegedly discharge tons of tailings per day in several rivers, rendering the rivers unusable for bathing and drinking. Beanal (P), a Indonesian, sued Freeport (D) in federal district court under the Alien Tort Statute ("ATS"), claiming that Freeport's (D) environmental abuses violated international law. Freeport (D) moved to dismiss Beanal's (P) complaint under Rule 12(b)(6) [demurrer/motion for summary judgment] of the Federal Rules of Civil Procedure. The district court granted Freeport's (D) motion without prejudice and with leave to amend.

■ ISSUE

Does a federal court have jurisdiction to hear a claim involving environmental abuses by a U.S. company in a foreign country?

■ DECISION AND RATIONALE

(Stewart, J.) No. Under the ATS, an alien may bring a claim for a tort committed in violation of international law or a treaty of the United States. International law is defined by customary usage, clearly articulated principles of the international community, judicial decisions, and jurists' writings. The ATS applies only to "shockingly egregious" violations of international law. Here, Beanal (P) has not shown any specific or discernable international environmental standards or regulations that Freeport (D) has violated. Beanal's (P) allegations do not show that Freeport's (D) mining operations constitute violations of international law. In addition, we do not want to interfere with another country's environmental practices that do not affect neighboring countries. Affirmed.

Analysis:

Beanal (P) cites the Rio Declaration to support his claim that Freeport (D) violated international law. However, the court rejects this argument because the Rio Declaration provides that countries have the right to exploit their own resources pursuant to their own environmental policies. The court is taking a very "hands off" approach, holding that what happens in another country is that country's business and is up to that country to address. The Rio Declaration also states that countries must ensure that activities within their jurisdiction do not cause damage to other countries. Therefore, Beanal's (P) case may have been permitted to go forward if he alleged that Freeport's (D) activities also caused damage outside of Indonesia.